WHAT FREEDOM ?

THE PERSISTENT CHALLENGE OF DIETRICH BONHOEFFER

WHAT FREEDOM ?
THE PERSISTENT CHALLENGE OF DIETRICH BONHOEFFER

Keith W. Clements

'To be free is to be in love, is to be in the truth of God. The one who loves because made free by the truth of God, is the most revolutionary person on earth......the upsetting of all values, the dynamite of human society...... the most dangerous of people.'

Dietrich Bonhoeffer, 1932

WIPF & STOCK · Eugene, Oregon

Wipf and Stock Publishers
199 W 8th Ave, Suite 3
Eugene, OR 97401

What Freedom?
The Persistent Challenge of Dietrich Bonhoeffer
By Clements, Keith

ISBN 13: 978-1-61097-126-3
Publication date 01/05/2011
Previously published by Bristol Baptist College Press, 1990

Contents

Preface

This book is in the nature of a file on Dietrich Bonhoeffer and the continuing challenge which he presents to the preaching, thinking, action and public witness of the Christian church today. 'File' indicates a common theme but discrete items. It is not yet another book attempting to deal with the whole of Bonhoeffer's life and thought. It is rather on the one hand an examination of certain aspects of this extraordinary theologian's life and work and the bearing of these on concrete issues we face today, especially in the 'western' world; and conversely, a discussion of a number of vital issues - as varied as east-west relations, the struggle in South Africa, and the credibility of Christianity itself - in the light of Bonhoeffer. One can only understand Bonhoeffer by trying to be concrete; and there is no greater challenge to Christian integrity over concrete human issues than that posed by Bonhoeffer.

One question above all dominates this file, and dominates this particular time in the west: our understanding of 'freedom.' I write just days after the breaching of the Berlin Wall, and at a time when still incalculable changes are sweeping through eastern Europe, shaking the foundations of our assumed viewpoints upon the world. We have been justly celebrating the promise of participatory democracies in the eastern bloc and in the Soviet Union itself. It may seem as though 'freedom' is now becoming so widely accepted as to become a closed issue. But the western notions of freedom as 'freedom of choice' and 'possibility of action', for all their intimate relationship with the Christian legacy, constitute the merest beginnings of liberty in the light of the freedom of *grace* and the freedom of *service*. If I were to identify one instance, apart from encounter with Bonhoeffer, as the germ of much of the material in this file, it would be a conversation with a Protestant pastor in the German Democratic Republic over ten years ago. He described his feelings when the Berlin Wall went up in the summer of 1961. His upbringing had been in the west, all his ties of family and experience were there, all his inclinations were westward. But, he said, the feeling of being trapped did not last long. In fact he came to regard the wall as a kind of blessing from God. For now, at last, after all the months of anxious wondering he knew where he was to be and what he was to do in his ministry, and with that he was content. If the pastors and congregations of the Democratic Republic have been instrumental in bringing about the eventual breakthrough in freedom, it is because during forty years they have already known a freedom which the state can neither give nor take away, the freedom of acknowledging the sovereignty of God's Word over all other claims to loyalty, and the freedom of service, seeking the welfare of the city without privileges and for no reward. Behind that attitude, both symbolically and in actual historical fact (for among the outstanding post-war Protestant leaders in East Germany have been his former students) stands the example and thought of Dietrich Bonhoeffer. Precisely because we are tempted to think that the quest for 'freedom' has reached its goal we need to listen again to Bonhoeffer's challenging questions as to what true freedom, especially the freedom of the church, comprises.

In part this file is the fruit of my earlier book *A Patriotism for Today: Love of Country in Dialogue with the Witness of Dietrich Bonhoeffer* (second edition, Collins 1986), which led me into discussions, correspondence, lectures and seminars with many individuals and groups, as varied as Welsh Nationalists and industrial chaplains, parish priests, polytechnic and sixth-form students, forces' chaplains and peace campaigners, pastors from both east and west Europe, and even deans of Anglican cathedrals. That book also may have had something to do with my being sent on delegations to both South Africa and the Soviet Union. Not least among the enriching encounters which has encouraged this further production was a seminar I was invited to lead at Eastern Baptist Seminary, Philadelphia, in the summer of 1988. Such wider experiences have, I hope, left their mark in these pages.

There are many, many individuals who deserve thanks for the way I have felt encouraged to pursue the lines explored here, especially in the rewarding fellowship of the International Bonhoeffer Society, details of which are supplied in an appendix for any reader who would like to enquire about participation in it. They will know who they are.

It is much more important to read Bonhoeffer himself, and for oneself, than to study books about him. This present book will have served its real purpose if it encourages some readers, at least, to turn to him for the first time, or to open his works again for further reflection. Most reviewers of *A Patriotism for Today* were generous. The single, eminently hostile critic commented that the best parts were the quotations from Bonhoeffer himself. I wholeheartedly agree! Bonhoeffer subsists too much in the present-day Christian consciousness at second-hand, and any encouragement towards direct encounter is to be welcomed.

As for the items themselves, most originated for specific occasions. Chapter 2 is a transcript of an interview with Eberhard and Renate Bethge which I recorded in October 1985 in preparing a BBC radio documentary on Bonhoeffer and the conspiracy against Hitler. To them, as always, I am deeply grateful for their enthusiastic encouragement and helpfulness, not to mention their willingness to allow the publication of this material in the first place. Chapter 3 was given as a paper to a study-day organized by the British section of the Bonhoeffer Society as part of the Remembrance Weekend at Coventry Cathedral in November 1988. Chapter 4 was prepared for a seminar of the Christian Campaign for Nuclear Disarmament and as one of the preparatory papers for the peace conference held in Budapest in December 1987. Chapter 5 was given to the Third International Bonhoeffer Conference in Hirschluch, German Democratic Republic, in 1984 and subsequently appeared in the *Journal of Theology for Southern Africa*, the editor of which has kindly given permission for its appearance here. Chapter 6 is a slightly revised version of a contribution to the Fourth International Bonhoeffer Conference in Amsterdam in 1988, which was presented in conjunction with a related paper by Professor John de Gruchy of Cape Town, South Africa. Chapter 8 was given as a paper to the Baptist Ministers' Fraternal in Bristol in 1988. Chapter 9 was a lecture given to the Vacation Term for Biblical Study in Oxford in 1987.

Bristol Baptist College
Advent 1989

1
Reading Bonhoeffer: Why and How

Somewhere in a basement in East Berlin there is probably a set of filing cabinets containing hundreds of dossiers on prisoners interrogated by the Gestapo during the last months of the Third Reich. One of the files will bear the name Dietrich Bonhoeffer. One day, perhaps, we shall see its contents. It will be intriguing to know just how this tall, heavily-built, innocent-looking, balding academic tried to convince his interrogators that he was just a simple Christian pastor trying to be a good German and help his country' s war-effort by going on some errands abroad for the *Abwehr*, the Military Intelligence. The Gestapo eventually came to know better than that. The *Abwehr* was in fact at the centre of the conspiracy against Hitler which culminated in the bomb-plot of July 20, 1944; and Dietrich Bonhoeffer's wartime journeys to Switzerland and Sweden were part and parcel of the conspirators' attempts to inform the allied powers of what was happening and to gain their support. So Bonhoeffer was finally hanged in the grey light of dawn at the execution camp at Flossenbürg on April 9th, 1945, barely a month before Nazi Germany's surrender.

In turn we know better than the Gestapo. The apparently naive pastor certainly possessed a deep and passionate faith. He read his Bible and said his prayers regularly. The piety was no veneer. But it was twinned with a brilliant and original theological mind, restlessly questioning conventional formulations and slogans, probing relentlessly into what the Bible *actually* says, what his own Lutheran tradition *really* stood for; seeing whole and making connexions where previously dichotomies had reigned, between divine revelation and the earthly, all-too-human community of the church, between faith and works, between prayer and politics, between God and the world, between Christians and Jews.

He overcame in himself, too, the dichotomy between intellect and activity - what in Christian contexts has often been a faithless divorce between theology and commitment. The fusion of life and thought is one of the chief fascinations in Bonhoeffer, and has assured his place in what Reinhold Niebuhr has called the twentieth century Acts of the Apostles. Those unfamiliar with his story may be grateful for a brief summary of his life. Those who know it may move on.

A life and death in outline

Dietrich Bonhoeffer was born in 1906 in Breslau (present-day Wroclaw in Poland). His father Karl was an eminent neurologist who in 1912 was appointed to a chair at Berlin University. Dietrich had a twin-sister Sabine, an older and a younger sister, and three older brothers. The family lived comfortably in the Berlin-Grunewald district, reflecting their aristocratic pedigree: servants, music, dances, a summer cottage in the Harz Mountains. Culture (Dietrich himself became an accomplished pianist early in life), good manners and good learning were the order of the day. Religion as a rule was not, though Dietrich's mother Paula was a devout Lutheran and encouraged a degree of family piety among the children.

The 1914-18 war left its mark on the Bonhoeffer family, as on so many others. The death of one of the sons, Walter, on the western front was a permanent grief. The oldest, Karl-Friedrich, survived the trenches to become a noted physicist. Klaus, five years Dietrich's senior, went into law.

Dietrich, already of independent mind, surprised everyone by deciding to be a theologian. He began his studies in 1923 at Tübingen, continuing from 1924 in Berlin. In 1927 - aged 21! - he produced his doctoral thesis *Sanctorum Communio*. This was a bold attempt to wed two seemingly alien theological approaches: on the one hand, that of Karl Barth (1886-1968) who had recently emphasized to revolutionary effect the 'wholly other' character of the God who transcends all finite existence - including religion - and who remains hidden from humankind except by his Word in Jesus Christ; and on the other hand, the 'liberal' approach of his own Berlin school, with its emphasis on the *human* aspects of faith, its history and sociological dimensions. Bonhoeffer wished to stress both that God is unknowable except through his Word to us, *and* that this revelation takes very human, concrete form in the community of the church. Indeed the church is 'Christ existing as community'. This dual emphasis upon the sovereign self-revelation of God and its 'earthing' in the real stuff of worldly life was the main theme which Bonhoeffer's theology played throughout his life, though with significant variations and modulations.

Already he was a great traveller. He had spent several months in Rome, where it was the sight of Roman Catholicism on full display in St Peter's that convinced him that Protestantism with its emphasis upon individual faith had much to learn about the church. In 1928 he went for a year as assistant pastor to the German emigrant congregation in Barcelona. On his return to Berlin he became an assistant university teacher and in 1930 completed another dissertation to qualify as a lecturer, *Act and Being*. Again it owed much to Karl Barth's emphasis upon God's sovereign majesty and freedom - but again with a qualification. God's freedom is supremely a freedom not *from* but *for* the world, in Jesus Christ. No sooner was this completed and accepted than Bonhoeffer was off again - this time for a year's study in New York at Union Theological Seminary. Here he was both disturbed and challenged by the Anglo-Saxon Protestant emphasis on 'open-mindedness' in contrast to his Teutonic background of intellectual rigour. But he was also impressed with Reinhold Niebuhr's profound insights into the nature of Christian social ethics, and no less with the deep social concern of the American churches. Above all, he became involved in the life of some of the black churches in Harlem, meeting for the first time the issues of racism and urban deprivation. Another challenge came from an unexpected quarter: a young French student, Jean Lasserre, became one of his closest friends and encouraged him to take seriously the commands of Jesus in the Sermon on the Mount as concrete forms of obedient discipleship: not, as Lutherans had been wont to treat them, as ideals of unattainable perfection with no practical import in the real world. Bonhoeffer, like other members of his family, had never been rabidly nationalist, despite losing his brother in 1918, and despite sharing the widespread German sense of injustice at the terms of the Versailles treaty. But neither had he dreamed of pacifism. To take up arms in defence of one's Fatherland was natural, honourable and right (Bonhoeffer during his year at Tübingen had even gone on military exercises with a student cadet corps). After his encounter with Lasserre and the Sermon on the

Mount, Bonhoeffer knew that the pacifist option could no longer be shrugged off.

In fact on his return home to Germany in 1931 Bonhoeffer became deeply drawn into the international peace movement of the churches when he became a German delegate to, and eventually a Youth Secretary of, the World Alliance for Promoting International Friendship through the Churches. This was at precisely the time when those German theologians who were adding their voices to the nationalist clamour were denouncing all such internationalist ecumenical activity as a betrayal of German interests. Meanwhile Bonhoeffer was fully involved as a university lecturer in Berlin, being occupied in 1932 with the topics of Creation and Sin, and in 1933 with Christology. All along, he was emphasizing in his own particular way Karl Barth's insistence that it is in and through Christ alone that God is known. The rising tide of National Socialism was being felt in the life and thought of the churches too. The so-called *Deutsche Christen* - German Christian movement - were calling for a truly 'German' or 'Aryan' Christianity based less on the revelation of God's Word in Jesus Christ, than on the 'orders of creation' such as people, race and nation. For such as Barth and Bonhoeffer, this was to confuse revelation with national 'renewal'.

Hitler came to power (by democratic means and to popular acclaim let it be remembered) in January 1933. There very quickly followed all the oppressive apparatus of the totalitarian regime. The churches were embroiled in controversy as the 'German Christians' called for the full 'aryanization' of the church - which meant in practice the expulsion of Jewish pastors from office and the production of a wholly 'Germanic' theology which recognized in Adolf Hitler the contemporary hand of God for the German people. Eventually those Protestants determined to resist the nazification of the church rallied together at the Free Synod held at Barmen, near Wuppertal in the Ruhr, in May 1934. The famous Barmen Confession - largely the work of Karl Barth - stated loud and clear that Jesus Christ, not any political leader or movement, was the one Word of God to be heard, trusted and obeyed in life and in death. Those who accepted this as the basis of belief of the German Evangelical (i.e. Protestant) Church constituted the 'Confessing Church' which throughout the Third Reich - whatever qualifications may be made of its political stance - represented the single most visible sign that the absolute claims of the Nazi state did not have total sway and met a point of denial.

Dietrich Bonhoeffer was not physically present at Barmen, but was in the confession heart and soul. For him the issue was utterly clear: the church is church only as she confesses Jesus Christ as the one lord of heaven and earth, above all other claims to sovereignty. It was an issue he was prepared to fight for both on the home and international, ecumenical fronts. 1934 saw him at the churches' peace conference at Fanö, Sweden, organized jointly by the World Alliance (see above) and the 'Life and Work' movement, and this provided the occasion for his most forthright call to the churches to proclaim God's command of peace among the nations.

1933-34 was an almost intolerably pressurized time for Bonhoeffer. He sought some relief from the conflicts at home (much to Karl Barth's annoyance) by accepting the invitation to the pastorate of the German Congregation in Sydenham, London, in the autumn of 1933. London however was no refuge from the church struggle. He was continually involved in discussions with the leadership of the Confessing Church (amassing huge bills in telephone calls and air fares as a result) and did much to gain support for the Confessing Church from the German pastors and congregations in Britain. More important still, he was able to feed inside information on the church struggle to interested ecumenical parties in England, above all to George Bell, Bishop of Chichester and Chairman of 'Life and Work', who became an intimate friend, counsellor and indeed a father in God to him.

Bonhoeffer's eye was always roving beyond the horizon. The German church struggle was revealing the incapacity of western Christianity in face of politicized evil. Did it really have any spiritual reserves left? He felt increasingly drawn towards India and the passive resistance methods of Gandhi, and was planning a visit there when a still more urgent summons came to return home. The Confessing Church was now having to set up its own training of ordinands, since the normal seminaries were being denied to their students by the official 'Reich' Church. Bonhoeffer took charge of a clandestine and illegal seminary which eventually housed itself in a former school building at Finkenwalde, near Stettin (now Szczecin in Poland) on the Baltic coast. He not only had the opportunity of teaching again - he no longer found the increasingly nazified universities congenial - but also was able to put into effect some cherished dreams of a Christian community life. Students found themselves not only attending seminars and lectures, but meditating on set texts of Scripture and even being invited to hear one another's confessions. Eventually Bonhoeffer was also able to establish a 'House of Brethren' alongside the seminary, occupied by ministers who could act as a kind of emergency team of pastors for the Confessing Church parishes under pressure from the authorities.

It was a creative as well as a fraught time for Bonhoeffer and two books emerged from the Finkenwalde experience. *The Cost of Discipleship* comprised many of his lectures on the Sermon on the Mount and other parts of the New Testament, stressing that grace as well as being 'free' is also costly, and that faith cannot be separated from obedience. Luther's teaching on justification by faith alone had been bowdlerised by Protestants into a recipe for inaction, and the results were all too apparent in the largely quiescent response of the German churches to Hitler. *Life Together* was a short but pungent reflection on the nature of Christian community.

The pressure was mounting on the Confessing Church. Already in 1935 Karl Barth had to leave his chair at Bonn University and return to his native Switzerland, when he refused to take the oath of allegiance to Hitler, as required of a professor. Pastors were harrassed and sometimes imprisoned. Several of Bonhoeffer's former students tasted life behind barbed wire for months at a time. Then in 1937 Martin Niemöller, outspoken preacher of the Berlin-Dahlem Church, was arrested and began his eight-year internment, becoming the most well-known symbol to the world of the Christian witness against the totalitarian state. That same year the Gestapo ordered the closure of the Finkenwalde seminary. Henceforth the work had to proceed in an even more covert way. Students were assigned to 'collective pastorates' in the remote rural areas of Further Pomerania, meeting together periodically for classes and mutual support. Bonhoeffer was assisted in this work by one of his first Finkenwalde students, Eberhard Bethge, by now his closest friend.

As war loomed nearer the tensions increased for Bonhoeffer. On the one hand his loyalty to the Confessing Church never wavered. By some he was regarded as a self-righteous fanatic but for him there could be no compromise. A church which, however slightly, admitted some kind of 'racial' basis into its constitution, and barred Jews from its pastoral office, was no longer the church of Jesus Christ, his word, his baptism, his forgiveness. On the other hand Bonhoeffer was increasingly troubled by the almost complete silence, even of the Confessing Church, on the persecution of the Jews in general. As early as 1933 he had raised with colleagues in Berlin the question of the Church's political witness on behalf of the oppressed. He knew people of Jewish descent among friends and relations. The day of reckoning would come, he felt sure, when the church no less than the nation as a whole would be under judgment for its silence and inaction. Another tension was still more acutely personal. He was liable for conscription. While he had never taken an absolutely unequivocal pacifist line, Bonhoeffer could not see himself ever being able to wear uniform in Hitler's army which could only serve an aggressive intent. But his attitude was almost unique in the Confessing Church and he was highly sensitive to the danger to which the Church might be exposed if he were to take a personal, conscientious stance. The Nazi propaganda regime would exploit it for all it was worth to discredit and perhaps eliminate the Confessing Church completely. A way out seemed to present itself in 1939, when ecumenical friends abroad secured an invitation for him to lecture in the United States. So in the summer of 1939 Bonhoeffer found himself once more in Union Seminary, New York.

He had hardly unpacked his luggage when he realised he had made a mistake. America was secure, kind, free and open to all he had to offer as a gifted theologian. But it was not home, and home despite all its uncertainties, frustrations and dangers was, he knew, where he had to be. His letter to Reinhold Niebuhr explaining his feelings has become a classic of faithful decision and obedience. He would have no right, after the war, to take part in rebuilding Christian life in Germany if he had not shared the intervening perils with his people. Christians in Germany were faced with the terrible alternative: praying for national victory which would mean the end of Christian civilization, or praying for the defeat of their country so that a Christian order could survive. Bonhoeffer knew which he must choose - but he must make the choice under the swastika, not at a safe distance abroad. So he returned, just before war broke out. He took up again the pastoral training work, now being carried out still more covertly in the east. Many of his former students were now in uniform, and many were to die in the rigours of the eastern front. Bonhoeffer himself began to be involved in another direction, the most venturesome and fateful of his life.

For some years Bonhoeffer had known that members of his extended family circle, including several in high places, were involved in discussions on the possibility of removing Hitler from office and replacing his regime with a non-Nazi (though probably rather traditional) government. Most eminent among these acquaintances was his brother-in-law Hans von Dohnanyi, a lawyer and civil servant in the Ministry of Justice, and only too well aware of the grim reality of Nazi government that operated behind the facade of the renewal of 'national greatness.' With the advent of war, the need for a *Putsch* became more urgent. It also became more difficult since the co-operation and commitment of highly-placed military commanders would be essential. On the military side the conspiracy found perfect camouflage in the Military Intelligence organization, the *Abwehr*, operated by Admiral Canaris.

Now simply by listening in and sharing in discussions with Dohnanyi and others, Bonhoeffer was effectively already an accomplice of the conspiracy (many were hanged in late 1944 for just that, or less). Events however moved him to more active engagement. For one, the threat of conscription still hung over him. In 1940 Dohnanyi proposed a solution. In order to carry out its ostensible aims of gathering information useful to the German war-effort, the *Abwehr* found a use for a wide variety of people to act as its agents, including people who might otherwise be thought suspect to the regime such as communist sympathisers and even Jews. Bonhoeffer with his numerous ecumenical contacts abroad could legitimately be taken on as an agent, using those contacts as sources of information. In fact, of course, from the point of view of the conspiracy those contacts would be most useful *outlets* of information.

So Bonhoeffer was taken on by the *Abwehr*. He continued in the employ of the Confessing Church, though by now banned from preaching and from working in Berlin, and having to report regularly to the police. The Church seconded him for 'theological work', which must have seemed like an indefinite sabbatical which he spent writing his *Ethics*, sometimes for long periods in the Benedictine monastery at Ettal in Bavaria. The *Ethics* is a superb example of theology in context, as Bonhoeffer seeks to make good the rift that had grown up in Protestant thought between piety and public life, between 'natural' life and the life of faith, between the relation to God and the relation to the world. We do not have God without the world, nor the world without God. Ethical action is a matter of concrete reality, not application of ideals but of free responsibility before God - even to the extent of being willing to 'become guilty' for the sake of others. The background of the plot to overthrow Hitler - by violence as that became necessary - is hardly stated but nothing is more obvious between the lines. The work was never completed.

Bonhoeffer's entry into the conspiracy was therefore not just an expedient to escape the possibility of conscription. He had an irrevocable commitment to it, of which *Ethics* is in large measure the exposition in Christian terms. The need for action became inescapable anyway, as he was fed with inside information about the atrocities on the eastern front and, presently, the 'final solution'. He took part in an *Abwehr* scheme to help a number of Jews escape into Switzerland. He undertook several journeys, mostly to Switzerland, to inform ecumenical colleagues about what was happening. Above all in 1942 he hurried to Sweden on hearing that George Bell was visiting there, and was able to pass to him detailed information about the plot with the request that this be relayed to the British government. Back in London the bishop saw the Foreign Minister Anthony Eden, but the allied governments felt unable to give any encouragement to the resistance. The conspirators had to go it alone.

Bonhoeffer was arrested (as was Hans von Dohnanyi) in Berlin in April 1943, and placed in the Tegel military prison. He was suspected, largely, of nothing more serious than continuing to evade military service (as yet the authorities had no suspicion of a plot to overthrow Hitler). His interrogations drifted on confusedly and finally ground to a halt. There began the last creative phase of Bonhoeffer's life, and theologically the most dramatic. As well as the 'official' letters he was able to write to his family, from the autumn of 1943 onwards he was able, through the offices of a friendly warder, to smuggle out letter after letter to his friend Eberhard Bethge. From April 1944 onwards these letters took a decidedly novel theological direction as he began to look at anew at the basic questions of 'Who is Jesus Christ for us today?' and how Christianity is to be interpreted in a 'non-religious way' for a world which has 'come of age'. The radical influence of these letters and other writings of the imprisoned Bonhoeffer on post-war theology needs no underlining here.

Bonhoeffer never married. There had been an engagement in younger life. A more permanent attachment grew during the war with the young daughter of an aristocratic family in Further Pomerania, Maria von Wedemeyer. Their engagement was made public just after Bonhoeffer's arrest! Separation from friends and loved ones was among the chief sufferings for the imprisoned Bonhoeffer, but even the theme of 'longing' he managed to transpose into a spiritually positive key.

On July 20 1944 the bomb plot against Hitler was finally attempted by Claus von Stauffenberg and other army officers - and miscarried. The unthinkable truth finally dawned on the regime, which now took its toll of revenge as network after network of collaborators and accomplices in the military, the civil service, the professions and the churches was revealed. Dozens were dealt with in the show-trials in the so-called 'People's Court' presided over by Judge Freisler, verbally abused and brutally hanged. Bonhoeffer and his immediate circle were not in real danger until the discovery of files incriminating Dohnanyi and his associates in the autumn of 1944. Bonhoeffer was then transferred to Gestapo Headquarters in Berlin and more thoroughly interrogated (though not tortured). In the New Year he was moved to Buchenwald concentration camp. The prospects of survival seemed to brighten as the American armour broke through southern Germany at the beginning of April. But with others Bonhoeffer was put on a southbound road transport. It reached Schönberg in Bavaria where on Low Sunday Bonhoeffer preached before his fellow prisoners for the last time. No sooner had he finished than he was taken away by the SS, but not before giving an English prisoner, Payne Best, a greeting to be passed to George Bell, and saying 'This is the end, for me the beginning.' He was taken to the extermination camp at Flossenbürg where with others he was placed before a summary court martial. Early next morning, April 9, he was hanged. By the end of the war his brother Klaus, and brothers-in-law Hans von Dohnanyi and Rüdiger Schleicher had likewise all paid the price for their 'civil courage.'

Why read Bonhoeffer?

It is tempting to say that any life-story such as outlined here must compel attention and a desire to make a first-hand encounter for oneself. We should of course remember that Bonhoeffer was but one figure from the story of the German opposition to Hitler, and in terms of accomplishment a relatively minor one. In terms of depth of involvement and dramatic escapade there are figures who will more rightfully come centre-stage. Nevertheless there is an intrinsic appeal in the story of a Bonhoeffer. It is at the simply human level a deeply stirring saga, whose appeal will not be confined to the Christian, or to those who look to him as a theological resource. One so socially privileged, so culturally rich, so gifted intellectually, who has every opportunity to enjoy what he has and to exploit it for his own fulfilment, yet who chooses to live without privileges, accepting risks and making ventures for justice at a time when so many compromised themselves - there is a universal appeal in this. He belongs not first to church history or to the Christian camp but to the human race, and he stands among those who, regardless of tradition or culture, represent the further possibilities of the human spirit.

Many, however, will want to know what he has to offer as a resource for Christian life and thought. I say 'Christian life and thought' rather than 'theology' not because the latter term is inappropriate, but because at face value it can convey a narrowly specialised academic interest. There is much in Bonhoeffer's writings which indeed - by his own intent - was for the specialist rather than the general reader. But one of the hallmarks of all his writing is that when it was 'academic' it was never abstract intellectualism for its own sake, and when it was more 'popular' it was never trivial. Even the same work can be read at more than one level, of equal importance. *The Cost of Discipleship* can be read as a searching devotional exercise on personal commitment to Christ, *and* as a major critique of the whole area of grace and law which has vexed the Christian west since the Reformation. *Life Together* can be read as a helpful manual on the practicalities of Christian community, *and* as a major question-raiser on the relationship between Scripture and worship, faith and psychology. The *Ethics* simply has to be read against the background of the conspiracy and its attempt to look for a new beginning of civic and Christian life amidst the ruins of the old society. Above all, *Letters and Papers from Prison* can be taken as both an extraordinary, refreshing and unselfconscious testimony on how to enjoy God and life when there seems so little to enjoy, and as a 'position paper' calling for a radical reassessment of western Christianity and society from a sophisticated theological and philosophical perspective. Intellectual alertness and spirituality, original thinking and concrete engagement are fused in a singular way.

Bonhoeffer's claim to continue to be taken seriously as a major resource for Christian theology and action is set in relief against the historical background of his century and ours. He focuses as do few others the issues raised by two tremendous developments.

The first is the Jewish holocaust. It *happened*. We know the dates when it occurred and where it was perpetrated as 'facts' of history. That it actually *happened*, in our time, in *our* Europe, in our *Christian* Europe, has barely begun to register with us. Two out of three European Jews were liquidated - one third of the world Jewish population. Yes, other peoples were brutally treated and often massacred by the Nazis. Yes, other atrocities and cases of genocide have been catalogued elsewhere this century. But nothing was so deliberate, so calculated, so efficiently carried out by bureaucracy and technology. It needed the age of the train and the timetable, the industrial chemist and the tidy-minded office-clerk who would not ask too many questions about what he was being asked to do. It is a sobering thought that on every overland journey one makes across Europe, several times one crosses the railway tracks where ran the transports to Auschwitz and Treblinka. The landscape looks as it did before. What mark has been left on Europe by it? It seems unreal in retrospect, and the temptation is always there to regard the holocaust as a sudden aberration, a blip on the screen of European rationality and enlightenment. Was it only an irrelevant excrescence, or was it rather a tumour born out of an inherent fault in the body, the culmination of processes and aspirations deeply embedded within the European mind? (I say European advisedly and not just 'German' because anti-semitism was neither a Nazi invention nor a German monopoly. People of several nationalities carried out the holocaust). Above all, the question of the responsibility of historical Christianity in the holocaust cannot be ducked. The matter of the 'preparation' for Auschwitz by means of centuries of Christian anti-semitism is a matter of some controversy. What is inescapable however is that there was a major, terrible and catastrophic failure by the Christian churches to prevent what happened. The failure may be historically explicable to some degree but that does not make it any less reprehensible.

The holocaust demands of Christians that they examine themselves, and allow others to examine them, to the roots of all their claims to be agents of God's mission in the world. It is a matter of integrity. Why have they allowed their faith - not only in the Hitler period but at other times and still today - to serve rather than to challenge the abuse of power, and to be drawn into mass hatred and violence? What does all their talk about 'building the kingdom of God' on earth amount to when they allowed the worst imaginable hell on earth to be established in their very midst? And what can they show as evidence that in the present world of conflicts and means of mass-destruction, they will act any better?

Bonhoeffer is vital to contemporary Christianity at this point. First, as a figure who established his own credentials beyond doubt, he demands that the Christian complicity in the holocaust - by silence and inaction as much as by overt 'anti-semitism' - be acknowledged. Indeed the first role he saw for the church in a post-Nazi Germany would be to confess of its own guilt, and then to invite people into the fellowship of confession. Second, the other side of the coin is that he is an enabler of this acknowledgment. He knew about grace and forgiveness, the new beginning in Christ. We are not left in our sins. This word of grace is not a cheap matter. There is no way to the liberation from guilt other than by way of acknowledging it. We are wrong to try to use Bonhoeffer as a shining, heroic figure to justify the role of Christianity under Hitler and in the modern world generally. He was not typical, that was the tragedy. His sacrifice throws the general Christian failure into even deeper relief. But his witness does point to an alternative Christianity, as does that of the others who acted similarly, and for whom Bonhoeffer serves as spokesperson.

On the one hand he compels an honesty, a readiness by Christians to stand under judgment rather than advertise the virtues of their religion. On the other hand he invites and encourages us to an exploration of what being Christian is all about, all over again. That is liberation.

The second great feature of our time is the collapse of traditional doctrines of God. Christian theology this century, and especially since the Second World War, has repeatedly been engulfed in controversy on the very meaning and designation of the term 'God'. Bonhoeffer is important because of his clear recognition that 'God' was becoming increasingly extraneous to human affairs and that many of the Christian attempts to rehabilitate God were in effect assaults on human dignity and maturity. Like all creative thinkers, he makes us look again at our tradition to ask if 'that' is really what it is saying. Above all,

Bonhoeffer makes us look at our Bibles again, and that is surely the mark of an effective theologian. Indeed his own theological renewal in prison came precisely out of an extensive re-reading of the Bible, especially the Old Testament. Is the Scripture really a 'religious' work telling us about how to get ready for heaven? Or is it about God's great cause of establishing his righteousness here on this earth? What have we done to the God of the Old Testament, the 'holy One in the midst'? At root much of the recent debate on God comes down to a choice: by 'God' do we mean one who exists objectively in his own reality, apart from us and this world? Or by 'God' do we mean a symbol, or personification, of the spiritual and ethical aspects of our own selves which find expression in the ideals by which we seek to live? The debates of the 1960's stirred up by Bishop John Robinson in Britain, and by the 'death of God' theologians in America and elsewhere, were fed by considerable use of Bonhoeffer's prison writings. In fact it is difficult to make Bonhoeffer into a clear-cut advocate of either a traditional or a non-theistic understanding of God. Bonhoeffer was not nearly so ready to rush into a reconstruction of the doctrine of God, as many of our radical theologians seem to have been. He was clear on certain fundamentals. Encounter with God is an experience of being transformed towards an 'existence for others', not a 'religious' relationship to a being who overwhelms us with supernatural power. He was clear too about where this encounter is to take place, namely in the world of everyday relationships, tasks, responsibilities and joys. He was clear also who could expect this encounter: the disciple of Jesus committed to following his way. As to what needs to be 'said' by the church about God and the great doctrines, Bonhoeffer was very hesitant. For the present, the 'secret discipline' of prayer and doing righteously must suffice for the church. Out of this a new theology would grow at the right time. Bonhoeffer therefore was not producing a new theology so much as feeling towards a new place, role and method of theology. Not a theology claiming intellectual and ecclesastical authority and therefore to be obeyed and 'applied' in actions; rather a theology claiming an integrity because it has grown out of faithful spirituality and action, the fruit of discipleship. Indeed, a genuinely lay theology, the work of the whole *laos* of the church. Bonhoeffer therefore should not be read for instant theological solutions to our contemporary dilemmas. He has, overtly, nothing to say on feminism or dialogue with other faiths or organ transplantation. Nor should we try to force him to produce answers, still less put our own answers on his lips. He is, like other great and creative figures in Christian thought and history, a crucial partner for dialogue as we wrestle with our contemporary issues. He is crucial especially as a guide who will continually remind us of the fundamental ground-rules for the theological exercise today: God met in encounter with the world by disciples of Jesus engaged, however humbly, in acts of righteousness and sustained by prayer. Fewer privileges for the church and theology - but therefore fewer burdens too. Within these parameters, the particular answers will be our affair, not his.

How to read Bonhoeffer

I said in the preface that it is more important to read Bonhoeffer than books about him. One cannot really understand Bonhoeffer, however, without taking into account the context in which he was writing - or rather contexts, for his situation changed dramatically several times in his career. One must beware of absolutizing what Bonhoeffer said at one particular point in his pilgrimage and saying 'This is the true Bonhoeffer.' It is a temptation, for example, to set *The Cost of Discipleship* with its peremptory call for obedience to Christ alone, and its sharp delimitation of the church from the world, over against the radically 'worldly' emphasis of the prison letters. The pietist can exalt the former and lament the latter's 'loss of faith'. The radical will dismiss the former as a narrow-minded enthusiasm but relish the 'maturity' of the prison letters. Neither is likely to comprehend fully either material. Each was addressed to a specific situation, with its own demands and responsibilities. Each took account of certain fundamental 'givens' of Christian faith. The two are not to be conflated, nor are they as antithetical as supposed.

While, therefore, to take Bonhoeffer seriously requires that he be read at first hand, it is very important to read with the aid of biographical and historical commentary. Pre-eminent here is the definitive biography by Bonhoeffer's closest friend and colleague Eberhard Bethge, *Dietrich Bonhoeffer: Theologian, Christian, Contemporary* (Collins 1970). Many will find a helpful introduction to Bonhoeffer and his context in Edwin Robertson's flowingly written biography *The Shame and the Sacrifice* (Hodder and Stoughton 1987). An excellent guide both to the context and development of Bonhoeffer's thought, with well-chosen selections from his major works under a single cover is John W. de Gruchy's *Dietrich Bonhoeffer. Witness to Jesus Christ* (Collins 1988).

All thinkers are illuminated for us in the light of their contexts. Bonhoeffer is more than usually so, precisely because he was so deeply engaged in that context. The *Ethics* for example is best read with the two-fold question: what light does this shed on Bonhoeffer's involvement in the conspiracy, and what light does that engagement shed on what Bonhoeffer is saying here? That being so, the reader might well ask whether all we are engaged in here is an observation of the interaction between Bonhoeffer and his context. What about our own context? Here in fact a strange paradox emerges. Bonhoeffer has such universal appeal precisely because of his inextricable engagement with his particular time, place and national crisis. Time and again, I have shared seminar and discussion sessions with students, ministers and others from contexts as widely different as Britain, Northern Ireland, West and East Germany, the Netherlands, Czechoslovakia, Australia, the United States and South Africa. The 'connexion' between his context and theirs - while so widely separated - has never been a problem. It has leapt like a spark of its own accord. Occasionally I have been asked whether, as in my own *A Patriotism for Today* for example, there is not a danger of wanting to draw too many parallels between Nazi Germany and wherever we happen to be today. That is of course a danger. (There is also the danger of ignoring whatever lessons may have to be learnt about abuse of power, racism, militarism and perverted national loyalty). But it misses the point, that the parallel to be explored is not simply that of the contexts, but that of *how* Bonhoeffer related to his, and how we should relate to ours.

Doing theology is often described today as a dialogue between the Bible, or the Christian tradition, and our contemporary context. A modification to this might be proposed, however. It can be illuminating to bring in a third party to the discussion, a historical situation other than our own, in which issues of belief, obedience and responsibility were critical for the church. It might be of comparative antiquity or of the recent past. What matters is that it is allowed to act as a further reference point in our search for the truth of belief and action here and now. We seek to listen to the Scripture and the tradition. It is instructive to find out how this was done in another context, or another crisis. To examine, and be examined by, the story of another historical situation can lend a wider perspective and a greater sense of objectivity to our enquiry. The dangers into which faith fell, the pressures to which it succumbed, or the opportunities that were taken, the witness that was made, all can help us discern more of what it means, in a concrete instance, to read or misread the Bible and the tradition. To use another analogy, it is to view the sources of our faith through the angle of another historical context than our own, and so to gain a kind of *binocular* vision towards the truth, of greater depth and perspective than our 'single eye' could afford.

The German church conflict, including the role of such as Dietrich Bonhoeffer, is one such historical witness which can be brought into the dialogue, another eyepiece to be brought to bear. It is a prime test-case of how theology fared in the encounter between the tradition and the demands of the hour. We study that situation not simply as an end in itself, or as a convenient escape from our own tasks (historians are sometimes diagnosed as insecure people who prefer judging the past rather than confronting the present), but so that we might the more critically engage with our world and more seriously utilize the tradition. To take an example, it will become obvious to the reader that several of the essays in this book take up the issue of 'freedom'. It is a word central to the vocabulary of religious devotion and much political rhetoric, especially in Britain and the United States today. But the German conflict, and Bonhoeffer's analysis, revealed it to be a highly ambiguous term which needs a good deal of theological qualification if it is to be preserved from misuse for oppressive political purposes, or self-justifying religious ends.

The ultimate Christian theological task is not to study Christian theologians, but to bring everything into subjection to Jesus Christ. He or she is a theologian who helps us do that. What matters in the end is not who Dietrich Bonhoeffer was and what he did, but his own question, 'Who is Jesus Christ for us today?' That he asked the question so sharply, is the most important reason for reading him, and our asking that same question in our own time and place provides the most productive way of reading him.

2

'It was not shame': The Bethges Remember

How close can we today get to Bonhoeffer as a person? No closer than those who knew him most intimately and whose lives and destinies were most deeply bound up with his own, and who can remember. In 1935 a young candidate for ordination in the Confessing Church arrived at the illegal seminary at Finkenwalde as one of the first batch of Dietrich Bonhoeffer's ministerial students. Eberhard Bethge, himself a son of the Lutheran manse but whose father had died some years before, regarded himself as a mere 'country boy' from Saxony, likely to be overshadowed by the sophisticated graduates from Berlin who had followed Bonhoeffer to Finkenwalde. Little did Bethge know that before long, when Bonhoeffer introduced the practice of mutual confession into the community of 'brothers under the Word', it would be Bethge whom Bonhoeffer would choose to listen to his own confession. Little did he know that he was to become Bonhoeffer's closest friend, assisting him in his responsibilities of theological training and accompanying him on many of his journeys around and outside Germany. Little did he know that when Bonhoeffer was eventually imprisoned in 1943 he would be the recipient of secret letters smuggled out of the cell in Tegel, letters which were to cause a unique disturbance to Christian thought in the post- war world and which now rank among the theological and spiritual treasures of the twentieth century.

Little did he know, either, that he was to marry Dietrich Bonhoeffer's niece! Next door to the Bonhoeffer family home in Berlin lived the Schleichers: Rüdiger (a lawyer in the Air Ministry) and his wife Ursula who was one of the Bonhoeffer daughters and so a sister of Dietrich.

Eberhard Bethge was naturally a frequent visitor to the Bonhoeffer family circle by the time of the Second World War, and it was to one of the Schleicher daughters, Renate, that he became engaged. They married in the summer of 1943, shortly after Dietrich Bonhoeffer was arrested. From prison Dietrich wrote a wedding sermon for them. Next year their first child was born, a son whom they named Dietrich after his great-uncle. For him, Bonhoeffer wrote a baptismal sermon containing many of the radical thoughts about the future of Christianity which by now were stirring within him. Both the wedding and baptismal sermons can be found in *Letters and Papers from Prison*.

After the war, Eberhard Bethge continued pastoral service within the Evangelical Church in Berlin. In 1953 he came to England as minister to the German Congregation in Sydenham, London, as his friend Bonhoeffer had done twenty years before. The original church building had been destroyed in the wartime blitz. It was largely Bethge's inspiration to build a new centre for worship and community life, and so close by the railway line at Forest Hill there now stands the Dietrich Bonhoeffer Kirche. The Bethges returned to Germany in 1961 when Eberhard took over the directorship of the Pastoral College of the Evangelical Church in the Rhineland. Now in (very active) retirement they live in a village near Bonn.

Some day, someone will write an account of the importance of friendship in intellectual and spiritual discovery. The friendship between Dietrich Bonhoeffer and Eberhard Bethge will have to figure in that account. Nor will it be confined to their relationship in life. From 1945 onwards Eberhard Bethge, without any conscious design or ambition, found himself the legatee of Bonhoeffer's writings, published and unpublished. He has given his own life and career over to the publication and interpretation of his friend's works, and what we now have and know of Bonhoeffer we owe to him more than to anyone else. Above all his definitive biography of Bonhoeffer is at once the indispensable tool for every serious student of Bonhoeffer, a crucial account of one of the most critical episodes in European Christian life and thought this century, and an inspiring testimony to faith and humanity at their highest.

All this has happened through considerable self-effacement on the part of Eberhard Bethge. He has always wanted not himself, but Bonhoeffer, to be in the spot-light. Moreover he has always been keenly interested in the light which others can throw on his friend. While at times prepared to challenge vigorously what he considers to be serious misunderstandings of Bonhoeffer and his circle, he has never pretended to own him. Again and again, those of us of younger generations who have sought help and guidance from him in our Bonhoeffer researches have been taken aback at his evident eagerness to learn from us! Simply to hear his questions, no less than listening to his reminiscences, has been a unique encouragement to us all.

This is equally true of Renate Bethge. She has the added advantage of having been childhood neighbour to her Uncle Dietrich, as well as, of course, sharing fully and intimately in the whole family life of the Bonhoeffers. The child's-eye-view is often one of great candour, and Renate Bethge is able to retrieve that early perspective as well as being able to reflect on the special social and cultural milieu of the family which was so significant for those relatives, like her own father Rüdiger Schleicher as well as her uncles Klaus and Dietrich Bonhoeffer and Hans von Dohnanyi, all of whom made the great venture and paid the ultimate price in the resistance.

In the autumn of 1985 I recorded several hours of interview with Eberhard and Renate Bethge in preparation for a BBC Radio 4 documentary on Bonhoeffer and the conspiracy against Hitler, which was broadcast in September 1986 as 'Striking the Serpent's Head'. The Bethges have kindly agreed to an edited transcript being published here. Their narrative constitutes a remarkable record of much of the background and many of the episodes surrounding Dietrich Bonhoeffer, the Confessing Church and the conspiracy, and of the theological and ethical issues which spring out of it. But also it allows the Bethges to tell their own remarkable story which is a crucial part of, and should not be completely overshadowed by, that of Dietrich Bonhoeffer himself. Theirs too is a story of great courage, immense risk and unswerving loyalty: yet all along too a story of humour, of determination to enjoy life whatever the odds, and of a faith which appears all the deeper for being modestly understated. It allows us to glimpse in personal and concrete form both the 'life together' and the 'existence for others' which were the quest of Dietrich Bonhoeffer.

* * * * *

Eberhard Bethge, is the Dietrich Bonhoeffer that people seem to be interested in, the Dietrich Bonhoeffer that you knew?

EB: Ha! It's always a certain selected Bonhoeffer who is presented or listened to. People were first of course very interested in that very courageous confessor of the Church Struggle, and in the man who wrote *The Cost of Discipleship*. And then they were interested in the man who could speak so well about prayer in *Life Together*. Then in the 1960s they would speak about the man of the 'non-religious interpretation' of the gospel in a 'world come of age', which sounded rather unfamiliar, as though it meant leaving Christianity - which is of course totally wrong. Then that discussion disappeared and from the late 1970s until now it has been replaced by the resister, the man making ethical, political decisions on the basis of his faith. That is still going on, and has nearly replaced the discussion about whether he was a 'liberal' or whether he was a theologian at all.

Now many people know Dietrich Bonhoeffer through his writings and probably think of him as a rather formidable person because of his strength of character, his academic brilliance and so on, but can you give us a picture of him as a human being - I mean what sort of a person was he like to be with?

EB: I met him first in 1935 when I was a candidate for the Confessing Church of my province in Prussia. So I met him as a leader of a theological seminary and expected him to be a great expert in theology, which he in fact was, and expected him to be a great fighter for the Confessing Church, which he was. But at our first meeting I couldn't make out which one was Dietrich Bonhoeffer in the group which I saw there, because he wasn't much older than we were ourselves, and he looked so 'sporty'. He was a rather strong and athletic man who liked playing games on the beach. The seminary first began in a little house near the beach on the Baltic coast, and every morning even in May we bathed in the very cold water. In the evening we used to relax and play some games, improvising our own games on the beach - throwing stones, running and so on. Bonhoeffer joined in from the very beginning and we soon found out that he wanted to win every contest! That was the first impression. The second was that apparently he knew so much about music, and was especially interested in it. Then too he displayed such great knowledge about German literature and told us he was astonished that we didn't know much of it. On Sundays in the seminary he felt he should read some good German literature with us, especially from the nineteenth century. These were very good things he had been familiar with, thanks to his family, ever since he was a young boy. So culturally he was very interesting. He played the overture *Der Rosenkavalier* by heart on the piano in a fascinating way. And I think it came from his family background that Sunday had to be given over not only to divine service but to games and reading - reading something other than your theological stuff. So it wasn't all the black atmosphere of the Church Struggle. Quite the opposite.

The third point was that he could be interested in each of us so personally. He would take us to walk with him on the beach and wanted to know everything about us. He was a great artist at asking questions, and we suddenly felt taken seriously in a way we hadn't expected or been used to from a German professor at the university. This leader of the seminary was soon able to build up an atmosphere in the house where everybody felt accepted and taken on one's own merits. You felt able to do more than you expected you could do, discuss better than you had expected to be able to discuss. So he was able to bring the best out of every person very quickly and we felt great.

Can you give me an example?

EB: I especially remember how each week one of the members of the seminary had to present a sermon to the class for discussion. Each of us young candidates had to do this and we were always afraid how we would come through. I was given Isaiah 53, the great Song of the Suffering Servant. I worked on it for weeks and was so afraid when I had to present it and read it in class. Afterwards, suddenly he praised my work which I hadn't expected at all. There were all his pupils from Berlin who had known him much longer already, who were supposed to be great theologians and I really felt like some kind of country boy. He praised it and gave me a kind of confidence that I could do something, which I have never forgotten.

Did he have a sense of humour?

EB: He had a very witty way. He would quickly discover double meanings in the sayings of important people, especially of theological colleagues or people in the government of the Confessing Church. His great friend of those years, Franz Hildebrandt, once made a whole collection of these. I still have that collection of funny mistakes, 'double meaning' phrases used unintentionally on very official occasions or in meetings of the church government, and he would send them to Dietrich and they would make great fun out of it . Dietrich had a great sense for the amusing situations caused by words which don't really belong together.

Renate, as his niece and next-door-neighbour, what would your own portrait of him be?

RB: Of course I remember him well because he had always been here - he was at home a lot especially in his last years after his work at Finkenwalde was prohibited. From 1940 he was not allowed to live in Berlin; but he could stay with his parents there, that was permitted. So, I mean, he was always near. As an uncle he was maybe closer to us than the other uncles because he was not married, and he was one of the youngest. He was always full of ideas and he was strong. He liked to make jokes. Of course he liked to play the piano, and I also liked to play the piano, and he was interested in how I did it and sometimes he told me something which I still remember when playing trios or suchlike. He very much liked playing chamber music - he could play everything at sight. When I play Mozart trios or Beethoven sonatas, violin sonatas also, I still remember very well how he had done this or that part in it.

The pious side never showed, you know! My father on Sundays liked to have a sermon. We had a bad kind of Nazi minister in our congregation, and so my parents didn't really go to church often. But basically my father liked something of this kind, and when Dietrich was there he asked him to give a little sermon, and he would then come over from the grandparents' house next door, but he was not especially fond of doing it. On Sundays also my father liked to accompany hymns on the piano. Dietrich would then also teach us hymns which he liked, which he had newly learnt or sung somewhere.

When we had English lessons in school he would come and talk English to us to see how much we could follow, and what we could answer, and then he was quite pleased if we could follow him and answer him in English. I still recall when he asked me something, and I said, *'Yes, I do'*, and not just 'Yes', he said, 'Oh, quite right!' Also he asked what we were reading, and he would suggest something we should read. He liked Konrad Ferdinand Meyer, a Swiss poet. He liked especially *Jürg Jenatsch*, a book he said I should read. I did, but at the time I did'nt really take to it! Also before he was put in prison, in the evenings, sometimes he just had a book in which he read poems for himself. Then he would read out a poem. So for instance from this Konrad Ferdinand Meyer I remember a poem, 'The Roman Fountain' which is very impressive, which describes how this fountain goes up and one after the other bowl takes it and gives it on, you know. I still remember that very well. It was just before he was taken to prison that he read this to us. Also, he liked funny poems and also during this last time he read poems from Christian Morgenstern, sometimes very funny poems - funny in a strange way, almost modern you could say.

He liked to play games. He liked bridge, for instance. He played very intensely. He was a very intense chess player also, but he didn't honour his nieces with this! He played with the nephews sometimes. Yes, of course table-tennis he liked but he didn't play this with the children, only if you were really good!

EB: I was rather amused later when I met his American friend Paul Lehmann. He described Bonhoeffer's ability at tennis and how he didn't want to play with bad players. But wherever possible on holidays and even just before the war in Further Pomerania, when we were really afraid the Gestapo would come, if possible he would go to a tennis court and play an hour of tennis with us.

Eberhard, when did you first know from Dietrich Bonhoeffer that he was not simply in the Confessing Church struggle, that there was a political conspiracy going on as well?

EB: I remember a situation in the summer of 1936, the first time he had taken me to Berlin, to his home. We then both went over to see his brother-in-law and his sister, Hans and Christine von Dohnanyi. He told me, 'Talk for a while with Christine for I have to talk something over with Hans and he wants to be alone with me.' I have such a vivid memory of that because I didn't know what to talk about with Christine all that time! But of course it was quite clear to me later on that they were talking about where the government was possibly failing, where it had weak points, or what could be done about it. So I was aware, especially from that point on, that Dietrich Bonhoeffer was involved in a much wider sense in opposition to the Hitler regime.

Was that your first encounter with Hans von Dohnanyi?

EB: He had come to Finkenwalde the previous year, in the late summer of 1935. Then, of course, I knew scarcely anything about it all. I simply learnt that this was Dietrich Bonhoeffer's brother-in-law, that he was in a high position in government in Berlin, that he apparently knew more than other people - especially churchmen - would know about political developments, and that he and Dietrich Bonhoeffer liked each other's company. He was a very careful person, and in a way you could feel his superiority a bit. He was the son of the great Hungarian composer so he could pretend he knew everything about that kind of cultural world, and of course he was an intellectual, a very quick-thinking, very exact and concise, reasoning man. Later on I was aware that he was a great help to all victims of Nazism, even in the church; that you could rely on him, that he was absolutely trustworthy. If he promised to do this or that, he would do it and you could count on that.

Renate, you were a young girl when all this was starting to happen - what was it like to grow up in a family of conspirators?

RB: Of course as a child, where you live, you think that is quite normal, wherever it is. I was seven when Hitler came to power and we knew from the beginning that the Nazis were very dangerous, and that we were not supposed to talk to others about things which were talked about in the family. When Hitler came to power I still remember very well how excited the family were and also worried, and that it was something very dangerous. And if it still needed something to prove it, it was the *Röhmputsch*, you know. Röhm, a friend of Hitler, was killed by the Nazis in June 1934 and by chance I was visiting my aunt, the younger sister of my mother and Dietrich, who lived near the barracks where many of these people were killed, and we heard the shots. My aunt told me that with each shot a person was being killed, a person whom somehow Hitler was angry about, who did not like Hitler. And so from the very beginning we knew that we had to be very careful. Also the family, very often they looked out of the door before talking, looked to see if somebody was listening, perhaps one of the maids or so on. A little later they put things over the 'phone because they thought somebody might perhaps listen in - it would be possible to listen through the 'phone. So from the beginning I knew that this was something special - there were Nazis about. On the other hand it seemed to me quite normal. Later I was in a way astonished that the family really acted so late, that this was all talk at the time, though it felt very much as if they were going to act very soon. They told us what Hitler was doing, above all the trouble with the Jews, that it was terrible how they maltreated Jews, that already Jews were being put into concentration camps and beaten up. So this was in the family from the beginning and I as a child really thought all the time they were planning something to get rid of Hitler from the government or to kill him.

Now many people would think of 'conspirators' as being highly cunning, devious, perhaps even callous sort of political people. But did your father, Rüdiger Schleicher, for instance, fit the normal picture of a conspirator?

RB: My father was perhaps a person who would fit least of all this picture of a conspirator. He was a very musical man, he had perfect pitch, he liked his violin. He was certainly not the type you mention for a conspirator. But nor would Dietrich fit that picture if you saw him - or Klaus. Hans von Dohnanyi seemed more cunning than the others, more hidden, you know. Dietrich, Klaus and my father, they came out quite openly. They grew very angry about Hitler and said - Klaus for instance said words about Hitler that were not otherwise used! Dietrich would never do that. Hans von Dohnanyi would never do that - he certainly was more restrained, he was more the type of person whom you could have imagined as a conspirator, thinking everything out; and he was of course the one who was mainly doing this planning. The others like Dietrich, Klaus and my father, they were more so shocked by this unlawfulness and all that the Nazis did to people, they somehow couldn't help but go into the conspiracy to do something - couldn't stand having such a government, such an unlawful and brutal government. So it was just something you couldn't help, without being a conspirator.

Eberhard, did this political dimension to Bonhoeffer's background surprise you at all at the time?

EB: It took quite a time to grasp because I was really a 'country boy', not so familiar with the idea that politically Hitler was wrong. We thought that he made mistakes - or his helpers made great mistakes - in moves against the church, and thought that we should fight with Hitler against the heretics who would 'nazify' the church. I was quite clear about that. But that it had a strong political dimension, that was not clear to me at the beginning. In that, I went through a deep and great education - not a direct one but an indirect one - under Dietrich Bonhoeffer.

So would you describe yourself at that early stage as typical of many Protestant students and churchmen?

EB: I would say that it was rather typical of them, especially for people who were not Berliners, who did not have their ear very near to the centre. There were rumours all over, but not having radios or the BBC in those days, in the country areas one could only read the local press. We thought Hitler was working out rather a good policy that started with Germany leaving the League of Nations in Geneva. We welcomed that of course and didn't see much of the problems behind it.

So what for you started to open your eyes to the political direction?

EB: I would say, looking at the Jewish question. Dietrich Bonhoeffer took it not only as a church matter whether church ministers should be Aryans - so-called - and not have Jewish ancestry. We looked at that only as a question of theological heresy. But that the Jew had to be helped and that you should not separate the question of Jews at large from the Aryan paragraph in the church - that became clear to us also in the summer of 1935. Bonhoeffer had friends in Berlin who very soon had to consider emigration, for instance, to Britain. Since he had been a pastor in London for quite a time, they came to Finkenwalde to ask him for help, how to find the way to emigrate. So suddenly there were Jews, or even Christians with Jewish ancestry, who were victims of the Nazi legislation. In the countryside we had not seen them personally, not really met them. Now we met them and suddenly it became real, it became concrete, what they had to suffer. So having looked at the Jewish problem as a question of heresy in the church, we now learnt to look at them as victims of Nazism.

Now in the Finkenwalde period, the time of writing THE COST OF DISCIPLESHIP, Dietrich Bonhoeffer must have appeared almost as a pacifist, musn't he?

EB: The old students and teachers from Berlin of the 1932 days, the time he was still teaching at the university, when they came to Finkenwalde they apparently knew about this side of Bonhoeffer's attitude and thinking. But we from the countryside, we had no idea and we expected him to be a good teacher of Lutheranism, of Reformation theology, and he was of course. But that this man at that time could have pacifist ideas - that we didn't imagine, and when we first discovered this, my friends and I were absolutely shocked, and thought it impossible that a good German Lutheran could have pacifist ideas. That was 'British' or 'western', but we supposed that these westerners were very bad theologians of course!

How did you make that shocking discovery?

EB: It was just on May 1, 1935, when we had been together about a week, no longer. Labour Day was being celebrated all over Germany and Hitler was due to make a speech in the morning from the Tempelhof Airport in Berlin. So we sat around the one little radio we had in Finkenwalde and listened to Hitler's speech, in which he put out the statement about introducing military conscription again in Germany. Most of us naively hailed this new legislation, saying that now we had an opportunity to show the Nazi officials in the villages and towns that we too were good patriots and not the bad traitors to the new Germany - they were accusing us of that in the Confessing Church all the time already. Dietrich sat there and was silent and didn't say anything. You could see that the announcement of conscription was an absolute problem for him and we asked him, 'Why? Why don't you agree with it?' He just said, 'Oh, let's have a talk about it.' That evening we sat together and for the first time I heard a very good, strongly Lutheran theologian, putting forward the idea that we should at least give an option to the possibility that you should refuse to take up arms. Of course we were reassured that this was not pacifism as a principle, but simply a call to listen to Jesus and the Sermon on the Mount; that we were not to defend ourselves. This was absolutely new in our Lutheran tradition after hundreds and hundreds of years; and in fact pacifists in Germany at that time were very, very few, and especially very few in the church (actually in 1939 there were one or two members of the official Church who refused to take up arms and they were considered to be 'enthusiasts' and so bad theologians). So Dietrich Bonhoeffer, being apparently influenced by western Christian pacifism from the time when he was in America and Britain, was absolutely alone. And so we resisted what he was saying that night.

So Bonhoeffer really based his pacifism on the Sermon on the Mount, taking it literally. Does this mean the Sermon on the Mount hadn't been taken so straightforwardly by German Lutherans up till then?

EB: According to the dominant German theology Jesus uttered the Sermon on the Mount in order to let us look into a mirror, to show us our sinful characters, and not to be taken literally at its word. And his book *The Cost of Discipleship* was the attempt not of an enthusiast, but of a Reformation theologian, to open up that simple obedience as the way of recovering the grace spoken of in Reformation theology.

So when Jesus spoke of turning the other cheek, he really did mean not returning violence with violence, did he?

EB: Yes. And he meant to say that this was not a weak attitude, but the strongest attitude you could take.

In that case, if Bonhoeffer was so committed to non-violence, why was he not prepared to be a conscientious objector in 1939, when he went to the United States, and during the war when he was engaged in the conspiracy? Wouldn't simple pacifism have been a much more straightforward way of Christian witness?

EB: That way, he would have solved the problem of a Christian who would like to show there's no blessing in taking up arms, there's only blessing in peace. But besides that very serious, very honourable position, the whole problem of the killing of thousands and thousands of Jews would not have been affected. Being German, and belonging to the kind of class who had furthered and nourished that anti-semitic atmosphere in which Hitler made it possible to come even to the Auschwitz solution, he had a responsibility. So giving that answer, or considering the whole question under the view of a straightforward pacifist principle, would have isolated this witness from the reality, that he was still accountable for the killing of the Jews. So the problem of radical, murderous anti-semitism would not be affected by any courageous step and act of refusing to take up arms. He would have solved a personal question of faith but he would not have solved the concrete reality of Germans in those days. He would have solved a personal, individual Christian question which would have absolutely stopped before the question of the holocaust, before the question of the elimination of a whole part of the German population, namely the Jews.

The conspiracy involved violence. Were the conspirators from the beginning actually wanting to eliminate Hitler, or merely to replace him and bring him to account?

EB: To stop him, that was the main point. Actually the leading people of the conspiracy in the first years (the end of the 1930s and the beginning of the 1940s) would have liked to imprison Hitler, to bring him to court or something like that, and not kill him straightaway. And still there were sections of the conspiracy who for even much longer considered not killing him, while there were others who were quite clear about the problem of putting him away, that the problem of stopping him could only be solved by killing him. In the winter around Christmas 1941, Hitler made himself commander-in-chief of the whole army. General von Brauchitsch till then had been commander. Hitler dismissed him and made himself the commander. From that point on the conspiracy had the problem as to who could give the command for the army to march - take the headquarters in Berlin and so on. You needed a high commander who would give the order to certain units of the troops to march. But then the supreme commander must be replaced. You can do that only when he is dead. So even some of the ones who for a long time held to the solution not to kill him, had in the end to agree that there was no other way to absolve them from the oath of loyalty, and so on.

But was there not here, some people might say, a contradiction with the tone of THE COST OF DISCIPLESHIP, which speaks about not using any methods of evil or anything like that?

EB: We didn't feel that way. I mean in a way we felt that *The Cost of Discipleship* was written in another situation. It was the word of a pastor, a theologian, to his own church. It was not written under the conditions that political people, responsible army leaders, responsible trades union leaders or so would have to solve in dealing with problems of public order and of injustice and so on - injustice at the level of the state.

Dietrich himself expressed the feeling in the letters from prison that maybe he had to write some chapters of *The Cost of Discipleship* again or differently, but he said at the time he would not repeal or withdraw *The Cost of Discipleship* because it was an attack on the Reformation churches in Germany which were just bodies of acclamation of the government - as they still are today.

When Dietrich made that memorable decision to come back from the United States in 1939, can you recall your reunion and what your own feelings were?

EB: Yes, I have vivid memories of that, if only because when he was away, I with some friends and others was responsible for his seminary which was being kept going in a small secret form in Further Pomerania, and I was so overloaded with responsibilities - he being away and the mail not doing too well in those days. He arrived back first in Britain and wrote from London that he would be coming. So I went and travelled to meet him before he got to Berlin. That was always a problem - Berlin was too excited a place, in the two houses of the Bonhoeffers and the Schleichers, to talk in peace and concentrate. There was not much rest there, though it was a very important and a very nice place. So in order to be really able to speak I had travelled from Berlin to Hanover and joined the train there and we had the whole ride from Hanover to Berlin which was about three hours, and talked and talked. I doubt whether in fact we talked about what his coming back really meant. Everybody knew. It meant having great hopes and doing the old work of the seminary - singing the *Lieder* and playing sports and meeting together. But what the conspiracy and maybe participation in it would mean, I at least had no real imagination what it would be like. And as you know, in a real organizational sense it was not until the autumn of 1940 that he became a member of the *Abwehr*, the intelligence service where the conspiracy was then centralized.

What sort of experience began to show you what conspiracy would mean?

EB: In June 1940 Dietrich was still an active employee of the Brethren Council of the Confessing Church and was accountable to them. When the seminary had been closed for the last time by the Gestapo in March 1940 he had been given special tasks by the Confessing Church. Now he was asked to carry out preaching and visitation work for the Confessing Church in East Prussia and, already being his assistant in the seminary, I went with him. So in June we had a journey of several weeks, near the city of Memel (formerly Lithuanian, then German, now in the Soviet Union). One Monday morning we had talked and given a Bible study to the Confessing pastors of that area in the far east of Germany. Memel is on the coast, on an inlet of the sea. There were some naval ships in the port looking rather warlike of course, and on the other side over there you could see, was a wonderful sunny beach, and we heard there was a coffee garden there. So we went over there in the afternoon, being free and wanting to have some coffee and cakes. We were just sitting there enjoying the coffee garden full of people. Suddenly through the loudspeaker came: 'Special announcement!' - which was always introduced by a fanfare like the opening of the Olympic Games today. And this special announcement came: 'France has capitulated!' Immediately there was uproar in the garden - everyone rising from their chairs, jumping on the chairs, raising their arms in the Nazi salute and singing the *Horst Wessel Lied*, together with *Deutschland, Deutschland über alles* (and I still cannot hear *Deutschland,*

Deutschland über alles today without thinking of that combination). And everybody raised his hand and sang loudly, and suddenly next to me I saw Dietrich also raising his arm in the Hitler salute, and murmuring the hymn too. And I was so paralysed that I did not move and I heard him suddenly say, 'Stand up! Are you crazy?'

The reason of course was that Dietrich had known for a long time about the preparations for stopping Hitler before France could be conquered. Now the capitulation of France was absolutely unexpected by the many experts in military matters. You must realize that with the fall of France, all hopes of overthrow of Hitler were put far away. Who would still co-operate if you had that unexpected military victory over France? Which General would now co-operate with the conspiracy? And one needed the army to stop Hitler! Instead the Generals were given their great estates for their conquests which fulfilled all those hopes which were so frustrated from the First World War. Now Hitler had done what the old people had not been able to do in the Marne battle. So all our hopes and imaginings of another future without Hitler were crushed. I was so full of that disappointment that I wasn't so quick and aware, and when we went out of the coffee garden, really down in our spirits, then Dietrich said to me - 'Are you crazy? Now is the time when we have to do quite other things than not raising our hands for the Hitler salute. That is not the testimony that is asked for now, but quite other things' - meaning dealing in secret, underground conspiracy.

So was Dietrich really saying, we must now pretend to be Nazis or at least 'good Germans'?

EB: Dietrich was already an accessory of the conspiracy, and from the point of sharing in it in an organized way, a kind of double life begins. You are suddenly thrown into the inner logic of underground activities in which you have to show yourself as a better patriot, as a better Nazi, than all the others; just as Hans Oster in the office of the Military Intelligence all the time had to show, on the surface, that he was one of the most dependable soldiers for the victory of Germany - in order to destroy it of course. And so Dietrich slowly came more and more into that kind of logic and understood that going into the conspiracy didn't permit any middle attitude. You cannot be partially a conspirator. Maybe your activities are very unimportant and so on, but you are drawn into the total community of the conspirators. You could not say

'I am a pastor, while you . . . It's not my business to kill.' Of course Dietrich himself would be no practical use at killing - he had not learnt to handle a pistol and so on - but clearly he had to take all the consequences, namely, for him to pretend to be a a Nazi. All that, he had to accept.

Did he find that easy?

EB: It was such a matter of course that you had to learn this, and very carefully. One instance was when Dietrich and Hans von Dohnanyi became aware from the end of 1942 that they were under special observation by the Gestapo. They had to make preparations in case they were imprisoned - how they would behave then, what they would say, what agree to, in order to lead the interrogators on the wrong track. They had to justify the fact that Dietrich was being employed by the Military Intelligence service so they drafted a letter, written by Dietrich and made to look as though he had written it in the summer or autumn of 1940. We even found some of the letter paper he had actually used in 1940 for writing his *Ethics* and for writing letters in those days. And then on his typewriter they made a long draft in which he talked about, in effect, 'How we talked a few days ago about whether I would be useful for the Military Intelligence, or not, and then I gave you information about certain relations I have to the ecumenical world and gave you some names; and in order to specify that once again I now put together a list of those whom I know, these names of great ecumenical people, in the United States, in Britain, in Roumania, in Greece, and so on.' He dated the letter sometime in 1940, and put what was supposed to be a copy of it on his desk so that the Gestapo should find it when they came searching, and they did. I still have his name and address list for the World Alliance for Promoting International Friendship through the churches and for 'Life and Work', and on the back cover, in his own handwriting, you can see he pencilled the names - like Visser't Hooft of the Netherlands - he was putting together for that letter. This was the kind of preparation for active conspiracy and for hiding the conspiracy at the same time: on the surface justifying the claim that he was working well for Hitler's victory. He was put in that situation all the time. It was a matter of course. The only problem was really to learn it properly and not to make a mistake in it.

Somewhere in his essay 'After Ten Years' Bonhoeffer asks 'Are we still of any use?' - having had to learn the arts of pretence and deceit. He was aware, then, of the moral dangers?

EB: Oh yes. In the *Ethics* he put that rather unique chapter where he formulated the 'acceptance of guilt' - the problems which arise in a situation in which you cannot refuse to take on guilt; when you realize that you have to take the consequences, yet it is necessary, it has to be done. There is a kind of involving yourself in guilt which is from the devil, and there's an involvement in guilt which is Christ-like or near to Christ. What do we mean, that Christ took our guilt on himself? He took that seriously, Dietrich Bonhoeffer.

Someone might say, 'Well, that's Christ's job - not the Christian's. According to the New Testament Christians have to be pure and spotless in a crooked world, not—'

EB: —Christians have to be . . . No, they have to acknowledge what is happening to victimized people and they have to accept their responsibility to try to save them, and not run away into purity and leave them. The purity is even worse then.

The victims in the case we're talking about were the Jews?

EB: Were the Jews. This is of course a problem. I am absolutely convinced that for Dietrich Bonhoeffer as for his family, the Jews were the main reason for sharing in the conspiracy. For instance when you read the record of the interrogations of Rüdiger Schleicher, Renate's father. Yes, when he had to agree before the Gestapo that he was wishing to replace the government, he gave as his reason: they had to because of the Jews. So it was for the whole family. For Dietrich there were very serious theological questions which involved taking concrete steps, and a new kind of teaching about the relation of Christians and Jews. But of course I can show you easily how many of the conspirators were still strongly anti-semitic Germans.

So there's a sort of paradox here that for Dietrich Bonhoeffer it was a question of being prepared to become guilty for the sake of others?

EB: Yes, not to refuse to become guilty, I would say. It's not a principle of becoming guilty or not. The wrong step had been taken much earlier in 1933 or 1934 when people could have avoided a situation in which such a thing becomes necessary. It is so now in South Africa, so many people, very good black and white Christians, know that if they could have succeeded five years ago they could have avoided what they still try to avoid now - revolution, violence. But there comes a point where it is impossible not to accept that situation which has gone too far. Otherwise you are under a devilish guilt - under a guilt of hell - where the guilt is not capable of being turned into an open door, into a new, reconciled and better peaceful world or community.

But were there any theological guidelines in the Lutheran tradition for actually plotting the murder of a lawful head of state?

EB: There's not of course a tradition of being educated into resistance, especially not into conspiratorial resistance, but I think Luther himself was very political and gave very straightforward advice to resist a prince or a duke who had become a traitor to God's mandate of government.

If Luther said that, why has the Lutheran Church, of which Dietrich Bonhoeffer was a product, on the whole been so quiescent - why has it been so subservient to governments in Germany?

EB: Luther himself said that when the relations with Rome had broken down he would have liked to hand over government of the Church to mature Christians. But he couldn't find them and as an emergency temporary solution he gave over the responsibility for church matters to the kings, dukes and princes. This emergency decision, meant to be temporary, became the solution for three or four centuries, and we became absolutely used to it so that the special solution became the general solution for ever. That was a very strong conditioning element in which even I myself was brought up. The Germans did not become democrats, the Christians in Germany did not become democrats in the Weimar Republic. Only now are they beginning, and as you have heard last week, for the first time in our whole church history the church has given out a memorandum that democratic government is the legitimate one on Christian principles. It needed four hundred years.

So, supposing that the plot had succeeded, supposing Hitler had been assassinated and that some form of government followed, how do you think Dietrich Bonhoeffer would have publicly justified his involvement in that?

EB: That's all speculation of course. Success is the only really convincing proof, and he would not have had too difficult a time giving justification, because apparently he would not have been wrong, but right.

But would everyone have accepted that he was right? Would there not have been a lot of Germans, a lot of Christians who would have been aghast at the thought that the head of state had been killed and that there had been Christian pastors involved in it? What do you think Dietrich Bonhoeffer's defence would have been if—

EB: -I resist a little bit your question because why has Dietrich Bonhoeffer to justify his attitude? The others who had not done anything, they have to justify their attitude. And it is not Dietrich Bonhoeffer who is before the court of good Christians today, who has to give reasons as to 'How could you do that?' Renate was once asked, I think it was in the United States, 'How could the good Christian, the great theologian Dietrich Bonhoeffer do such a thing?' and she said, 'Oh, you are absolutely wrong with your way of asking the question. You have to turn the question round and ask, "How could he *not* have done it?"'

In view of what was happening to the Jews?

EB: Of course, in view of what was happening to the Jews. Not to do anything, not to lift your hand for the Jews, this was a much bigger guilt, quite another guilt to the guilt of stopping the leader and his perpetrators!

So that really to have done nothing would have preserved his own innocence but it would have made him guilty of the—

EB: —I mean this is the real motive all the time: how could he as a member of this kind of educated, responsible, political family of Germany - how could he sit down and let these things go on being done all the time? It is not a question so much of 'How could we do such a thing?', making a resolution and so on. The question is: 'How can I still bear to be made an accomplice of the crimes and then claim the name of Christ, claim the gospel for me?' That's all poison and that's all betrayal of Christ. God's name is being held in contempt by sitting on one side and doing nothing. If you try to hold to the name of God by avoiding all that, you are only betraying yourself.

Would you say this is fine for a thinker as responsible and careful as Dietrich Bonhoeffer was, but rather a dangerous line of thought which by less responsible people could justify any sort of revolution?

EB: Yes of course, and that happens. You cannot be responsible for every misuse of Bonhoeffer all over the world, which is of course being done all the time. There are associations for birth control and other things, in Australia for example, and now they use the name of Dietrich Bonhoeffer. But I cannot be the policeman and try to hinder all that. What else in history has been named after Martin Luther or even Jesus Christ and misused such names? Only by studying carefully and being thrown a little bit more into that figure and the circumstances under which he lived and thought and acted will one be corrected. And one must not be too careful with that or too full of anxiety - if you are really being drawn into the problems and to that kind of person, it will correct itself.

Would it be true to say that Dietrich Bonhoeffer and perhaps some of the other conspirators actually thought of the risks they were taking, and their final sacrifice, as some kind of atonement for Germany's guilt?

EB: Yes. I remember an evening in Sakrow, where the Dohnanyi family lived, early in the war. We were just sitting together at the fireside, and Hans von Dohnanyi, who had certain elements of piety even then, asked Dietrich, 'What about Jesus' saying, "Whoever takes up the sword will perish by the sword"? What about us? - we are taking up the sword.' And Dietrich answered, 'Yes, that's true. And Jesus' word about whoever takes up the sword will die by the sword is valid. It's still valid for us now. The time needs exactly those people who do that, and let Jesus' saying be true. We take the sword and are prepared to perish by it. So, of course, taking up guilt means accepting the consequences of it. Maybe God will save us but first of all you must be prepared to accept the consequences.' He meant of course it needs exactly those people who accept Jesus' word - the truth of it and so the consequences of it, of perishing. That Germany needs at this moment of its history exactly these kinds of Christians, and that is what being Christian means.

So from the autumn of 1940 Dietrich Bonhoeffer was engaged in the conspiracy and writing his Ethics and so on - what were you yourself up to during that time?

EB: But Dietrich was officially still a kind of theological adviser to the Brethren Council of the Confessing Church in the north of Germany - Prussia so to say. And I myself was finishing the seminary work in the spring of 1940. Being an illegal pastor ordained by the Confessing Church, not being accepted by the official Church, I could not just get a pastorate somewhere. Then I was accepted as an employee of the Gossner Mission Society in Berlin which had their special missionary field in India. The leader of that missionary work was a very good friend, still a leader in the Confessing Church, Pastor Lockies, in Berlin. So I was working in Berlin for the missionary society, raising funds in all kinds of ways, which gave me still the opportunity to be together with Dietrich. When he was in Berlin I was in Berlin, we met and shared his room in the Marienburger Allee. So the contact was never really interrupted. Sometimes we didn't meet for quite a while, therefore there are letters between Dietrich and myself because I was away, but basically I was with him all the time. He and Hans von Dohnanyi helped me to escape military service for a while, to be free from it on the grounds that I was doing some important church work, and even to be taken on as a member of the Military Intelligence service myself when it became very dangerous to be sent to Russia as a normal soldier.

I was once a little bit more important in the conspiracy than even I at that moment knew. That was when Hans von Dohnanyi in the beginning of 1943 had to go and visit the headquarters of the middle front army in Russia, where the famous Tresckow and Schlabrendorff were preparing for an attempt on Hitler's life by putting a bomb on his aircraft (with an English detonator which didn't work, you know!). Hans von Dohnanyi was planning this from his office in Berlin. He had to take a train from Berlin to East Prussia, and then go by air. And in the evening I had to drive Hans von Dohnanyi and his luggage from the Bonhoeffer house to the station, in the car belonging to Dietrich's father (being a doctor and medical professor he was still permitted a car). And in his luggage there was some of the explosive - which I didn't know till later.

It sounds as though the Bonhoeffer family house was itself a headquarters for the conspiracy - presumably important meetings did take place there?

EB: Actually the two houses in the Marienburger Allee, which are still there - numbers 43 and 42 - the one that the Bonhoeffer parents had built in 1935 and the Schleichers' house, these were the centre for the conspiratorial participation of the large Bonhoeffer family. But of course there was outside, near Potsdam, the von Dohnanyis' house, and then some houses of other friends, for instance a son of the famous theologian Adolf von Harnack, who was a great flautist and always organized house-music, where we played the Brandenburg Concertos by Bach. In the Fourth Brandenburg he took the first flute part and I the second. Several times these people would pretend to be meeting there for music, but actually talked over things.

So was the music used as a kind of cover, or was it also a necessity?

EB: The music was both. It was a necessity because we had been in it so much for years and years and enjoyed it so much. But partly of course coming with the instruments under the arm, it was a good cover.

And Dietrich played on some of these evenings?

EB: Dietrich of course was the best pianist in the great family. He was a great player of Beethoven but he was a very sensitive accompanist when his mother used to sing the great songs of Löwe, especially about the two grenadiers coming from Moscow in the Napoleonic War. Dietrich had been into this absolutely since his youth. Later on my wife had to take over and she'd have loved that same ability.

Dietrich was arrested on April 5 1943 - were you with him then?

EB: Renate and I were already engaged and we were preparing for our wedding. On April 4 - that was a Sunday - Renate and I had travelled to my mother's place about 100 kilometres away from Berlin and had come back maybe either the evening of that Sunday or on the Monday morning. We went to 42 Marienburger Allee. Dietrich came over from his parents' house, telling us that he had rung Christel von Dohnanyi and strange voices had answered the call, so he knew now what was happening. First Hans was imprisoned, then Christel in her house, and he too had now to expect the black Mercedes with the commissars. So he had a great meal over at the Schleichers' - my future mother-in-law prepared it for him - and we talked and waited there together. About 4 o'clock Dietrich's father came over from number 43 and said, 'Dietrich, there are two gentlemen who would like to speak to you, they are in your room upstairs where they are searching.' We went over and Dietrich met them there and a few minutes later they came down, and he had to get into the black Mercedes and disappear. That was his last moment of liberty.

And what happened to you yourself, then?

EB: When Dietrich was imprisoned I was still a civilian, serving the missionary society, and on the other hand freed from military service for the Military Intelligence run by Admiral Canaris's office. Which meant that when Dietrich was imprisoned and the danger was that they would show that Canaris had saved several church people from military service, the accusation would go to the very dangerous point of not being in the army and so destroying the German morale. So I had suddenly to produce proofs that there was real justification in my being taken into the Military Intelligence service lists, and with some friends in Dohnanyi's office I quickly had to organize a journey to Switzerland, pretending that I would visit our related Swiss missionary society and try to find out what was happening in India, what was happening with the Japanese coming over the mountains into India - who would co-operate, who would not, and so on. Missionary societies still working there might have been useful for that. I got a visa, I got money and everything and I had the great opportunity to meet Karl Barth in Basel and to report to him, and later on to Visser't Hooft in Geneva, what had really happened with Dietrich's imprisonment, and with Hans von Dohnanyi, what the circumstances really were; and on the other hand, to collect news from the missionary societies about what the Japanese were doing in China and in their conquest of the whole Far East. I still have the documents of my notes. Then I came home. By the way I bought the gold wedding ring - I couldn't buy that in Germany - in Switzerland on that occasion.

Then I sat down with Klaus Bonhoeffer and for several evenings we worked on a report to the Military Intelligence service which would give good reasons for my trying to work for them, finding out what was happening in the neutral countries and in the Far East, in war matters, and that report I still have here in my files. It was of course 'not good enough' and I was soon dismissed in the summer and became a normal soldier. But still then, old friends worked it so that it wouldn't just mean being sent to the eastern front and disappearing in Russia, but being sent to Italy where I was a normal soldier from the winter of 1943 to 1944. I was in a little unit with the task of counter espionage - I was the clerk of the unit because I was the only one who could write properly on a typewriter and so could make reports.

How did you keep contact with Dietrich?

EB: First of all of course, the first half-year of his imprisonment from April to November or so, he totally avoided mentioning me and I totally avoided showing any relation to him. When he was writing official letters out of Tegel prison he would ask after Renate which meant of course he was asking also what was going on with me. But then when the first main hearings were over (this was of course still in 1943, long before the crisis brought about by the July 20 plot in 1944), in the autumn he began this smuggled correspondence with me, the first letter I think in November 1943 and then very regularly, sometimes several letters a week. The smuggling was never discovered, and I and my wife and my mother, we preserved the letters, and they were the basis for the later *Letters and Papers from Prison* which started that whole new theological discussion. But I still have them here, the originals.

You were able to meet, though?

EB: Oh yes. In 1944 after my son was born, when I came on leave to baptize him and so on, then we prepared several meetings in prison. Dietrich had developed a relation to the Kommandant and to the guards so that he could give information to us through them. For instance, 'Please come on Wednesday morning, when there will be a very good man on guard, he will let you in.' Of course I was rather afraid of meeting him at first. How should I behave to him? But he took it away when we first met and everything was as it had always been. The second time one of the best guards he had - at that time it was a normal military prison, not Gestapo - took me into the prison, put me into his cell and after a few minutes the door opened and Dietrich came in, and he let us be alone together in that cell for a whole hour, where we could talk over many, many things.

What did you talk about in that meeting?

EB: I can't remember any specific statements but it was absolutely natural of course that the opportunity was there to exchange all we knew about the other hearings, especially Hans von Dohnanyi's, as far as we had messages from him: what he was being asked about, what Dietrich should agree to, what he shouldn't, and things like that. So particulars about interrogations, particulars about how to handle the possible trial, and so on. This of course was already prepared before the prison time - what means could be used to inform each other. We knew that when in custody in a military prison you were allowed to receive food from your family, you were allowed to receive reading stuff, books and so on. Knowing that, we had to prepare a method of telling Dietrich or Hans for instance, 'When you get one of our books with a line under your name in the book, as the owner, then there's a message in that book and the message will be put in so that, starting at the end, each third or fourth page will have a small pencil point under one letter.' And so through the whole book there could be written a whole sentence by that method, and they could use the same method to communicate with us in turn. It was a very, very difficult and tiring task to find out whether it really was a point made by a pencil or a point made by a fly! It was then of course agreed that if you deciphered the message then you would eradicate all the points as soon as possible. Just recently I found a book where someone had forgotten to do this, where maybe even one of the nephews or nieces had been set to work deciphering and had made strokes indicating 'Here is a point, there is a point.' There, Dietrich had written, 'Everything is OK, no involvement of P.' - which meant Justus Perels, one of our friends in the Confessing Church who was involved in the plot too. So, in effect, 'Tell him that he is not figuring in the interrogations' - which was important to know.

But this information exchanged in that meeting in the cell was of course most important. Then of course he would ask a lot of things: how I was doing in Italy as a soldier; about my visit to Rome and seeing the Laocoon, had it anything to do with the suffering of Christ or what the artists of the antique time of the Greeks would have meant to say in it.

Were you still really hopeful about the outcome of the conspiracy? I mean in your heart of hearts were you all still believing that it could come off, or was it now simply a matter of survival?

EB: First of course, before July 20 1944, you had to spread optimism in yourself, in your own heart and especially to the others. There were several conspirators who were greatly gifted. Today they are considered to be dreamers. They were not. It was a matter of survival and a matter of success too, not to spread that poisoning pessimism about the whole thing. So it was a matter of course to persuade yourself. And of course when it was delayed again and again there was in any case the feeling 'Success or not success, we have to do it - for Germany, for the future' and so on. You must never give up hope for survival and finding a way through.

Dietrich quite clearly did not give up hope himself. He tried things, gave them up, hoped another way. Even when he was transferred from the military prison to Himmler's Gestapo cellars there were times when he developed hope because now the interrogators, in the winter of 1944-45, were of course interested in having news about the English for instance: what Bishop Bell and his acquaintances in Government and Parliament really would say, whether there were sources of information, whether there were even ways of communicating or so. The interrogator - Huppenkothen was his name - was in charge to find out the bad things people like Bonhoeffer had done. But secondly, he had taken over the business of Canaris's office, which had been dissolved. He had to be interested in finding out new ways of espionage, of using knowledge that churchmen like Dietrich Bonhoeffer might have had. He had to be interested in Dietrich's acquaintances in England and whether they could still be used even in war, and so this double role comes out. Generally they were treated badly but sometimes they were treated like gentlemen. Dietrich was offered cigarettes, he was a great smoker during interrogations. And sometimes there must have been an atmosphere not as hostile as before July 20. Before then, his interrogator had been the Luftwaffe Colonel Roeder who was always hostile because he had to show that he was a good Nazi. The Gestapo interrogator did not have to show that he was a good Nazi! He was much freer in handling it. In any case Dietrich was never treated as badly as others - his personality did not permit that.

So during such sessions Dietrich would have played the role of trying to help?

EB: Very much so, yes.

It must have been quite an experience for you on July 20 1944, hearing of what happened that day.

E.B.: On the evening of July 20 I was with my unit in Italy. I was sitting there - I had to make a report to our unit on the news every evening at mealtime - so I was the first to hear about the plot that evening, that it had failed, and of course you can understand I knew what it was like. I knew the names of all who were involved - now it had failed. What about home - my wife - her parents - Dietrich himself and the others? I had to go up to the meal at 7 o'clock, where we were about twelve to fourteen soldiers. The officer was a major, a nice Austrian. He came in and stood at the end of the table, took out his pistol, put it on the table and said: '*Heil Hitler*! There has been an awful attempt on Hitler's life. Whoever says a word against Hitler here, I will shoot him down on the spot.' Then we sat down and we tried to eat our meal. As soon as possible I excused myself and went to bed, and it was a terrible evening of course. I couldn't say anything. There were some friends in the unit who were anti-Nazi - they were away just that night, so I was totally alone. Then after a few weeks I was still getting letters from Dietrich in prison. I got letters from my wife which told me that up till now nothing had happened. In fact it took another two months before Dietrich was taken from Tegel prison, where really nothing had been found out so far, and was put into the Prinz-Albrecht-Strasse Gestapo headquarters. My father-in-law Rüdiger Schleicher was imprisoned, and so was Klaus Bonhoeffer.

Then, one day at the end of October a signal came to our unit. Each evening about 6 o'clock the driver came from Mantua with the mail. That very nice - but Nazi - Austrian major had once given me the authority to open even the secret letters to him and put them out ready on his desk for him. This evening, there was this telegram: the order, 'Bethge has to be arrested and brought to Berlin under heavy guard.' I had of course half expected such a thing, but I went first to my luggage where there were still some of Dietrich's letters smuggled out of prison. These I burnt. Then I put all my luggage in order and got rid of everything that could be dangerous for Dietrich's hearings and mine. And then I went to one corporal who was rather friendly to me and I opened up myself to him and told him what the telegram said. He said, 'Eberhard, there's only one solution: you disappear. Go to the partisans in the mountains. ' I replied, 'Maybe right, but I can't do that. I have a young wife over there, the baby and my old mother, and they would take hold of them if I were to disappear - I can't do that.' Then I went to the officer and told him. He said, 'Oh, Bethge, what has happened here?' I told him that maybe my father-in-law had been accused of participating in some resistance and that it might be that they just wanted to get hold of the whole family and interrogate me too. So he said, 'Oh, we'll send you to Berlin but let's do it tomorrow and you'll be back with us in two weeks' time.' I knew better of course. Then that journey to Berlin began - and that's a story in itself.

How long did it take?

EB: Several days. I was given the heavy guard, actually two corporals of my unit, who were asked to bring me to Gestapo Headquarters. They were old Bavarian people from Munich, and so we went slowly through the Alps which took two days. When we arrived at Munich they said, 'Oh, first we go to our wives and families', and so we used up another night there. And with air raids all over Germany there was always justification for being late. So we stayed in Munich and after another day we started on the train to Berlin. Coming nearer to Berlin, I said to my two corporals, who were very friendly, 'Now what are we going to do? I don't suppose you'll take me straight away from the station to the Kurfürstenstrasse. Let's go first to my wife's home and see them. They'll make you a wonderful meal after the long night journey.' So we did. It was a dark autumn day and of course expecting that the houses might be watched by the Gestapo, we had to find out and we approached slowly. My mother-in-law made a great meal for the two corporals and I went into another room with Renate to be informed about the latest developments with Klaus's and Rüdiger's interrogations, and tried to determine what the main point in my own hearings was likely to be - whether they would ask about my father-in-law Rüdiger, which would not have been too bad, or whether they knew about the relation between Dietrich and me. Now as a prisoner one could ask one's family for toilet articles. So we decided that if I asked for a toothbrush it meant that my father-in-law was the centre-point of my interrogations. If I asked for a towel or something it would mean that Dietrich was.

But in fact for a few weeks I could not give any message because they just let me sit there in the prison and only after two or three weeks did they start interrogating me. Then, actually what they knew of course was my relation to the Schleicher household, and nearly nothing about my relation to Dietrich, which in fact saved me from a lot of dangers. I could make clear to the Gestapo why I was in that house - because my fiancée was there! I had to agree to a statement about this. My trial would have been set for May 15 1945, but that was too late. Then when the Soviets got near our prison the Gestapo disappeared and their prisoners suddenly were free - though the Gestapo had killed many, even during the last days.

Did the Gestapo ever get close to your friendship with Dietrich?

EB: There was one occasion. The interrogations would start with this point or that. Then suddenly the commissar put a file in front of me and said, 'Do you recognize that?' It was supposed to be statements by Dietrich and of his case, with his signature. That was of course a most dangerous moment, especially since I was not very courageous or quick and so on. But that moment I was able to say with apparent credibility 'I don't'. From my first interrogation I already knew the protocol. Notes of the interrogation were taken by a secretary, the final version being formulated mostly by the commissar and dictated by him, not by oneself. Seven copies were made and one had to sign them, so that they could be distributed to other groups of interrogators where things could be found out. But then he put the file away and didn't continue to ask about it much longer.

What would have happened if they had found that you were a close friend of Dietrich?

EB: Oh, they would of course have insisted on much more interrogation. In this hearing, I had to agree that certain talks had happened in the Schleicher house, about the dangers of this war, of losing the war, about another government. Yes, then I had to agree that if I came across Jews I would meet them and as a Christian pastor would even try, if asked, to baptize them, or something like that, which was bad enough. But of course it put me in what in fact was a truthful position, it put me a little bit on the margin, and I was a marginal figure in the whole thing.

Would you say that Bonhoeffer was prepared to put at risk even his credibility as a Christian?

EB: Yes, yes as a Christian. For instance that letter I described earlier, written in 1942 and dated 1940 to deceive the Gestapo - it used all the names of his ecumenical experiences, the greatest names of the ecumenical world of those days, which normally would be a very doubtful thing of course. But you reach a point in history when things have gone so far that even that doesn't count. Oh yes, when you imagine his isolation on the evening of July 20 when the message came that the plot had failed - in Tegel he had good information and could listen to the radio with some of the guards - he soon knew what had happened and the greatest hopes were totally crushed, Hitler was going on. He was even again the victor and now the whole attempt of the last year's conspiracy was in vain. Everything had become even worse. Not only for Germany, but also his personal, very private hopes of marrying his fiancée soon - they were virtually at an end. But evidently in his prison cell he had that very Bonhoefferian method of at once thinking not only on yourself but thinking of others. The letter he wrote next day, July 21, I was so eager to get. And when it came it meant so much to me, because first of all it said that nothing really dangerous has happened - nothing has really changed with me. And of course I still love that letter nearly most of all because so many emotions were involved, so many dangers speak out of it, and so much of conquering and victory over these troubles and sorrows. I've still got the original here in my archive. As you can see, the paper's a little bit destroyed and I was able to save it by putting it into Japanese paper, so I hope it really is saved. It's written on July 21, it's a Friday, the day after the plot had happened and failed, and just the first sentences you can feel . . . there - *'Heute - (Heute!) - will ich Dir nur einen kurzen Gruss schicken. Ich denke, Du wirst in Gedanken so oft und viel hier bei uns sein, dass Du Dich über jedes Lebenszeichen freust, auch wenn das theologische Gespräch einmal ruht. . .'* [All I want to do today is to send you a short greeting. I expect you are often here with us in your thoughts and are always glad of any sign of life, even if the theological discussion stops for a moment']. And then he goes on - the Bible verses he has read and is remembering and quoting for himself the great hymns of Paul Gerhardt. And then giving a kind of review of his whole life as a Christian and where he came to his insights on the 'this-worldliness' of the Christian faith. So it is very personal. It is full of the anxieties in the background, and full of conquering them by his biographical review and sharing that with someone, and thinking that all of us outside his cell were all in the same situation - 'please think of this'. And then there comes that great word about what faith really is.

Renate, what was it like in your family when the arrests began?

RB: Yes, I was already married then - on paper. I had just finished my school exams, a year earlier than usual, and would have been drafted very soon into war-service with the *Arbeitsdienst*, and in order to free me from that I was allowed to marry. So when Dietrich was imprisoned we had our proper marriage soon afterwards. At the same time Hans von Dohnanyi - and Christel von Dohnanyi at first - was also put in prison. The Dohnanyi children were our own age and so they were very close to us and this really was a shock when both the parents of the Dohnanyi cousins disappeared. In a way one had been aware for a very long time, and as I said earlier you had to be careful what you said, so that from the beginning there was clearly a danger that this would happen. But now when it happened of course it was very bad, and yet there was never a kind of lamenting, with anybody. One just had the feeling that it had happened and I must say we were even proud about it, because of course we knew people who were against

Hitler. You knew that the people who were important in your mind would agree; that they would think of our people as being in prison for something which they had done against the government, and think 'This is really the right thing to do and perhaps I should have done something also.'

So it was terrible in a way yet it was not shame, not at all, that they were in prison, but of course one was very worried what would happen to them. Yet soon one had hope because Hans von Dohnanyi and his wife had thought everything out well beforehand together with Dietrich. Christine, Hans's wife, she knew a very, very great deal but she played the stupid little housewife very well and always gave very stupid answers so that they really thought she was stupid. So after five weeks she came out again. So one had hope when she came out that they wouldn't really find anything out. But first of course it was awful. And later when the others were put in prison, after July 20 1944, when the cousin Paul von Hase was killed and all these other people were killed, this was then quite a different feeling. One was frightened now that putting more and more people into prison they would really find something out, also about Hans and Dietrich, so that everyone was now in danger. That was very bad.

Then when Klaus Bonhoeffer and my father were taken to prison, one didn't think that perhaps they would find out too much. With Eberhard we didn't think it was dangerous at all, yet my father then got his death sentence together with Klaus in February. So of course all this time was very, very difficult. It must have been terrible for my grandparents because most of those arrested had smaller children and nobody got money anymore, and there were the air raids at the same time. So it was a very hard time in the family. Then we tried to get food for the people in prison. We only had our food-stamps which was very difficult, but then I must say it was astonishing how many people just gave us some of their food stamps. There were travel stamps for instance with which you could buy not only in the shop where you were registered, but anywhere. We got sent travel stamps for food by people. There were a lot of people who, when they heard, would send this kind of thing to my mother or to my grandparents, so that somehow we could always provide the food which we took then to the prison.

Did you know that your father had been sentenced to death?

RB: Yes, we knew that. We knew that he had his trial on this day and then we heard in the evening about his death sentence. And this of course was quite a shock, the death sentence for my father and also for Klaus. Theirs was the same trial the same day.

A strange thing happened. My father's brother who was a doctor in the army came right away when he heard about the death-sentence and wanted to go to the office of Freisler, the highest lawyer in the *Volksgericht* [People's Court] where the trials had taken place. An air-raid came and he sat in a basement there - in a shelter - and suddenly it was called out 'Doctor please! Doctor please! Something has happened.' So he went out and he was led to - Freisler! He'd apparently been hit by a bomb, and my uncle then tended him and said, 'I can't do anything, he's dead.' And it was Freisler. When he heard that, he said, 'This is the man whose last death sentence yesterday went unlawfully against my brother.'

The family still had links with a few non-Nazis in the background, through Christel von Dohnanyi. So these people said - after this had happened to Freisler - maybe some people don't want to have anything to do with it because many of them are superstitious, so that there's a good chance for Rüdiger if you ask for mercy. But then there was the danger that at the same time if we got mercy for my father the others in this group from the trial would be killed right away if they had the death sentence. So there was always the question, 'Shall we go on with this appeal for mercy? How dangerous is it?' Christel Dohnanyi found out how dangerous it was and so we held back a little on this plea for mercy. It was all drawn out until the end of the war and of course at the very end they just shot these people, and also shot some other people who had not even had a sentence but were known to be very strong anti-Nazis. We had hoped even after this death sentence that maybe the end of the war would come before they could be killed.

So was it some time before you heard that your father and Klaus had been killed?

RB: Yes, that was some time. Nobody of course told us, nobody knew, it was in the turmoil of the very end when they did it. After his release Eberhard went round in Berlin to ask here and there. Then he found a man from the prison who had been in one of the two groups - one of six and another of seven - of prisoners who had been driven away, having been told that they were being taken to another prison.

Quite near the prison, they were shot. But there was this one man who was not actually killed, somehow the bullet went through his mouth and he just fell down to the ground. They thought everybody was dead and the Nazis went off. And so when they had disappeared he just somehow tied something round his neck and went home, and really was all right again. And from him Eberhard got the whole story of all that happened. So we knew exactly how it went. Only later did we find out where these dead people had been brought to, and where in the end they were buried. There was a house where dead people who had been found anywhere were put, and of course in these last days of the war there were quite a lot. There was a large bomb crater in a cemetery right next to this house, and there they had buried them together with other people who were killed at the end. This was difficult to find out but Eberhard managed to.

Can you recall Eberhard's release?

RB: Yes of course. Really, with Eberhard we were not so concerned, not so worried, because he had been a soldier and he had been a bit more marginal. He was of course also in danger when he was in Italy as a soldier, so when he came to prison I was not so worried, in a way I was very glad to have him near! Of course you were worried . . . Yes, when he came out that was marvellous. I had a baby already at that time, and I lived with the Dohnanyis because of the baby - they lived a little further out of Berlin at Sakrow, a bus ride away. So Eberhard of course wanted to get to me but he didn't make it. He rang that he had tried to get out to the Dohnanyis but the bridge over the Havel was hit so there was no way to come to us. So Eberhard was staying with my mother and I was staying with my aunt. Of course I was very happy when I heard that he was out but there was my father and Klaus, who, so we had heard, had been taken to a prison elsewhere. So at the same time we were filled with worry. And then at this time the Russians were just arriving. So that was quite a turmoil - not a pure joy when he came home, because of all the other bad things which happened. And then at the very end my parents' house was bombed, while Eberhard was already there; it got a heavy grenade in it. So of course we were very happy about Eberhard but at the same time all the four other men, they didn't return. The longer it took, the more sure you were. Eberhard then made it later on to Sakrow where we stayed for about two more months and then we went back to Marienburger Allee.

When did you actually hear that Dietrich had been executed?

EB: Up to the middle of July we were still in doubt and so had great hopes that he might have survived somewhere in south Germany . In the meantime, as I said, I had been freed by the Soviets and in May and June had found out what had been the fate of Klaus Bonhoeffer and Rüdiger Schleicher, who had been with me in the same prison. We had found out nothing about Hans von Dohnanyi and really no message about Dietrich. The message about him went from Schlabrendorff, who escaped from Flossenbürg through the Alps to Italy where the surviving Martin Niemöller and others were, and from there to Geneva, and from Geneva to London, and came to George Bell and Bonhoeffer's colleagues in the German pastorate. They arranged with Dietrich's twin sister Sabine, who had emigrated to England, the memorial service at Holy Trinity Church, Kingsway, in London, at the end of July. By the way, the liturgy and so on was printed by the BBC because the service was being broadcast and on the back of one copy all the participants signed their names: George Bell, Forell and others, and it is very dear to me. Through the BBC transmitting that service to Berlin, we heard on the radio that for sure now Dietrich had been killed. At the same time Gisevius, a member of the German resistance movement who lived in Switzerland had come to Berlin and told us too.

Can you recall your feelings?

EB: One was prepared for such a thing for quite a time. And since we were now sure about Klaus and Rüdiger, what could we have hoped for Dietrich? Shall I say that . . . it's difficult to say . . . for me personally I felt at once a responsibility for Dietrich's heritage, and now being married to his niece and living near the Marienburger Allee - the two houses - and already putting in order Dietrich's papers left in his room, getting precious pieces from his mother and father, it meant that there was a continuation of the whole spirit of Dietrich and that household. This was there through my marriage with Renate of course, and living in that family as one of the few men now left who could help the afflicted families in some way, I was so involved and busy that there wasn't much time to sink into deep depression.

Isn't it a rather strange irony that because you were able to keep your friendship with Dietrich Bonhoeffer a secret from the Gestapo, and so survive, you were able to make known Dietrich Bonhoeffer to us later on?

EB: Or you can put the same thing another way. My relation to Renate saved me really. It gave me a good excuse during the hearings. And it made me the the natural heir of Dietrich's writings. There was for me no difficulty in access to Dietrich's archive - or what has now become his archive.

So looking back after forty years, what do you think is the continuing significance of the conspiracy for Germany - and indeed for other countries who were involved in the war?

EB: Isn't it the great German example? In our history we do not have many examples showing that qualities of humanity cannot be destroyed, and that belongs to the way Dietrich Bonhoeffer went to his death. In a full sense he is that kind of martyr who went freely into his own death and did not allow his death to be sheer black destruction. I think it is important not only for me but for our Church and for Germans that Dietrich Bonhoeffer was already thinking along these lines and then actually did it. Death for him was not just a cruel, senseless destruction of human being without any free will, but he was able to make that horrible Flossenbürg death into an act of his free will. It was a free entering into death, and in this way made out of a death which is a witness for more death, a witness for life.

Is that what he meant in his last reported words to Payne Best, 'This is the end, for me the beginning'?

E.B.: Maybe not all, but certainly part of it.

3
Peacemaker and Liberator

I begin with a story, which for me has become a kind of parable of involvement in peace issues. In February 1987 I spent a week in Moscow, a guest of the Baptists of the Soviet Union who were holding a Peace Seminar just prior to President Gorbachev's famous international Peace Forum. On Sunday morning, with the other British guest, I was taken to a Baptist church in a village among the birch woods and snow drifts just outside Moscow. I preached (only one of the five sermons at that service) through an interpreter. Afterwards there were the warm greetings typical of Russian people, the bear hugs and kisses from the men, fervent handshakes from the women. I shall always remember the old lady who came up to me, wrinkled face beaming under her shawl. She simply pointed to my heart, and then to her own.That seemed to say it all: we belong together, as part of the one body of Christ, not to mention the one human family and people for peace. Between herself and myself there was a whole history of apartness, a whole cultural and linguistic and political divide. But she has transcended it with a single, simple gesture.

A day or so later, during the seminar itself, I got into conversation with a Russian Baptist who could speak English - and there the problems began! He wanted to know, in the wake of the Rejkjavik summit meeting, how any one could possibly doubt the genuine desire of the Soviet President and people for peace. I do not usually find myself in the role of ambassador for the present occupants of either 10 Downing Street or the White House, nor did I become such on this occasion. But I found myself pushed into having to say why, in the west, many people do fear a 'Soviet threat'; that memories of Hungary 1956, Czechoslovakia 1968 and Afghanistan 1980, do not easily die away. He was baffled. I became frustrated. Complexities reared their head. How much easier if he too could speak no English and we could simply smile and make friendly gestures over the coffee.

Peace-making and human liberation need heartfelt commitment. They are the pearl of great price. They also plunge us into bewildering complexities in the political, social and economic fields. They are a matter of simple moral affirmation, welling from our gut humanity into spontaneous gestures, and pose highly technical challenges in decision-making. They require the innocence of doves and the wisdom of serpents. Moral commitment without being simplistic, realism without being evasive - someone who embodies these has to be listened to.

That is why I find the thought and witness of Dietrich Bonhoeffer so magnetic. In 1939 he could write to his brother Karl-Friedrich of the all-or-nothing nature of the struggle being waged by the minority Confessing Church: 'I do not know anything that is worth our whole-hearted commitment today, unless it is this cause. The main point is, not how many are in it, but that there are at least some.'[1] Equally, and with no loss of integrity, he could write in his *Ethics* that 'Telling the truth is not solely a matter of moral character; it is also a matter of correct appreciation of real situations and of serious reflection upon them. The more complex the actual situations of a man's life, the more responsible and the more difficult will be his task of "telling the truth"'.[2] In her novel *Last Score* Storm Jameson has one of her more perceptive characters saying: 'Nothing is of the least importance except being able to love. It's frightfully difficult - unless like Christ you have a talent for it. Nowadays we're so clever and unloving we shall probably kill everyone in the world - which is not worse than killing one child but, if there's no one left to repent, more malicious and stupid'.[3] Bonhoeffer for me is prophetic because in his writings and life, he held to that kind of simple insight without being simplistic, amid all the tensions and contradictions of the church struggle and the political resistance.

Tensions and conflicts are familiar to anyone who even begins active involvement in justice and peace issues. Who among us, campaigning for world development, has not felt uneasy about the tensions between charity and political change? Which of us, expressing solidarity with the struggle to end unjust rule in Southern Africa, has not winced at the accusation of being self-righteous from a safe distance? How many of us, calling for the overcoming of fear as an obstacle to disarmament, have not actually feared for ourselves when charged with our lack of patriotism? Peace-making can be a notably unpeaceful experience. We are unlikely to get very far unless we are able to handle creatively the often warring emotions and impulses within ourselves. Here again Bonhoeffer is instructive. He knew only too well about living with tensions, and in one of his most penetrating prison letters to Eberhard Bethge he speaks about the way in which faith enables a diversity of emotions (note, emotions or feelings, not ideas!) to co-exist in a harmony or 'polyphony'. Being a musician, he exploits the metaphor for all it is worth. Faith in God is the *cantus firmus*, the basic melody, to which all the other levels of life, in freedom, can be in counterpoint.[4] And he goes on in another letter, to complain of the many people in prison who cannot harbour conflicting emotions at the same time - they are swayed either by fear, or greed, or pride:

> They miss the fullness of life and the wholeness of an independent existence . . . By contrast, Christianity puts us into many different dimensions of life at the same time; we make room in ourselves, to some extent, for God and the whole world. We rejoice with those who rejoice, and weep with those who weep; we are anxious. . . about our life, but at the same time we must think about things much more important than life itself. When the alert goes, for instance: as soon as we turn our minds from worrying about our own safety to the task of helping other people to keep calm, the situation is completely changed; life isn't pushed back into a single dimension, but is kept multi-dimensional and polyphonous.[5]

There is material here for a spirituality of peace-making and liberation. So often action and witness are vitiated by the assumption that purity of heart means only to feel one thing, whereas as Kierkegaard put it (not to mention Jesus in Gethsemane), it is to *will* one thing - a very different matter.

Take tomorrow, for example, Remembrance Sunday. Time and again clergy of all denominations, and of all ages, say how mixed their feelings are on this occasion, and there are some who try to duck out of the observance altogether. They feel caught between their repugnance at what can easily be a militaristic and chauvinistic occasion, and their desire to witness nonetheless to the gospel of reconciliation; between the pastoral needs of those in their congregations who do literally remember the fallen, and the impatient desire of younger members to forget the old world of battles long ago, and to campaign for peace today. Between red poppy and white. The complex of feelings is indeed formidable, but not new. It was well-known to Dietrich Bonhoeffer, as is clear from the lecture to his students in the seminary at Finkenwalde, on the conduct of the German Remembrance Day. Bonhoeffer, we should remember, was at this time strongly pacifist in tendency, had lost an elder brother in the 1914-18 War, and never forgot the devastating grief borne by his mother at this loss. Moreover, the German Remembrance Day had originally been known as *Volkstrauertag* - People's Day of Mourning - but under Hitler it became *Heldengedenktag*, Heroes' Remembrance Day. Bonhoeffer insisted that the day still be kept with all solemnity amidst the crude chauvinistic and ideological pressures. 'Whoever speaks only mockingly or moralistically about 1914-18 makes his words not worth believing'[6]. The preacher on that day, said Bonhoeffer, must begin with consolation for the mourners and injured, and thankfulness for the sacrifices made. So it is 'From pride and grief through Christ to repentance' - and the note of repentance is itself many textured:

> Repentance - since God is so good, preserving us even despite and through 1914-18. Repentance - because we know in the event of the World War that our world is a lost world, because war is, according to the Word of the Lord, the omen of the final break-up of the world under God's assize. Repentance - because war is a temptation of our belief in God and robs many of their faith. Repentance - for war is sin against God's gospel of peace. Repentance - since Christianity and the churches in general frivolously make themselves accomplices in crime, by blessing war and pronouncing it righteous before God. . . . Repentance - because Christians oppose Christians, because the World War was a war of 'Christian' peoples amongst each other. 'Christ in the trenches' - that means judgment on a godless world. But also the infinite love of God, which enters into this godlessness and has borne all sin. And also the faith in this divine mercy in the cross of Christ, where there is forgiveness.[7]

As well as illustrating Bonhoeffer's 'polyphonous' understanding of life, that quotation conveniently summarizes his whole theological rejection of war. But we need to look, positively, at his understanding of peace and liberation.

Bonhoeffer as peacemaker

Bonhoeffer as peacemaker is the sophisticated young German theologian who at Union Seminary, New York, during 1930-31, prompted by his new-found friend the young French pastor and pacifist Jean Lasserre, was stopped in his tracks by the Sermon on the Mount. Bonhoeffer as peacemaker is the enthusiastic (to his seniors, tiresomely so) youth secretary of the World Alliance for Promoting International Friendship Through the Churches from 1931 onwards, sharing in conferences in England, Germany, Czechosolovakia and elsewhere, and eventually serving on the committee of the Ecumenical

Council for Life and Work, chaired by his spiritual father in God, George Bell, Bishop of Chichester. Bonhoeffer as peacemaker is the young German who loved his country deeply, yet who dared to face the outcry from those nationalist Christians and theologians who regarded any involvement in these internationalist ecumenical activities as treachery to the Fatherland. Bonhoeffer the peacemaker is the young man who, during the ecumenical peace conference at Fanö in 1934, while relaxing on the beach was asked what he would do if war broke out, and, picking up a handful of sand and letting it run through his fingers said, 'I will pray that God will give me the strength not to take up arms.' Bonhoeffer the peacemaker is the Director of the Confessing Church Seminary at Finkenwalde, who in May 1935 sat with his students listening on the radio to Hitler 's speech announcing the introduction of military conscription, and who did not share his students' glee at this news, to their bewilderment. Bonhoeffer the peacemaker is the one who, ever so gently, suggested to those ordinands, who were anxious to prove that service in the Confessing Church did not signify any lack of patriotism, that the pacifist way should at least be considered a valid Christian option. Bonhoeffer the peacemaker is the author of *The Cost of Discipleship*, first given as lectures in the seminary, insisting that Jesus' commands in the Sermon on the Mount are to be obeyed concretely, that grace is costly: '

> *Blessed are the peacemakers: for they shall be called the children of God.'* The followers of Jesus have been called to peace. When he called them they found their peace, for he is their peace. But now they are told that they must not only have peace but make it. And to that end they renounce all violence and tumult. In the cause of Christ nothing is to be gained by such methods. His kingdom is one of peace, and the mutual greeting of his flock is a greeting of peace. His disciples keep the peace by choosing to endure suffering rather than inflict it on others. They maintain fellowship where others would break it off. They renounce all self-assertion, and quietly suffer in the face of hatred and wrong. In so doing they overcome evil with good, and establish the peace of God in the midst of a world of war and hate.[8]

Bonhoeffer the peacemaker is the one who in 1939 determined to avoid conscription into Hitler's aggressive war machine by going to the United States in that fateful visit of a few weeks. Bonhoeffer the peacemaker is the one who, writing his *Ethics* during the Second World War, exposed the singularly godless nature of modern warfare, in terms which it is hard to realise were penned before the advent of atomic weapons. In previous ages, he writes, war between Christian peoples had been seen as a method of seeking divine arbitration over conflicting issues, and therefore certain rules for the conduct of war were at least theoretically recognized. But loss of faith, loss of any sense of God's judgment in history, allows total war which 'makes use of all conceivable means which may possibly serve the purpose of national self-preservation', 'in which everything, even crime, is justified if it serves to further our own cause, and in which the enemy, whether he be armed or defenceless, is treated as a criminal.'[9]

In the portrait of Bonhoeffer the peacemaker, one feature above all stands out. Bonhoeffer the peacemaker was Bonhoeffer the ecumenical churchman. For him, peace was not just an item on the agenda of the international ecumenical movement: peace actually was what the gathering together of the scattered members of the Body of Christ was all about. Time and again during the early 1930s he challenged the ecumenical organizations to regard themselves, far more seriously than they were doing, as the visible manifestation of the church of Christ, and to speak and act accordingly. He laid down his starkest challenge to the Fanö Peace Conference in 1934:

> There shall be peace because of the church of Christ, for the sake of which the world exists. And this church of Christ lives at one and the same time in all peoples, yet beyond all boundaries, whether national, political, social or racial. And the brothers who make up this church are bound together, through the commandment of the one Lord Christ, whose Word they hear, more inseparably than men are bound by all the ties of common history, of blood, of class and of language. All these ties, which are part of our world, are valid ties, not indifferent; but in the presence of Christ they are not ultimate bonds. For the members of the ecumenical church, in so far as they hold to Christ, his word, his commandment of peace is more holy, more inviolable than the most revered words and works of the natural world.[10]

Over fifty years later, Bonhoeffer's challenge sounds no less exciting - or disturbing - than it must have done then. Most Christians, it has to be frankly recognized, see themselves as primarily citizens of their respective nation-states who happen to be members of their particular churches, rather than as first and foremost members of the *una sancta*, the one holy, catholic and apostolic church in its diaspora among the nations. There are also immensely powerful political forces with vested interests in keeping the religious consciousness confined within the sense of national identity. Mrs Margaret Thatcher recently assumed that confinement in her speech, delivered in Bruges, on the European community. 'Visit the great churches and cathedrals of Britain,' said the Prime Minister, listing the historic glories of the British scene: 'all bear witness to the cultural riches which we have drawn from Europe - and Europeans from us.' A little more reflection on the original purpose of those buildings is in order, however, and it hardly supports a mentality which would view Europe from behind the battlements of an 'island fortress.' The great cathedrals were not just 'cultural riches' built for latter-day tourists. They were built to the glory of a God whose creative and redemptive love gathered into a single piece heaven and earth and everything in it, a vision embodied in the soaring unity of stone and glass. This unifying view of Christendom pre-dated any concern with 'national identity'. It was striking that in Mrs Thatcher's speech, there was the barest passing reference to 'Christendom', and no mention at all of Christianity as the living faith which has been the single most unifying element in European history. It would be interesting to know what she would make of Bonhoeffer's assertion that 'the form of Christ is the unity of the western nations and that for this reason no single one of these nations can exist by itself or even be conceived as existing by itself'[11]. To take seriously the transnational nature of the one Christian church considerably relativizes the 'east and west' mind-set as well as the status of national identity, as will perhaps be seen as the new Europe struggles to take shape in the age of Glasnost. As Jan Milic Lochman, the Czech theologian with the rare distinction of having lived, studied and worked in both east and west, states: 'both parts of Europe represent radically secularized cultures, be it militant official atheism in the East or practical irreligiosity in the relativistic West.'[12]

If we are to take Bonhoeffer's challenge seriously today, it will mean recognizing that the very existence of the Christian Church in both east and west, rich north and poor south, is meant to be the Holy Spirit's spontaneous gesture. Or in the more theologically respectable language of today, the church is a sign upon the earth, a witness to the new humanity in the midst of the old. In asking for the church to be radically transformed, Bonhoeffer the peace-making ecumenist is simply wanting the church to believe in itself for what it really is, and that will involve questioning all complicity in national self-interest. Suppose, for example, one Sunday morning a typical congregation singing 'The Church's one foundation Is Jesus Christ her Lord' were to be stopped in mid-verse and asked whether they really believed in the lines:

> Elect from every nation
> Yet one o'er all the earth

- suppose the minister was to ask them how this was to be reconciled with their acquiescence in policies of mass-destruction towards peoples where an even higher proportion of the population than in Britain was in church at that very moment (namely the USSR) one can imagine the effect. Why, to my knowledge, did no church leader of any denomination in the United Kingdom correct Mrs Thatcher for concluding her address to the General Assembly of the Church of Scotland earlier this year [1988] by extolling the virtues of the hymn 'I vow to thee, my country'? In the light of the doctrine of the one, holy catholic and apostolic church, and in the light of any commitment to ecumenism (which must mean a concern for the church of the *oikumene*, the church of the whole inhabited earth) such sentiments are not merely heretical but pagan. If the response is that such issues are on the merely symbolic level, that is to miss the point that one of the reasons for the present strength of the 'new right' in politics is its profound understanding, and skilful manipulation, of the symbols and imagery by which people at large are motivated, especially in the areas of national loyalty and religion. We must rescue our cathedrals, our hymns, and our bibles, we must retrieve our whole Christian tradition which is being hi-jacked by a sinister new form of nationalism. Remember the last recorded words of Bonhoeffer the peace-maker, to Captain Payne Best as he was led off to his last and fatal interrogation, his message to Bishop George Bell: 'Tell him . . . with him I believe in the principle of our universal Christian brotherhood which rises above all national interests, and that our victory is certain.' Brothers and sisters, he is placing great hopes and confidence in us, over forty years on!

Bonhoeffer the liberator

Bonhoeffer the liberator is the one who stated that only one who cries out for the Jews has the right to sing Gregorian chant. Bonhoeffer the liberator is the one who made that momentous decision to return from the safety of New York in the summer of 1939, to share in all the trials of his people in war. Bonhoeffer the liberator is the Lutheran who suspended the typical Lutheran doctrine of unquestioning obedience to the state authorities as ordained of God, and instead acted out of a sense of civil courage and free responsibility for the good of his oppressed neighbours. Bonhoeffer the liberator is the one who thus joined the employ of the *Abwehr* in 1940 as a member of the resistance committed to the overthrow of Hitler and to negotiating a just peace with the allies. Bonhoeffer the liberator is the one who was prepared to accept that this conspiracy would eventually entail violence. We are therefore quite entitled to ask, 'Is Bonhoeffer the liberator the same person as Bonhoeffer the peacemaker?' Did his entry into the conspiracy signify that - as I recall one reviewer putting it - he 'slipped' from his earlier pacifism? This is not just a question of Bonhoeffer biography, of course. It is a personal focusing of the wider tension between the quest for peace and the demands of justice, the kind of question which is daily facing so many in Latin and Central America and in Southern Africa. 'I am mad enough still to believe in non-violence', a friend who is a black pastor in South Africa tells me.

It is, first, important to note that from the beginning Dietrich Bonhoeffer warned against talking of 'peace' in an unqualified sense. In those early 1930s days of his involvement in the ecumenical peace movement, he had hard things to say against nationalists - especially from his own country - who were elevating 'nation', 'race' and 'people' into inviolable and sacred 'orders of creation' which must be preserved at all costs. This pseudo-theology, he argued, provided the justification for war. But equally, and in a discomforting way, he had sharp criticisms of those Christians who, especially in the Anglo-Saxon world (Britain and the United States) made 'peace' an ideal in itself, and thus another 'order of creation'. Both the nationalist and the naive internationalist were guilty of divorcing their ideals from the issues of truth and justice. The gospel certainly declares against war, said Bonhoeffer, but may equally allow pursuit of conflict where truth and justice are at stake. 'Struggle is not an order of creation, but it can be an order of preservation for Christ's new creation. Struggle can in some cases guarantee openness for the revelation in Christ better than external peace, in that it breaks apart the hardened, self-enclosed order.'[13]

The moment when those words really came alive for me was in September 1985 when, in Khotso House, then headquarters of the South African Council of Churches in Johannesburg, I was present at the public launching of the now famous *Kairos Document*. That 'Challenge to the Church' inveighs against the cheap use of the word 'reconciliation', which in the South African context all too often is a demand for peace without justice, a cloak for the continuance of oppression under the pretext of 'law and order'. It states:

> In our situation in South Africa today it would be totally un-Christian to plead for reconciliation and peace before the present injustices have been removed. Any such plea plays into the hands of the oppressor by trying to persuade those of us who are

oppressed to accept our oppression and to become reconciled to the intolerable crimes that are committed against us. That is not Christian reconciliation, it is sin. It is asking us to become accomplices in our own oppression, to become servants of the devil. No reconciliation is possible in South Africa without justice. [14]

It is too much to say that Bonhoeffer has inspired the *Kairos Document* (though he has inspired not a few of its signatories), but he certainly would have understood it! He would have understood it, first, let us be under no illusions, as a young German in the latter days of the Weimar Republic, who, though no nationalist, shared the smarting at the injustice of the Versailles Treaty. When Bonhoeffer in his early ecumenical days talked of the struggle for truth and justice he was including the necessity of British, French and American Christians realizing just how Germans like himself felt - and how that particular injustice was contributing to the rise of Nazism. There is in fact an unmistakeable line of continuity from that Bonhoeffer, through the Bonhoeffer who shared the life of blacks in New York's ghettoes during 1930-31, through the pastor-lecturer who took on a confirmation-class in a working-class area of Berlin, through the Bonhoeffer who as early as 1933 was raising questions about the Church's political responsibility for the oppressed Jews, right through to the Bonhoeffer who grieved that his Church - even his Confessing Church - had not opened its mouth for the dumb, and who in the end felt it his duty to join in the conspiracy. It is quite wrong to see Bonhoeffer as a kind of proto-liberation theologian. But one can see why he has been an important stimulus to many liberation theologians of today. He, the academic of aristocratic background, discovered that things look very different among the oppressed. It was a view he summed up in that little paper written shortly before his arrest in 1943, 'After Ten Years', where he speaks of the incomparable value of the experience brought by the conspiracy, in sharing 'the view from below':

We have for once learnt to see the great events of world history from below, from the perspective of the outcast, the suspects, the maltreated, the powerless, the oppressed, the reviled - in short, from the perspective of those who suffer.[15]

But what about the violence issue? Was Bonhoeffer the conspirator being inconsistent with the earlier days of *The Cost of Discipleship*? He who had said he would pray for strength not to take up arms had implicitly done so - against his own country's leader. But *The Cost of Discipleship* was about Christians refusing to use violence in their own defence and interests. It was not addressing the later, hideous situation of the systematic annihilation of a whole people, the holocaust. Yes, Bonhoeffer knew he was incurring guilt by involvement in the conspiracy. But he knew he would incur even more guilt by pursuing an innocent detachment. His was the kind of bearing of guilt he writes about in his *Ethics*, the becoming guilty for the sake of others, refusing to make any claims of self-justification, and placing oneself solely before God in free responsibility.[16]

Peace, liberation . . . and community

It is clear that to call Bonhoeffer a peace-maker needs qualifying by the title liberator. And if we had put it the other way round , to call him a liberator first we should have had to qualify that by his concern for peace. That prompts us to ask: is there yet another concern, which embraces his commitment both to peace and to justice? Finding the right formula for this relationship is, again, not just a Bonhoeffer question. It is the question of humanity's chances in the modern world. Peace, unqualified, can be another term for silent oppression. Liberation, unqualified, can be another way of expressing a form of superiority. An Aboriginal Australian woman has written:

If you have come
to help me
you are wasting
your time
But
if you have come
because
your liberation
is bound up
with mine
then let us work
together.[17]

The term is - community. Listen to this narrative about two young people on the verge of falling in love:

Suddenly he said, surprised at himself, 'I think that all of that will come by itself, Renate.' These words were like a liberation for both of them.

What came by itself was that the two got into a really free and easy conversation. They didn't question each other; what each wanted to say of one's life, one's views, one's closest friends, was to be said freely. In this way one of those rare and happy conversations came about in which each word is taken as the free gift of the one to the other. As it goes with gift giving, first there are only small, groping signs, timid unspoken questions as it were, as to whether the other is ready to receive a gift - unwanted gifts humiliate giver and recipient - but the acceptance of one's gift is the greatest gift the giver receives. Precisely because everything depends on the inner freedom of the giver and the recipient no one who is aware of that fact gives or takes everything all at once. It is a slow, free process of mutual bonding.

Now what would Dietrich Bonhoeffer the sophisticated theologian have thought of this little piece of romantic fiction? Quite a lot, since he himself wrote it in prison, as part of his attempted novel![18] He was simply putting in another key a central theme of his entire theology and career. 'Life Together' was not just the title of Bonhoeffer's great little book on community life in the seminary. It was the core of his view of the sociality of human existence in his early study on the church, *Sanctorum Communio* - the church is 'Christ existing as community' - through to the *Ethics* and the prison letters. In that attempted novel written in prison, one of the main characters, Major von Brake, says: 'For me the main question for people and nations is whether or not they have learned to live with other people and nations. To me that is more important than all their ideas, thoughts and convictions'[19]. Peace and liberation can cohere only in community, and Bonhoeffer here makes clear that this is ultimately true not only in the interpersonal realm but in the international too. This thought is quite subversive of our normal cast of mind when thinking of national loyalty and identity. The existence of a community is conventionally thought of as discrete and self-sufficient, with an identity already known to itself. Such self-affirmation is entirely justified when the community is gravely threatened and its rights disregarded by a powerful aggressor (hence the motivation of, for example, black consciousness in Southern Africa). But there can be no real peace or real freedom where the otherness of other peoples is regarded simply as alienation or threat. In the biblical witness, nothing is more striking than, on the one hand, the particular calling of Israel as a distinct people, and on the other hand the crucial role of the 'stranger', the foreigner, in the life of that people. It is the stranger and the sojourner [20] who remind Israel of her real identity, that she too was a slave in the land of Egypt, that she owes everything to the liberating compassion of the Exodus God. It is the Moabite Ruth who in remaining with her mother-in-law come what may, becomes both a picture and a means of God's faithfulness to his people. It is the Roman centurion who illustrates for Jesus true Israelite faith, and the Samaritan who fulfils the great commandment. The precise kind of awareness which the foreigner prompts can be extremely various . On occasion it can be the painful exposure of the community's own endemic failures to pursue truth and justice. But in whatever way, the community needs the 'foreigner' to become aware of who it is, rather than to be reminded of what it is not.

Indeed, in Bonhoeffer's novel the young girl Renate with whom the chief character Christoph is falling in love is, unexpectedly, a South African. A main theme of this attempted fiction is the nature of German society, and what it means to be German. It would seem that Bonhoeffer has felt the need to introduce a complete stranger into the plot, because he, through Christoph, needs a stranger with whom he can converse about his homeland. Christoph resolves to be her guide to Germany. It is only as he sets about imagining this interpretative task, that he realises how elusive 'Germany' is, how many Germanies, good and less good, there seem to be. It is in meeting her that he meets his own people and land anew.

That the 'stranger' may be highly necessary to the community and its self-understanding was thus no strange thought to Dietrich Bonhoeffer. In the final analysis it is bound up with his understanding of Jesus Christ. European Christian identity, in Bonhoeffer's eyes, was too important to be left to the Christians. It is the Jew who 'keeps open the question of Christ'[21] - how we still have to learn that there is a mission of the Jews to Christianity! Bonhoeffer's Christ, like Luther's, was a strange Christ, and 'must provoke contradiction and hostility'. 'He goes incognito, a beggar among beggars, as an outcast among outcasts, as despairing among the despairing, as dying among the dying. He also goes as sinner among the sinners, yet . . . as sinless among sinners.'[22] This Christ who is the strangest of strangers to all communities, is the one who is utterly for us, in all our communities. He himself is our true community. No alienation, no enmity is greater than that between the world and God, which he overcame on the cross. That is why there is hope for community even between the human communities that seem strangest to each other. That hope does not smother, but can enable, struggles for truth and justice to be pursued with the utmost vigour and sides to be taken with the most passionate conviction in the here and now, yet without self-destructive hatred of the other. Wouldn't it be good to know for whom Bonhoeffer was praying as he knelt at the scaffold at Flossenbürg? In March this year, when Desmond Tutu, Allan Boesak and other South African Church leaders produced that prophetic and defiant call to President Botha to rescind the banning of black rights' organizations, few probably noticed the final phrase of their letter: God bless you.

The revolutionary implications of taking up these insights into community lie on the agenda of those who would seek, with Dietrich Bonhoeffer, a church for peacemaking and liberation among the nations today. The day we can meet sisters and brothers from different nationalities, from different cultures, from different political systems, neither aggressively nor defensively, but with a sense of mutual dependence for discovering (rather than just asserting) who we are, we shall be experiencing both peace and liberation: including that most profound liberation, liberation from the accursed treadmill of self-justification, the liberation which is at the heart of the gospel (Cf Romans 5.1ff). What polyphony there will be in the music we shall make then!

4
The Confessing Church Tradition and its Relation to Patriotism in a Nuclear Age

'Christians in this country will have to form a Confessing Church in order to protest against the blasphemy of nuclear weapons.' This kind of remark, not infrequently heard these days, testifies to the persistence of a 'Confessing Church tradition' in the modern Christian consciousness. Of course there has only been one church which has actually worn the title as its name, the Confessing Church (*Die Bekennende Kirche*) of Germany. Formed in 1934, it comprised those congregations, pastors and members of the Evangelical (that is, Protestant) Church who determined to resist the nazification of church order and Christian doctrine. With Karl Barth as its leading theological inspiration, Martin Niemöller as its chief symbol of resistance through his eight-year imprisonment, and Dietrich Bonhoeffer - who ventured into the political conspiracy against Hitler - its most famous child and martyr, the German Confessing Church provides one of the most evocative historical images of the corporate Christian conscience refusing to render unto Caesar that which belongs to God. The 'Confessing Church tradition' largely clusters round this instance.

Its roots in the sixteenth-century Reformation, however, need to be noted. The early Reformers made a distinction between essential, highly significant matters of faith and practice on the one hand, and *adiaphora*, neutral or insignificant matters, on the other. But, as for example in the Formula of Concord (1577), it was recognized that in certain extreme conditions matters of church order and custom which in 'normal' circumstances might be considered to be *adiaphora* could assume great significance, nothing less than the gospel itself being at stake. In such a time, 'the congregation of God, yes, every Christian, but especially the preachers of the Word' were required to make public confession by word as well as deed. Galatians 2 - where Paul recalls his rebuke to Peter for refusing to eat with gentiles - was cited as one such instance where what might seemingly be a matter of mere custom involved a decision for or against the gospel itself. In Reformation tradition the matter has been summarized thus: *in statu confessionis nil adiaphoron* (in a situation of confession there are no neutral matters).

In 1934 in Germany, the year after Hitler's accession, matters of church order and pastoral office suddenly no longer remained *adiaphora*. The so-called German Christians, a movement formed by the fusion of various pro-Nazi groups of Protestant provenance, were campaigning for the *Gleichshaltung* (conformation) of the Evangelical Church to the new German order. The Führer-principle was to be introduced into church government and, most ominously, so was the programme of 'aryanization'. No-one of Jewish 'race' would be allowed to hold pastoral office. It was in opposition to such measures that the Pastors' Emergency League had been formed under Martin Niemöller and that, in May 1934, the national Confessing Synod meeting at Barmen in the Ruhr unanimously adopted the Barmen Theological Declaration, effectively the founding charter of the Confessing Church. Its basic claim was that only on such terms could the German Evangelical Church - which is what the Confessing Church claimed to be in truth - remain true to its own constitution. Not race, not the imposition of political principle or ideology, but faith in God's revelation in Christ constituted that Church. Whatever may be said about the Confessing Church - and it was some of its founders and most ardent supporters who were later to be foremost among its critics - it did represent throughout the Third Reich a denial of the satisfaction of the complete claims of the totalitarian state.

It is largely out of the German Church Struggle that there has entered contemporary currency the technical-sounding phrase *status confessionis*, to indicate a situation where a stand has to be taken by the church on specific issues, not simply on 'moral' grounds but out of a conviction that the very gospel of Christ will otherwise be denied or fatally compromised. In the Third Reich, to have allowed the 'Aryan clause' into the church constitution, even though it would have affected relatively very few persons directly, would have meant that Jesus Christ was no longer believed to be Lord of that church, and that baptism and faith in the forgiveness of sins were no longer the basis of unity in that church. The *status confessionis* has been invoked in a number of subsequent cases, most notably on the issue of racism. The World Lutheran Federation in 1977 declared a *status confessionis* in relation to apartheid, the essence of the church being felt to be at issue. The World Alliance of Reformed Churches made a similar declaration in 1982. In South Africa itself the example of the German Confessing Church has provided a powerfully symbolic case-study of Christian resistance to state oppression supported by religious justification, and the Dutch Reformed Mission Church, with other groups, has condemned apartheid as a heresy and called for a *status confessionis* to be recognized. In fact the existence of a 'confessing church' movement in South Africa has been taken for granted by many there for over 25 years.[1] The *status confessionis* has also been invoked in relation to nuclear arms. In 1958 Karl Barth called for a church confession in view of the 'godless' character of nuclear weaponry which effectively denies all three articles of the Christian creed. In 1981 the Reformieter Bund Churches of the German Federal Republic declared that a *status confessionis* had been provoked by the marshalling of weapons amounting to 'a blasphemy destroying all life.' A heated controversy ensued with the other Protestant Churches of West Germany which illustrated the problems involved in invoking 'confession' in relation to specific issues with a major political bearing. Among the critics of the RB statement were many, for example, who agreed with the condemnation of nuclear weapons as a necessary part of the ethical, indeed prophetic, witness of the church, but who felt that to claim that it was an issue whereby the church's faith itself was under trial was an over-dramatization - indeed one which would obscure for many people both the ethical and technical aspects of disarmament. The debate revealed the difficulty that there are no clear, objective criteria as to when in any particular case events have moved so far as to warrant the term *status confessionis*. (It should also be noted that in the Netherlands the Reformed Church had previously issued a number of very forthright declarations on nuclear arms to the point of stating that the church's faith was being put to the test by the issue, but not specifically invoking the *status confessionis*).

Nevertheless, to be within the 'Confessing Church tradition' does not require exact conformity to the technicalities of correct theological terminology. We may say that in essence a 'confessing church': -

- identifies the kingdom of God in contradistinction to all the principalities and powers of this world;
- by word and deed declares its obedient faith to be in that kingdom alone;

- and, in face of whatever wrath its witness provokes from the world, entrusts its safety and future solely to God.

Wherever a Christian community acts and speaks and prays in this way, or acknowledges that in its own situation it may be called upon to do so and behaves consistently with that possibility, or acknowledges in repentance that it has failed to do so when the *kairos* dawned in the past, it may be said to be within the 'Confessing Church tradition' regardless of the exact form its 'confession' takes. Notice, however, the qualifying terms used in our summary of 'confessing' criteria: *in contradistinction to all*. . .; in that kingdom *alone*; . . . *solely* to God. Crucial to confession is its decisiveness (Latin *de-cidere*, to cut away), the choice of an either / or, the bold leap to the *one* object of faith and loyalty above all else. Such determined single-mindedness, such ruthless (one might say puritanical) passion to find the one thing needful, is the passion of a community to rediscover and to reassert its own identity. It is like a person subjected to all manner of assumptions, threats, cajolery and flattery to conform to the images and roles desired by family, friends or teachers, suddenly crying out 'I'm not any of these - I'm me!' Only, in the church's case, the 'I'm me' is expressed in terms of reference to the One 'whose we are and whom we serve.'

But to speak of a community desiring to rediscover and to reassert its identity is, taken as it stands, and recalling actual historical experience as distinct from theoretical idealizing, to speak less of the Christian Church than of the nation-state in the modern world. Reinhold Niebuhr's words require very little qualification over half a century since he wrote:

> The modern nation is the human group of strongest social cohesion, of most undisputed social authority and of most clearly defined membership. The church may have challenged its pre-eminence in the Middle Ages, and the economic class may compete with it for the loyalty of man in our own day; yet it remains, as it has been since the seventeenth century, the most absolute of all human associations.[2]

That is a fact which generations of peace-campaigners have deplored this century, but one that has bluntly refused to go away on that account. Time and again Christian organizations and conferences devoted to peace have stressed the 'absurdity' of the idea of war between civilized nations, and have hoped in the deterrent effect of the bitter experiences of suffering in recent wars as a safeguard against future follies. Time and again all this has proved wishful thinking once a time of international crisis occurs, when the bonds of national solidarity reassert themselves and patriotic fervour sweeps all before it. Surveying the ecumenical peace movement of the inter-war years, J.S. Conway concludes soberly:

> In the eyes of many of its critics the Christian peace movement in the twentieth century has been the refuge of idealists or utopians whose theology was weak, whose politics were naive and unrealistic, and whose public advocacy was inadequate. These pacifists failed to recognize that the social function of the mainline churches, and of the educated bourgeoisie which upheld them, was largely, if unconsciously, preservative of the existing social order, with an attendant attachment to the nation state and its apparatus of military defence forces, whose use could be justified in time of crisis.[3]

Exceedingly deep and powerful dynamics are at work in human collective loyalties, especially at the level of a people and nation. Nor can this be viewed wholly negatively. To be identified with a particular community with its peculiar mix of land, language, custom, historical experience and tradition, is indeed one of the most enriching elements in any person's social awareness. Conversely, it is largely through the development of a definable 'national community' with its concomitant political apparatus and legal system, that the organization of so much that we take for granted as good and valuable becomes possible, from an educational system to a national health service to a football league. One cannot just be 'human' in an undefined way, shapeless and abstract, and this applies to us socially as well as individually. Nationality is part of our earthiness, and there is about as much point in passing moral sentence upon it in the abstract as there is in condemning, say, sexuality per se. The question is that of diagnosing where national feelings of identity and loyalty become destructive instead of preservative, death-dealing instead of life-enriching. At least two such critical points may be recognized.

One such point is where nationhood becomes absolutized as a value of ultimate concern for its own sake. Thus:

> I vow to thee, my country - all earthly things above -
> Entire and whole and perfect, the service of my love,
> The love that asks no question . . .
>
> *(Cecil Spring Rice, 1859-1918)*

> Whoever is prepared to make the national cause his own to such an extent that he knows no higher ideal than the welfare of his nation: whoever has understood our great national anthem 'Deutschland *über* alles', to mean that nothing in this wide world surpasses in his eyes this Germany, people and land - that man is a [National] Socialist.[4]
>
> *(Adolf Hitler, 1889-1945)*

Theologically, this is to equate the national cause with the kingdom of God. The equation can take a number of forms, some overtly religious as in the notion of a 'chosen people' with a triumphalist, messianic mission to the rest of the world. Just before and during the Third Reich, the absolutization of nation and the sanctification of unquestioning patriotism was given theological justification by those Protestant theologians who elevated race and nation to the status of 'orders of creation', that is, structures of human existence which are of original and eternal significance as ordained by God, and therefore to be maintained in all their 'purity' by whatever means possible. As Dietrich Bonhoeffer observed this was exactly the theology which provided the justification for war. Bonhoeffer was too much of a realist to deny the reality of national existence (and he never attempted to disown his Germanness) but he recognized the vital theological distinction between an 'order of creation' and an *order of preservation*. The latter is a phenomenon which God, by his providential care, permits to arise within human history for the sustenance of human life. The nation is one such order of preservation. Its existence however is not unconditional since it is not itself an ultimate item in the divine purpose. Its role is to provide a matrix of community as a preparation for what is ultimate, namely the gospel itself. Should the nation or any other order of preservation prove to become totally closed to the reception of the gospel then it falls under the divine judgment and it may be removed. Bonhoeffer himself knew that as war approached Christians in Germany would 'face the terrible alternative of willing the defeat of their nation in order that Christian civilization may survive, or willing the victory of their nation and thereby destroying our civilization.'[5]

That perhaps was the sharpest-ever expression of the contradiction by the 'Confessing Church tradition' of conventional patriotism in our time. We should note, however, that far from distancing himself from his country, Bonhoeffer in writing these words was conveying his decision to return to Germany from America, to enter into the most intimate and fateful solidarity with his people as their crisis deepened. We shall mention this aspect of a 'confessing patriotism' again later.

A second critical point in the perversion or 'demonization' of national identity and loyalty occurs when loyalty to nation effectively depends upon the threatening 'enemy-image' of another nation or group of nations. The 'enemy' provides the justification for one's own nation-state in its present form. The evil empire of the Soviet Union supplies the grand rationale for everything that the Pentagon, NATO and the 'Free World' aspire to achieve for the maintenance of their own 'security'. The converse happens too of course. It is not simply that the 'enemy' is open to criticism or even condemnation, but that the enemy on principle is never allowed to be other than a menace. The requirement to believe the worst about the other side means that there is in reality very little genuine attachment to the reality of one's own country, let alone any ability to examine it in critical love. A spurious patriotism is masquerading as 'love of country'. In fact what is being covered up by such chauvinism is a deep insecurity due to a lack of positive identity in oneself.

The 'Confessing Church' stand is a flagrant declaration of a specifically Christian identity and obedience. We may take the Barmen Declaration of 1934 as our case-study. In six relatively brief paragraphs, each introduced by appropriate scriptural texts, it asserts that:

(1) Jesus Christ alone is God's Word of revelation;

(2) Christ's forgiveness and sanctifying grace cover all areas of life;

(3) the Church is to conform to the law of Christ and is not to be subjected to ideological or political pressures in its order or teaching;

(4) its ministry has to reflect the servant-pattern of Christ;

(5) church and state are not interchangeable in their roles;

(6) the Word and work of the Lord can never be conscripted into alien purposes.

The Barmen Declaration was not, overtly, a political statement in opposition to the Nazi regime. Indeed many of its signatories had initially welcomed the accession of Hitler and the leadership of the Church was frequently at pains to give give assurance that, on secular and political as distinct from ecclesiastical matters, there was no question of disloyalty to the state as such. Much controversy has ensued about the accusation that, for all its courage, the Confessing Church simply eventuated in another exercise in ecclesiastical self-preservation, saying to the state 'Hands off the Church!' but not going on to cry 'Hands off the Jews!' Did the fault lie with Barmen? Or was it that Barmen, which could have provided the basis for a distinctly political stand (especially paragraph 2) was betrayed into the hands of conservative ecclesiastics? The latter was certainly the view of Barth and Bonhoeffer.

Be that as it may, the Confessing Church was certainly accused of national disloyalty by those who thought that the swastika and the cross could hang over the same altar. If there is any single statement which for all time sums up the 'Confessing Church tradition ' it is surely the first paragraph of the Barmen Declaration. As magnificent as it is simple, after quoting John 14.6 and 10.1, 9 it affirms:

> Jesus Christ, as he is attested to us in Holy Scripture, is the one Word of God which we have to hear, and which we have to trust and obey in life and in death.
>
> We reject the false doctrine that the Church could and should recognize as a source of its proclamation, beyond and besides this one truth of God, yet other events, powers, historic figures, and truths, as God's revelation.[6]

In contrast to the self-assertiveness of national chauvinism the 'Confessing Church' affirms not itself but Jesus Christ. Its identity lies in Christ alone. (One cannot help recalling the Fleet Street columnist of the 'Gotcha' mentality who during the Falklands War bitterly demanded to know why 'the Church of England' was not 'supporting England'). Something of the power of the Barmen statement is, however, lost in English. In German the verb 'to hear', *hören*, is a very close cousin to the verb 'to belong to', *gehören*, and indeed sounds close to 'to obey', *gehörchen*. Heinrich Vogel, who as a young pastor actually attended the Barmen Synod (and sat next to Karl Barth during part of the proceedings) is quite clear that the explicit mention of hearing and obeying in this paragraph was deliberately evocative of *belonging* [7].

Christ is the one to whom we belong, the statement is saying. To him we belong in a far more radical and fundamental way than we even belong to our own kith and kin, people or nation. This is because our belonging to him is not established by anything in ourselves to which we can lay claim, or to anything we have done or achieved, but by what he has done for us in his utter grace.

The confession of Christ as the 'one Word', at once both confirms the deep human need for 'belonging' and at the same time undercuts the false claims to a final 'belonging' made by the provisional structures of human existence such as race, clan or nation. The Christ to whom we belong is the one who died for all, in whom there is neither Jew nor Greek, slave or free. This narrow, exclusivist confession is therefore a defile which immediately widens into a panorama embracing the whole earth. Our oneness with Christ brings a solidarity with all. As Vogel puts it, the first Barmen paragraph implies that 'we, who belong to him, belong together, and even that through him, who belongs to all people, we belong to all humankind.'[8]

Such a notion of belonging will qualify, in the severest way, conventional patriotism which, in both secular and religious guises, assumes as Conway says an 'attachment to the nation state and its apparatus of military defence forces' as the ultimate frame of reference. Not that the German Confessing Church as a whole, at the time, saw this as clearly as did Bonhoeffer, for whom the Confessing Church was not just the authentic Evangelical Church of Germany but the representative, in and to Germany, of the *una sancta*, the universal Church of Jesus Christ, God's sign amid the world of nations of a new heaven and a new earth. As he told the Fanö ecumenical peace conference in 1934, 'There shall be peace because of the church of Christ . . .'[9] The ecumenical community is a peace community. For members of the body of Christ to make war against each other is to take up arms against Christ himself.

Bonhoeffer is doing two things with us here. He is bringing us back to that simple question: primarily British, or Christian? To confess Jesus Christ as Lord of lords qualifies all other claims to loyalty, including country, and signifies a bond with the *una sancta*, the universal community which exists among the nations and which points to the new creation lying beyond them. And is not this the meaning of what is already being affirmed in worship? Every time belief in the catholic church is confessed in the creed, every time we sing of the church being 'one o'er all the earth', patriotism is being put in its proper perspective, national sovereignty is being placed in its relative position, national security is being reminded that here we have no abiding city. But Bonhoeffer is also tormenting us. For where do we find the ecumenical community, the *una sancta*, in as concrete and tangible form as can rival that of the nation state today? What hope is there of British Christians sensing a solidarity with the whole *oikumene* when there is relatively little sense of church across denominational barriers at home, as yet?

Perhaps that is to despair too quickly, or at least to choose the wrong route to that sense of ecumenical solidarity. When Karl Barth visited England in 1937 he was asked how Christians here could best help the

Confessing Christians of Germany. His answer was to say that, apart from their prayers, the only real help would be to declare 'with as much publicity and solemnity as was done in Barmen itself' that, that confession was their confession of faith as well. [10]

To what extent this was ever done by any of the British churches is not clear. Perhaps it would have provoked too searching a critique of the role of the British churches in national life. The confession of Jesus Christ as the sole Lord, to whom we belong by faith, means that absolutization of country 'all earthly things above' is to be unmasked as idolatry. The confession of Jesus Christ who belongs to all by his grace means that a claim of allegiance to the state which depends upon fear of others has to be recognized as inherently sinful. The possession of weapons of total annihilation will ipso facto be seen by many as signs that a nation, or alliance of nations, is already along the road of self-deification and untruth. If the state of armed conflict or readiness for such conflict is felt by Christians to be compelling them to acquiesce in idolatry and in the bearing of false witness against their neighbours, then indeed a *status confessionis* will exist for them . But to repeat what was said earlier, to 'confess' is more than pointing out a moral error. It is to say that it is impossible to maintain Christian belief by acquiescence in the situation. A confessing stance on nuclear weapons would have to declare the specific ways in which the creed is mocked, and belief in the doctrines of creation, incarnation, reconciliation, the church and sanctification are denied by them.

It is also important to recognize that 'belonging to Christ' and loyalty to the *una sancta* are not to be set over against national loyalty so as simply to form a kind of 'ecclesiastical' (or ecumenical!) patriotism. Belonging to the nation and belonging to the universal church are not isolated alternatives, for the church is not, any more than the nation, an end in itself. It is a sign of the end, the whole *oikumene* made new in Christ. We referred earlier to a 'confessing patriotism'. The 'confessing church' does not detach itself from and above the nation, still less indulge in a fit of moralizing wisdom from above. It 'seeks the welfare of the city' and intercedes on its behalf before God. [11]

It is deeply identified with the people's predicaments. The most necessary confession which the church may have to make - the most offensive yet the most beneficial - is the confession of the nation's guilt and of the church's own share in that guilt (as the Confessing Church of Germany did at the end of the Second World War in 1945 at Stuttgart, and indeed also as did the penitential liturgy devised at the time of the Munich crisis in 1938, not to mention the blunt confession prepared by Bonhoeffer to be read from pulpits in the event of a successful coup against Hitler). The 'confessing church' declares that it belongs to Christ alone, which means that it will remain identified with the nation after the manner of Christ: not in the unthinking subservience of blind loyalty, but in the humble solidarity of intercessory grace. 'Would that even today you knew the things that make for peace' (Luke 19.42). If it stands for the repudiation of the old forms of patriotism, equally it can signify the birth of a new way of loving the country.

5

Religious Liberty or Christian Freedom? Bonhoeffer, Barmen and Anglo-Saxon Individualism

In the summer of 1939, pending his dramatic return to Germany, Dietrich Bonhoeffer reflected on American Christianity in his essay 'Protestantism without Reformation': 'America calls herself the land of the free. Under this term today she understands the right of the individual to independent thought, speech and action. In this context, religious freedom is, for the American, an obvious possession . . . Thus freedom here means possibility, the possibility of an unhindered activity given by the world to the church'[1]

Much of what he wrote could apply also to British Christianity, and indeed to the British social, cultural and political ethos generally.

We must be free or die, who speak the tongue
That Shakespeare spake.

Wordsworth wrote those lines. During the 1914-18 War young men climbed out of the trenches to their deaths reciting them. But even before they were written, English people sensed them. An English historian has justly observed:

> The freedom of Englishmen was held to be the object of the English law, it was the subject of the constitutional struggles of the seventeenth century. It was enforced, if also menaced, by the Puritan, claiming for himself a freedom which he believed to be endorsed by God. The Established Church believed that it protected freedom when it tried to check the forces of superstition and enthusiasm, and acknowledge the rights of human reason; the Dissenter believed that he vindicated it when he attacked the privileges of the Established Church. The manufacturer and the Liberal claimed it against the State in the nineteenth century, and the social reformer and the trade unionist against the manufacturer. [2]

The meaning of freedom as 'possibility' (to use Bonhoeffer's phrase) has indeed become a *sine qua non* of British life, not least in its religious aspects. Vital here has been the role of the dissenting churches, or nonconformists as they later came to be called, or Free Churches as they have preferred to call themselves since the later nineteenth century. Descended from the Separatist groups which dissociated themselves from the Church of England under Elizabeth I and James I, Congregationalists, Baptists and Unitarians (together with the Methodists of later times) unfurled the banner of religious liberty under the ramparts of state religion. And, in distinction from continental Anabaptist groups, they did not retreat from the godless world into a society of their own making. True , many felt compelled to make their spiritual fortunes (and in due course their material fortunes as well) in the wide open spaces of the New World. But many stayed, claiming the right to be English and to participate fully in civil life while worshipping in an order different to that in the Established Church. Debarred from many positions of civil and judicial office until the nineteenth century (not until nearly 1830 could non-Anglicans sit in Parliament), and suffering a variety of social disabilities as well, the dissenters nevertheless found a variety of outlets for their creative energy. For instance, the innovative and entrepreneurial use of coal-based technology in the eighteenth century, which gave birth to the industrial revolution in England, was to a significant degree a dissenting phenomenon.

In England therefore the religious dissent which refused to emigrate quietly, or to retreat into into a self-enclosed ghetto, repeatedly staked out its right to exist in the midst of the body politic. It armed itself with the idea of religious liberty - for all, of whatever belief or persuasion. One of the earliest statements of this came from the leader of the first Baptist congregation on English soil, Thomas Helwys, in 1612:

> Our Lord the King is but an earthly King, and he hath no authority as a King but in earthly causes, and if the King's people be obedient and true subjects, obeying all human laws made by the King, our Lord the King can require no more: for men's religion to God is betwixt God and themselves: the King shall not answer for it, neither may the King be judge between God and Man. Let them be heretics, Turks, Jews, or whatsoever, it appertains not to the earthly power to punish them in the least measure. [3]

In such a belief we can recognize part of the seed-bed of such later notions as 'liberty of conscience' and 'rights of man' which came to fruition in the eighteenth century and were enshrined in the American Constitution. They also became enshrined in their homeland, Britain, but in a rather different way. Britain has no written constitution, no charter of essential liberties spelled out in plain language. Instead she has a story - and like most stories it grows in the telling - of the progressive struggle for the realization of such liberty. For that reason the notions of 'liberty' and 'religious liberty' can be more emotive for the British than for most people. When such issues are raised the liberty-loving Briton does not call to mind a piece of paper or parchment, but scenes of clandestine meetings in hay-lofts, arrests at night, imprisonments in foul dungeons, public hangings or burnings at the stake, deportations . . . and eventual hard-won concessions.

Further, and crucial to this present study, such a story has not been a matter of remote history for twentieth-century Britain. To understand the consciousness of any generation we have to understand what that generation remembers of its recent past. In Britain, in the 1930s, many leading Free Churchmen remembered vividly the struggles with the Established Church on issues such as education around the turn of the century, when some nonconformists had been prepared to suffer imprisonment or the distraint of their goods, rather than pay their rates for the maintenance of Church of England schools. This issue was but the last in a whole series of grievances which had soured inter-denominational relationships in the later nineteenth century. Equally, not a few Anglicans were by now uneasy in their consciences over the ways in which their Church had stubbornly and sometimes arrogantly clung on to its social privileges. Moreover, during 1926-28 Parliament had rejected the proposed revision of the Anglican Prayer Book, which would have allowed worship and devotion of a more Catholic nature in the established Church. High (or 'Anglo-Catholic') Anglicans, poles apart from Free Churchmen theologically, in some cases felt as bitterly as the Free Churchmen that liberty of conviction and conscience were being trampled on by the state (and it is worth remembering that in England the Catholic no less than the Puritan tradition contains much martyrology).

For a variety of complex historical causes, therefore, and in different ways according to one's particular religious tradition, 'religious liberty' was a precious concept to English churchmen - and still is. For Protestants especially of course, implicit in the notion is the importance of individuality which many assumed - and still assume - to be the great discovery of the Reformation. 'Here I stand. I can do no other': Luther had brought the individual conscience out of medieval darkness into the light of day. Thus the British, no less than the American, Anglo-Saxon is liable to find Bonhoeffer's remarks on 'unreformed Protestantism' somewhat surprising and thought-provoking. He charges our individualism with being untheological:

> The freedom of the church is not where it has possibilities, but only where the Gospel really and in its own power makes room for itself on earth, even and precisely when no such possibilities are offered to it. The essential freedom of the church is not a gift of the world to the church, but the freedom of the Word of God itself to gain a hearing.[4]

It is in the concrete preaching of the Word, regardless of external opportunities or constraints, that Christian freedom exists. 'But where thanks for institutional freedom must be rendered by the sacrifice of preaching, the church is in chains, even if it believes itself to be free.'[5]

To what particular situation was Bonhoeffer alluding in this last quotation? It is hard not to imagine pictures of German ecclesiastics flitting through his mind, suavely justifying their loyalty to the Reich Church Committees in terms of the guaranteed pulpit and the opportunities of 'influence' - yet by their silence on the 'Aryan' issue betraying an enslavement to the principalities and powers. Equally it could have applied to the rather tragic situation of the small Free Church communities in Germany, who had enthusiastically welcomed Hitler's accession, not least because they did gain certain securities and privileges in the early years of the new Reich. German Baptists vehemently told their puzzled British counterparts that they now enjoyed more liberty than at any previous period in their hundred-year history - and their numbers actually grew in the Nazi period. But, more disturbingly, it can be taken as an indictment of American Protestantism and (by extension, in view of our earlier analysis) the British as well. If religious liberty, and liberty of conscience in general, becomes an ideology in its own right, arrogating to itself an ultimate and absolute significance and so displacing the gospel itself, then the church has once again surrendered itself to an idea of this world instead of the living Lord, to immanence instead of transcendence. Individual liberty itself becomes the truth, instead of a creation and servant of the truth.

The kind of questions which Bonhoeffer was putting to Anglo-Saxon Protestantism can be seen to be still more apposite if we briefly look at the way in which the German Church Struggle was viewed by sympathizers outside Germany. The interest taken by foreign observers in the Church Struggle from 1933 onwards constitutes in fact one of the most important chapters in ecumenical history. It also provides a a classic illustration of the difficulties of assessing the actual issues involved in a conflict occurring in a particular context, when viewed from a very different social and religious milieu. In brief, many Anglo-Saxons rightly supported the Confessing Church but for the wrong reasons - or at least for reasons which many in the Confessing Church found a little difficult to understand. This can be well illustrated in the case of British churchmen, especially in the way they interpreted the Barmen Declaration.

In Britain the London *Times* took a major role in publishing accounts of the goings-on in Germany. George Bell, Bishop of Chichester and Chairman of 'Life and Work' was instrumental here, and as we now know one of his prime sources of information was Dietrich Bonhoeffer who in the autumn of 1933 arrived in London as pastor of the German congregation there. Much comment in the religious press was derivative from that in the *Times*. In what follows I shall be drawing upon reports which figured prominently in the weekly *Baptist Times* [6]. To some extent British Baptists had certain independent sources of information, notably J. H. Rushbrooke, Secretary of the Baptist World Alliance, who was a frequent visitor to Germany and who on at least one occasion attended Niemöller's church in Dahlem.

In the Baptists' journal some of the main contours of the struggle can be recognized from the early summer of 1933 onwards, namely:

(i) The campaign to unite the various *Land* churches into a single Reich Church, and the German Christians' campaign to introduce the Aryan clause into the church constitution.

(ii) The heavy- handed coercive measures imposed on the Evangelical Church, notably the dictatorial administration of Reich Bishop Ludwig Müller, and the use of state commissars.

(iii) The resistance to these coercive methods, the questioning of the legality of many of Müller's actions, the protests by increasing numbers of pastors at these measures, and at the dismissal of pastors of Jewish ancestry.

(iv) The actual dismissal (albeit temporary) of some protesting pastors.

From the British vantage-point the struggle quickly became identified as a contest between 'Hitlerism' and 'Protestantism'. 'Protestantism alone has successfully resisted Hitler's dictatorship and survived in the struggle', declared the *Baptist Times* of December 14 1933. And a few weeks later: 'The Evangelical party protests against the policy of identifying religion and nationalism and complains that Christians have not now the right to meet in the land of Luther.' Clearly the German struggle was being viewed through the spectacles of the English history of state control versus liberty of conscience. That there was state imposition in the Church Struggle is not in doubt. But there was much less concern in Britain with what the Confessing Christians were standing for than with what they seemed to be protesting against.

For British Baptists the German scene was raising peculiarly delicate issues in view of the Congress of the Baptist World Alliance to be held in Berlin in August 1934. In Britain - and still more in the United States - doubts were expressed as to the wisdom of the venue. The chief concern was whether freedom of speech could be guaranteed at the meetings, and a prominent British Baptist articulated the doubts thus:

> Baptists by conviction and tradition are opposed to the State control of religion. They stand for liberty and for the sacredness of personality. Their witness is worldwide and cannot be silenced in any nation, even though some adherents . . . may waver in their allegiance and be attracted by the glamour of the religion of nationalism. [7]

In other words, would the Berlin Congress be allowed to speak its mind on issues of its own choosing, including nationalism and race ? In fact the Congress did meet as planned, drawing an attendance of 8,000 including 300 from Britain and many from the United States. Further, it was not silent. Even a resolution on anti-semitism was carried. German reporting of the event was, however, decidedly selective. The Nazi government gave it the freedom to speak but not to be heard. Just over two months before that event the second Barmen Synod had met, and the now famous Declaration, inspired by Karl Barth, had been drawn up. Within a very short time a translation of it appeared in the London *Times*. The ecumenical world - for a moment at least- sat up and watched keenly. Something primeval seemed to be stirring again within Christendom, as in the fourth or sixteenth centuries. The Fourth Evangelist, St Paul, Athanasius, Luther and Calvin all seemed suddenly to have been summoned by Barth into the twentieth century to say 'Jesus Christ, as he is testified to us in Holy Scripture, is the one Word of God. . .' [8]

But what did English Protestantism of the time make of this? M.E. Aubrey, Secretary of the Baptist Union, speaking at a youth meeting of the Baptist Congress in Berlin, stated:

> We stand for liberty of conscience in all matters of faith, liberty to speak and worship as the Spirit of God directs us, and we stand for a free, unfettered Church. A Church that is not free to go as God directs it cannot carry out its task of saving humanity. To bind the Church is to tie the hands of God. We stand by the noble declaration of the Synod of Barmen which ended on June 1.[9]

This is precisely the view of 'freedom' which Bonhoeffer was to treat so mercilessly in his 1939 New York essay! Anglo-Saxon Protestantism saw human freedom as a condition for obedience, for the individual and for the church. Bonhoeffer saw freedom as precisely that which comes *through* obedience, regardless of external conditions. The church that believes is *always* 'free to go as God directs it' (Aubrey's words) 'even and precisely when no such possibilities are offered to it' (Bonhoeffer's words). Bonhoeffer's understanding of freedom was ultimately a theological one, grounded in the sole true freedom of God in his speech and action for man, and thus man being truly free only in relation to God and to others. Freedom as an inherent possession or right of the isolated individual was therefore an inadequate concept for him.[10]

In reading Barmen as a statement about religious liberty Aubrey was typically Anglo-Saxon. There is in fact nothing about 'religious liberty' in the Barmen Declaration, but everything about obedience to the Word of Christ. But a conflict involving church and state could be seen from Britain only as a conflict *about* church and state and the state's desire to infringe 'rights of conscience.' Nor was it only Free Churchmen who were confused on this score. One of the most substantial contemporary British accounts of the Church Struggle was by A.S. Duncan-Jones, Dean of Chichester. It was informative and detailed - yet entitled *The Struggle for Religious Freedom in Germany.*[11]. Possibly the publisher thought that only such a title would sell well in Britain!

Bonhoeffer himself was in England during 1933-35. Other than his behind-the-scenes conversations with George Bell, there were too many preoccupations to allow him to address English theologians and church people. Interestingly, though, in giving an address to the students at Richmond Methodist College, near London, he chose as his theme 'The Nature of Authority'[12]. But even so the British could not claim much excuse for not knowing what was really at stake in Germany after certain events in 1937. That year saw the Oxford 'Life and Work' Conference on Church, Community and State. The German invitations had gone to the Confessing Church but the delegates were refused permission to travel. At least their absence proved to be an eloquent one. Moreover that year Karl Barth visited Britain and addressed gatherings of churchmen in London and Scotland. Barth made no secret of his misgivings about so much concern with the 'liberty' issue. When asked what the British churches could do to 'aid' the Confessing Church, he first of all dismissed protest resolutions and petitions as completely futile and counter-productive as far as their effect on the Nazi regime was concerned. He continued:

> The fact that 'freedom of conscience' and 'freedom of the Church' are approved in Britain and that all atrocities are detested and that these views find ready expression is well known in Germany; but it makes not the slightest impression on the National Socialists, or they do not comprehend it. And the Confessional [sic] Church is not thereby helped, because the fight is not about the freedom, but about the necessary bondage, of the conscience; and not about the freedom, but about the substance, of the Church, i.e. about the preservation, rediscovery and authentication of the true Christian faith. It is not waiting to hear the voice of the British citizen saying once again what every stout Briton has been saying for many centuries, but the voice of the British Christian, the voice of the Church in Britain, saying now that which can only be said in the Holy Spirit, only in recollection of what the Holy Scriptures say. [13]

Barth insisted that the core of the struggle was about the content of the Christian revelation, the response to the Nazi claim that alongside the revelation of God in Christ there was a revelation in nature, history etc. This was the matter of Barmen. He went on:

> Dear brothers and friends in the Church of Great Britain and of all other countries, the only real help, apart from your prayers, which you can render the German Church, would consist in this: in declaring with as much publicity and solemnity as was done in Barmen itself that in your conviction also, a conviction arising from Holy Scripture, this statement with its positive and negative content is the right and necessary expression of the Christian faith for our day and therefore also your confession of faith.[14]

Barth referred to the way in which the reforming churches of the sixteenth century helped each other by reciprocally recognizing their confessions. In the contemporary situation the churches abroad could make it known that they are one with the Confessing Church 'not in disapprobation of Hitler and his methods and aims, not in the idea of freedom of conscience or of the Church, but in the theological presuppositions of the conflict it is waging . . .' [15].

Barth in London in 1937 and Bonhoeffer in New York in 1939 were effectively speaking on behalf of each other - and both on behalf of the inner meaning of Barmen. In the meantime, the English religious press repeatedly illustrated Eberhard Bethge's comment: 'The concern of the western ecumenicals was to a large extent determined by practical - that is to say, political - considerations; consequently, when the struggle became a tedious contest for the Confession, their interest flagged, to flare up again as soon as there was any sensational news of police action in Germany.' [16.] Indeed, so powerful was the pull of the ideology of religious freedom that at their Annual Assembly in 1938 the British Baptists even subsumed the issue of persecution of the Jews in Germany under a resolution on 'religious liberty'.

It is one of the paradoxes in Bonhoeffer that he argued most forcefully with those to whom he felt most indebted. This was so with his own early attitude to Barth, and it was true also of his relationship with the Anglo-Saxon world. Bonhoeffer's strictures on the Anglo-Saxon individualistic view of freedom and conscience should not be construed as a Teutonic attempt to dismiss these values altogether. America and Britain were crucial to Bonhoeffer's career, both in his life and his thought. In 1930-31 the openness of the New York cultural and theological atmosphere was enriching to him in so many ways. Would, for example, the encounter with Jean Lasserre have been as influential on him in any other context than this one? And in England, supremely in his meetings with George Bell, Bonhoeffer experienced the trust between persons that can only grow as they allow each other to be themselves; which means the right to a degree of privacy, hiddenness and reserve. In one of his prison letters to Eberhard Bethge he was to defend this English 'reserve' against the charge of hypocrisy in contrast to German 'honesty' - 'I believe we Germans have never properly grasped the meaning of "concealment" . . .' [17] Without rejecting these values as such, Bonhoeffer's concern was that the Anglo-Saxon world should not confuse them with the ultimate truth of the gospel itself. The gospel is not the innate liberty of the individual, but the forgiveness of sins by the freely gracious and liberating God. The gospel is not the 'sacredness of personality' but the incarnation of Jesus Christ who eschewed his own 'independence' in order to unite with sinners in bearing their guilt. The Anglo-Saxon values cannot be accounted for without the historical involvement of the gospel in the west, but neither can they simply be equated with that gospel. The need to keep both the relationship and the distinction clear is as urgent today as it was in the

1930s for today the ideological divide between west and east is too readily seen - in the west - as the divide between individual liberty and totalitarian oppression, which means for many Anglo-Saxons the divide between Christianity and atheism.

Bonhoeffer's dialogue with the Anglo-Saxons, far from being interrupted by the Second World War, reached a new depth of sensitivity during the darkest days of that conflict. Bonhoeffer the conspirator remained an ecumenist - indeed it was his ecumenical experience abroad which made him of service to the resistance and enabled the *Abwehr* to recruit him as an agent with ostensibly useful contacts whereby relevant information could be gleaned for German military intelligence. On one of his visits to Geneva in 1941 Bonhoeffer was shown by W.A. Visser't Hooft a copy of William Paton's *The Church and the New Order* and copies of the *Christian Newsletter* edited by J.H. Oldham, in which the problems of reconstruction in Europe after the war were already being discussed by British Christians. Bonhoeffer at once saw that much of the thinking in the British churches was of a much more positive nature than that being broadcast nightly to Germany by the BBC. Bonhoeffer and Visser't Hooft, in response, jointly wrote a paper, 'The Church and the New Order in Europe', which sought to reply to sympathetic circles in the Anglo-Saxon world by giving an accurate picture of Germany from a non-Nazi perspective, and of the kind of situation likely to be found after an allied victory. Above all it welcomed Paton's call for a clear statement from the allied leaders as to what, apart from the defeat of Germany, their war-aims were. The absence of such a clearly-stated policy was simply feeding the Nazi propaganda machine and was clearly discouraging the German army which was the only group capable of effective action against the regime. But the chief importance of the paper lay in its exposure of certain awkward factors in the current and future German situation which liberal British opinion was apt to overlook:

> The Anglo-Saxon world summarizes the struggle against the omnipotence of the State in the word 'freedom'. And Paton gives us a charter of human 'rights and liberties' which are to provide the norm of action by the State. But these expressions must, as Paton indicates, 'be translated into terms which relate them more closely to the life of other peoples.' For freedom is too negative a word to be used in a situation where all order has been destroyed. [18]

In a country lying in social and political chaos one could not speak of the rights of individuals as if these could subsist independently of a firm - and probably authoritarian - basis of order for a time. 'Democracy can only grow in a soil which has been prepared by a long spiritual tradition.' [19] This was not a concession to state absolutism but a requirement that the state itself act in accordance with law.

Anglo-Saxons still have problems in assessing the situations of countries which do not measure up to their own canons of democracy, especially newly-independent nations in the Third World. It is not readily seen that the values they cherish require a context as a plant requires soil. In Britain itself, as a matter of fact, a continuing debate is taking place as to how far 'individual liberty' is inherently and universally applicable in the social and political sphere. It is one thing to say that there should be 'freedom of speech' for all, regardless of belief. But should that extend, for instance, to the fascist and racist National Front who, given power to govern, would severely curtail that freedom? In practice our attitudes to such groups involve judgments as to the likelihood of their extending their power and influence, and not simply their intrinsic rightness or wrongness. Questions of power lurk beneath even the most libertarian of consciences.

Questions of order were central to Bonhoeffer throughout the war years as he wrestled with the questions of 'rights' and freedom in the *Ethics* and, later, in some of his attempts at writing fiction in prison. What he returns to again and again is his lifelong emphasis on community, on learning to live together as people and nations. [20]. There is recognized here a need for safeguarding what the Anglo-Saxons cherish. There is also stated a requirement for what they are not always ready to give, the use of freedom not in preserving individual apartness but in expressing solidarity. Underlying all is the christological motif of Jesus Christ who is with others and for others, and only as such is he the Christ. Freedom for Bonhoeffer could only mean freedom-in-relationship, which is different from both Anglo-Saxon individualism and from his own country's lapse into mass subservience to authority. And, as the later prison letters show, freedom-in-relationship is also different from the dogmatizing tendencies which the Confessing Church tended to exhibit after Barmen. The Barmen Declaration could have been the spring-board for authentic Christian witness. Instead it became a plank on which the preacher stood mouthing the traditional formulae of orthodoxy, and eventually it became the barrier on which was pinned the notice addressed to the world: 'No entry'. Bonhoeffer's criticism of the Confessing orthodoxy and what he saw as Barth's 'positivism of revelation' implies a renewed recognition of, if not the individual, then the 'personal' dimension in faith: 'Generally in the Confessing Church: standing up for the church's "cause", but little personal faith in Jesus Christ.'[21]

> What do we really believe? I mean, believe in such a way that we stake our lives on it? . . . "What must I believe?" is the wrong question . . . Karl Barth and the Confessing Church have encouraged us to entrench ourselves persistently behind the "faith of the church" and evade the honest question as to what we ourselves really believe. . . To say that it is the church's business, not mine, may be a clerical evasion, and outsiders always regard it as such. It is much the same with the dialectical assertion that I do not control my own faith, and that it is therefore not for me to say what my faith is.[22]

But again, it was honesty not before one's own isolated conscience but before Jesus Christ, which Bonhoeffer ultimately had in view. That is why Anglo-Saxon Christianity still needs Bonhoeffer's searching questions. We still talk, in conservative or radical fashion, a great deal about the value of the individual and his or her freedom, need for security, meaning, fulfilment and so on . . . and surprisingly little about Jesus Christ who freely gave up all these for us.

6

The Freedom of the Church: Bonhoeffer and the Free Church Tradition

What significance does the thought of Dietrich Bonhoeffer have for the Free Church tradition, and vice versa? My question is prompted by a vested interest. I write as an English Baptist, who feels deeply rooted in his tradition - dating back virtually to the English Reformation itself - yet who is also aware that in the British as in other contexts searching questions are being asked of all churches concerning the nature of Christian witness in the social and political sphere. To ask serious questions about the Free Church tradition means asking, sooner or later: what does it mean for the church to be 'free'?

It was out of English 'Separatism' in the early seventeenth century that Independency (later known as Congregationalism) was born. Here, the church exists in two modes: the universal church of all Christ's people, and the particular congregation or gathered church, comprising only the committed believers who have 'as the Lord's free people joined themselves, by a covenant of the Lord, into a Church Estate of the Gospel to walk in all his ways made known, or to be made known, according to their best endeavours whatsoever it would cost them' [1]. Moreover it was in one of the English Separatist groups that had sought refuge in Amsterdam, the congregation from Gainsborough led by John Smythe, that a further step along the Independent road was taken which was to be of immense significance: the rejection of infant baptism - frequently identified as the *sine qua non* of a state church - in favour of 'believers' baptism'. The extent to which Smythe and his congregation were influenced by the already-existing Mennonite communities in Holland who were the direct legatees of the

Anbaptist wing of the radical Reformation, is not clear. But in 1609 they constituted the first English Baptist Congregation. Under the leadership of Thomas Helwys a number from this community returned to England in 1612 to form the first Baptist congregation on English soil, in London.

The Congregational and Baptist churches, emphasizing as they do the primacy of Scripture, the gathered church principle, the requirement of personal faith in Christ for church membership, the right to freedom of conscience in religion and the complete independence of church from state, were to be of immense significance in the development not only of Protestantism but also of western democracy, first in England and then in North America, whither many of the early adherents sailed to seek their freedom. In Anglo-Saxon circles, by 'Free Church' is generally meant this gathered-church, state-free tradition (joined significantly by Methodism after the Evangelical Revival in the eighteenth century). It was a tradition which became a crucial bearer of the Reformed faith beyond the European continent, providing a means whereby the social potentialities of Calvinism were released in the creation of an open, activist and libertarian society: 'A Free Church in a free society.'

What does it mean for a church to be 'free'? Further, what is the relation between a church which claims to be 'free', and the liberation of people at large? Can the church which is 'gathered' from society, and is independent of the state, really have any ethical contribution to make to the public issues affecting the society from which it distinguishes itself so clearly? Once Dietrich Bonhoeffer is brought into the debate a whole host of further questions jump up like iron filings onto a magnet. How far did this German Lutheran, reared in the *Volkskirche* of the Reformation, really appreciate the Free Church possibility? How does the 'Confessing Church' which Bonhoeffer sought so ardently, relate to the gathered 'Free Church'? In his last prison writings, especially in the 'Outline for a Book', in those concrete proposals for a new form for the church [2], was he not coming close to the Free Church pattern? Or, no less than other patterns, when weighed in Bonhoeffer's balance is the Free Church tradition found wanting? What significance, for example, should be attached to his critique of American Protestantism and its emphasis upon 'freedom'?

Sanctorum Communio: national church, gathered church, confessing church.

Any encounter with Bonhoeffer's ecclesiology must begin with *Sanctorum Communio,* his doctoral thesis of 1927. What experience or comprehension would the young Berlin theologian have had of the 'Free Church'? In terms of our Anglo-Saxon understanding, very little on the face of it. He might well have thought of the radical reformation groups still anathematized in Lutheran catechetics as 'Anabaptists', though represented in modern Germany by the Mennonites; or of the Moravians, offshoots of Lutheran pietism in the eighteenth century. Equally, however, he might have had in mind the Protestant churches which had seceded from the historic *Volkskirche* over doctrinal issues and thus separated from the 'establishment', such as the Old Reformed Churches (c.1700), the Old Lutherans (1830), or the Evangelical Lutheran Free Church of Saxony (1860). By the same token of course the Old Catholic Church which was formed through rejection of the decrees of the Vatican Council of 1870, was technically a 'free' church.

The 'Free Churches' of an Anglo-Saxon type had not made their appearance in Germany until relatively modern times, in the first half of the nineteenth century. The Baptist movement, for example, began in Hamburg in 1834. Significantly, this and other Free Church developments in Germany owed much to British and (especially) American support. For two decades or more the Free Church movements met with considerable opposition from both church and state authorities in Germany (a factor not without significance in influencing the stance of those Free Churches in the Nazi Period - see below). For a time the Baptist movement in Hamburg was dubbed 'the English faith', and *Methodismus* became a synonym for that most Lutheran term of abuse, 'Enthusiasm.' As relative latecomers to the German scene they bore no comparison with the way in which English 'noncomformity' had been a powerful force, socio-political as well as religious, in British history. They were always to remain a minority on continental soil. But with their emphasis on evangelism they were able to implant within German Protestantism the gathered church principle and to make the plea for the independence of religion from state control or patronage. In Wilhelmine Germany of course that was a vain dream. Ostensibly the Weimar Republic offered more hope for that principle, but the Free Churches found that in practice the great *Volkskirche* still behaved as in the old establishment days [3] (a situation not unlike that found in British overseas colonies where the Anglican Church often assumed rights and privileges which it had at home as the 'Church of England').

When the young Dietrich Bonhoeffer thought of 'Free Churches', therefore, he probably also had in mind these small, rather pietistic groups claiming to be the real inheritors of the Reformation doctrines of justification by faith and *sola scriptura*, and claiming to be really putting these into effect, unlike the Evangelical *Volkskirche* which was trapped in rationalism and liberalism. Indeed the Free Churches often made the claim that if the German Evangelical Church had really maintained its missionary zeal to its own people, their formation would not have been necessary. Seen from the outside there was more than a suggestion of spiritual elitism and exclusivism about the German Free Churches, which in turn only led to 'official' church leaders and theologians being still more dismissive of them.

There was however at least one notable exception. Ernst Troeltsch in his massive *The Social Teaching of the Christian Churches* [4] gave a remarkably full place to the radical Reformation groups and the later Free Churches (displaying an unusual knowledge of English-speaking church history) in his sociological survey. Troeltsch is now perhaps best known for his distinction between the 'Church type' and 'Sect type' of Christianity:

> The Church is an institution which has been endowed with grace and salvation as the result of the work of Redemption; it is able to receive the masses, and to adjust itself to the world, because, to a certain extent, it can afford to ignore the need for subjective holiness for the sake of the objective treasures of grace and of redemption.
>
> The sect is a voluntary society, composed of strict and definite Christian believers bound to each other by the fact that all have experienced 'the new birth'. These 'believers' live apart from the world, are limited to small groups, emphasize the law instead of grace, and in varying degrees within their own circle set up the Christian order, based on love; all this is done in preparation for and expectation of the coming kingdom of God. [5]

There is nothing pejorative in Troeltsch's usage of 'sect'. Indeed his historical-philosophical judgment was that, in balance with the church-type and mystical-type, sect-Christianity was a vital and necessary form of Christian community. Moreover, bearing in mind when he was writing (early in this century) he offers an intriguing prophecy that Lutheranism 'is being slowly drawn into the forward march of the Protestant social doctrines, and is being influenced by Ascetic Protestantism. This process of development will increase when, as we may expect with certainty, it is no longer supported by the State.'[6]

However, Troeltsch is primarily of interest to us here in being one of Bonhoeffer's main sources in his attempt to do both theological and sociological justice to the church. In *Sanctorum Communio* Bonhoeffer expounds a view of the Church wherein revelation is concretized in human community - it is Christ existing as community. That means a heavy theological investment in (very!) human, historical communities which bear the name 'church'. Indeed as a good Lutheran Bonhoeffer freely admits that in its visible historical form the church has many more 'nominal members' than 'members of the kingdom':

> It is present, in other words, as a national Church *(Volkskirche)* and not as a 'gathered' church *(Freiwilligkeitskirche)*. How can a church that, as a human community, is by its very nature a community of wills, at the same time be a national church? Such is the sociological formulation of the problem of the empirical church.[7]

Bonhoeffer, however, is not dismissing the principle of the gathered church, but simply defending the existence of a national church. And, as he proceeds to make clear, the justification of the national church lies *precisely in its capacity to enable a gathered church to arise*. The link between the two is the Word, for it is in the preaching of the Word that the church truly gathers:

> The sanctorum communio, which by its nature presents itself as a national church, equally demands the gathered church, and continually establishes itself as such; that is, the sanctorum communio sustains the others, as it were, in whom the possibility of becoming 'effective' members of the church is dormant, by virtue of the Word which constitutes it and which it preaches.[8]

Here we are a long way from the 'gathered church' in the Free Church sense of a committed membership since Bonhoeffer maintains the traditional Lutheran principle that a person can be assumed to be a possible member 'as long as he has made no conscious retractation.' But the dynamics of the relation between national and gathered churches, as introduced by Bonhoeffer, are crucial. The national church is not justified per se, but only as having the potential for the visible, gathered church under the Word. It was thus a remarkable and prophetic insight for him now to state, six years before Hitler's accession and seven years before the Barmen Synod:

> Now for the church there is a point in time when it may not be a national church any longer, and this point is reached when it can no longer see in its national form any way of fighting its way through to becoming a gathered church. But such a step would in the event spring from church politics and not from dogmatics. It does, however, show

that the church's essential character is that of a gathered church.[9]

Still Bonhoeffer refuses to disengage from the historical *Volkskirche*, inveighing against the 'many presumptuous attempts at purifying the church from the formation of the perfectionist sects of the early church to those of the Anabaptists and pietists.'[10] His argument is that it is precisely in this world of sin and death, and hence of historical ambiguity, that God is at work in his hidden way. 'The church is meant to let the tares grow in its garden, for where else can it find the criterion of knowing and judging which of its members are tares?'[11] It is an attitude found again about fifteen years later in *Ethics*, in the passages dealing with judgment (The Pharisee), and still more clearly in the criticism of 'stupidly importunate reformers' and ideologues with their 'idealizing failure, which substitute an abstract notion of good for the unity of creaturely life before the Creator.'[12]

In *Sanctorum Communio*, however, the cruciality of the Word for the identity of the Christian community has injected a kind of restlessness into Bonhoeffer's reformed ecclesiology (and here an interesting comparison could be made with Schleiermacher). It results in his rejection of Troeltsch's church/sect distinction, on theological grounds. The Christian sect, too, has the Word (and so has the Roman Catholic community), whatever important sociological differences in structure there may be between these communities. Moreover, the necessary tension between the national and the gathered church returns as an insistent refrain. So, on the one hand, Bonhoeffer repeats his defence of the historic *Volkskirche* despite - indeed because of - its innate conservatism: 'as an organically developed historical power it possesses greater firmness and lasting power than the voluntary association: historically sterile periods can be withstood by the national church, whereas the gathered church is ruined by such a time'[13] (incidentally a judgment which an English dissenter, especially with the eighteenth century in view, will contest vigorously). On the other hand comes the ominous and prophetic warning:

> . . . we can now affirm that the national church and the gathered church belong together, and that it is all too obvious to-day that a national church, which is not continually pressing forward to be a confessing church, is in the greatest inner peril. There is a moment when the church dare not continue to be a national church, and this moment has come when the national church can no longer see how it can win through to being a gathered church . . . but on the contrary is moving into complete petrifaction and emptiness in the use of its forms, with evil effects on the living members as well. We have to-day reached the point where such questions must be decided. We are more than

ever grateful for the grace of the national church, but we are also more than ever keeping our eyes open for the danger of its complete degeneration. [14]

'Gathered church', 'confessing church', are here being drawn close together if not identified. The author was clearly being theologically prepared for the coming Church Struggle[15]. He was also being equipped for a critical yet open and creative encounter with the ecumenical community, and not least with the Free Church life he was to meet in the United States and Britain. There is, however, another important theme, found later in the *Ethics*, which has a vital bearing on how we are to understand both the distinction of the church from the world and the relation of the church to the world, which takes cognizance of the 'gathered' nature of the church yet implies that any notion of 'gathering' is by itself inadequate apart from a christological base.

Gathering for others: the church as deputy

Throughout Bonhoeffer's *Ethics* there is an attempt to overcome 'thinking in two spheres.' On the Pauline model, in Christ (II Corinthians 5.19) God has reconciled the world to himself, and whatever else might need to be said about the world in its sinfulness and godlessness, it is the world which God loves and has somehow 'made one' with himself in the incarnation, death and resurrection of Jesus Christ. Because of the reconciling, mediatorial work of Jesus Christ, one cannot have God without the world, nor the world without God whose rightful rule over the world is manifest in Jesus Christ. It is important to recognize that already, prior to the prison writings, Bonhoeffer is seeking on this christocentric basis to explicate what he calls a 'genuine worldliness' [16]. What then on this unitive view happens to the church as a distinct entity vis à vis the world? And especially, what happens to any notion of a 'gathered church' which, in the Free Church tradition, has been powerfully motivated by a desire to distinguish the people of God from citizenship in general, and an office of the state in particular?

Bonhoeffer makes several assaults on this problem in *Ethics*. In addition to discussing the exclusive and inclusive aspects of Christ's call, he includes the church as one of the divine 'mandates' in which God-given human responsibility is to be exercised along with marriage, labour and government [17]. He discusses the respective roles of government (note, government, not 'state'!). He asks in what sense the church is entitled and obliged to deliver a word to the 'world'. In no case does he rush to disavow his traditional Lutheran insistence on the distinctness of the 'spheres', but seeks to uncover the positive relation between them in the light of the ultimate unity established between all things in Christ. There is one section especially, however, where Bonhoeffer achieves a notable integration between the church as 'gathered' and a total view of humanity as under the lordship of the reconciling Christ. In 'The Commandment of God in the Church' [18] Bonhoeffer insists that it is the one Christ who is Lord and Saviour of the world, whom the church always proclaims. There is not one word for the church and another for the world. Christ is Lord and Saviour of his people and of the whole world, and the church proclaims his commandment 'by summoning all men to fellowship with him.' In Jesus Christ God took upon himself bodily all human being. Henceforth divine being cannot be found otherwise than in human form, and man is free to be man before God. 'The "Christian" element is not now something which lies beyond the human element.' And in view of the incarnation 'to live as man before God can mean only to exist not for oneself but for God and for other men.' Similarly the cross of Christ marks both the godlessness of the world and its reconciliation, and apart from the crucified Redeemer the reality of the world is not grasped, no true 'worldliness' is possible. Further, it is under the lordship of the risen and ascended Christ that the liberation of creation takes place, for he is the Lord in whom all created things find their true origin, goal and essence. His law is their own true being, therefore, and in his commandment they are neither subject to an alien law thrust upon them, nor are they left to some arbitrary autonomy.

The sum of the matter is that 'Jesus Christ's claim to lordship, which is proclaimed by the church, means at the same time the emancipation of family, culture and government for the realization of their own essential character which has its foundation in Christ.'[19] Bonhoeffer immediately rejects one possible interpretation of this, namely, a dominion of the church over society and world. The church does have its own specific mandate: to proclaim the revelation of God in Jesus Christ. But first, this proclamation being the proclamation concerning him in whom God took manhood upon himself, means a community of response to that word:

In Jesus Christ is the new humanity, the congregation of God. In Jesus Christ the word of God and the congregation of God are indissolubly linked together. Through Jesus Christ the word of God and the congregation of God are inseparably united.

Consequently, wherever Jesus Christ is proclaimed in accordance with the divine mandate, there, too, there is always the congregation. In the first instance this means only that men are there who accept the word concerning Christ, and who believe it and acquiesce in it, unlike others who do not accept it but reject it. It means, then, that men are there who allow that to happen to themselves which properly, as an act of God, should happen to all men; it means that men are there who stand as deputies for the other men, for the whole world. [20]

The church is a particular community with its particular law, or discipline relating to itself. But the law which governs its own life cannot and must not be imposed on the worldly order, for then it would be an alien rule. And conversely 'the law of a worldly order cannot and must not ever become the law of this community.' The church is a means to an end, which is not to dominate or govern society but to proclaim to society the one true Lord of its life. But in fulfilling this instrumental purpose, paradoxically, the church becomes the goal and centre of all God's dealing with the world:

The concept of deputyship characterizes this twofold relationship most clearly. The Christian congregation stands at the point at which the whole world ought to be standing; to this extent it serves as deputy for the world and exists for the sake of the world. On the other hand, the world achieves its own fulfilment at the point at which the congregation stands. The earth is the 'new creation', the 'new creature', the goal of the ways of God on earth. The congregation stands in this twofold relation of deputyship entirely in the fellowship and disciplehood of its Lord, who was Christ precisely in this, that he existed not for his own sake but wholly for the sake of the world.[21]

There is, then, a proper life of the community as a 'self-contained' entity (and here Bonhoeffer has sharp criticism to make of the pastorally and liturgically sparse nature of much Protestantism as compared with Roman Catholic spirituality and discipline), but only on behalf of the world. In writing of the need to insist on the church being free from the alien law of the world order, Bonhoeffer was of course writing with the Barmen Confession behind him. He was also equally, if not consciously, writing with the Free Church tradition at his elbow. But in drawing his notion of deputyship into his ecclesiology - and in a way which was to be continued in the prison theology - he was transcending that usual notion of the 'free' church. For the Free Church tradition, while vigorously (and some of us will think justifiably) asserting the distinction of church from world, has been vulnerable to losing interest in the world as such, so long as that 'independency' is maintained. It has been prone to conceiving itself pietistically as the ark of salvation, the only interest which the world now has being that of a 'mission field' ('We remain missionaries!' was the German Baptists' slogan during the early days of the Third Reich[21]). Or, it is content to acquiesce in any socio-political system which leaves it alone. But, according to Bonhoeffer, the fact that the church is the representative of the world before God, not just the antithesis to that world, need have no deleterious consequences for the church's own sense of identity. Indeed when deputyship is seen as the expression of the form of Christ himself, that identity comes to fulfilment. Equally, it has to be said, this later ecclesiology of Bonhoeffer not only transcends the usual 'Free Church' understanding, but takes us beyond his own earlier understanding of the essentially 'gathered' nature of the church in *Sanctorum Communio*. There, Bonhoeffer had seen the *Volkskirche* as an expression of the fact that the Word is intended for all people. Now, it is much more the content of that Word which is to convey that goal, a content to be embodied within the concrete life of the church as deputy 'for the world.'

Bonhoeffer and the Free Church tradition today: A British perspective

A theological understanding of the nature of the church and its relationship to the whole of humanity remains high on the agenda, especially in ecumenical discussion [23]. In Faith and Order enquiry over the past thirty years the debate has been both deepened and enriched by the full-scale entry of the Eastern Orthodox Churches, providing a milieu rather different to that known by Bonhoeffer where the parameters were still largely the western ones of the Roman and post-Reformation churches. Given the eastern comprehension of the church as the divinely given, eternal community without essential change or development it would be interesting to know of an Orthodox response to *Sanctorum Communio*. But the contemporary ecumenical scene is also increasingly shaped by the experiences of Third World Christianity where the questions revolve around the issue of how far Christianity is implicated in, and how far it can be both free from and liberating others from, the structural sins of economic and political oppression, racism and militarism. The Free Church tradition of the west, if honest, feels as vulnerable as any other Christian tradition when faced with the question, 'Today, are you free enough to liberate the poor and imprisoned of your own and others' societies?' On the one hand much history supports the Free Church case in the English-speaking world. The democratization of society, the rights to religious and political liberty, the campaign against slavery and the slave trade, the early trades union movement in Britain, the movement towards universal suffrage - all these were part of the classic Free Church witness. At its best the Free Church movement has asserted the implications for everyone in society of the 'crown rights of the Redeemer.' It has declared that, Christ being head of the church, no earthly power should be allowed to lay hands on the visible community of his kingdom, or to come between any person and his or her God. Equally, Christ being the true Lord of human society (a belief stemming especially from the Calvinist root in its heritage), it has at its best dealt roughly with all claims to absolutist authority in society, and has vigorously asserted that the strongest safeguard against the corrupting concentration of power is that the will of the people as expressed in Parliament should be sovereign.

Moreover, is not the presence of any community which visibly and concretely by its very existence testifies to the distinctness of the body of Christ from the state, making a much-needed witness? Have not disastrous confusions flowed from the near identification of God and Caesar, of heavenly kingdom and earthly despotism, which has characterised so much of post-Constantinian Christian history? Is not a supposed dependence of Christianity upon the support of the state an implied statement of disbelief in the power of the Holy Spirit? Has not the 'establishment' of Christianity weakened its integrity as much as it has promoted its 'influence' in the world? Apologists among our Lutheran friends, at least, will have their answer ready: Luther would have been more than willing, at first, to have entrusted the destiny of the church to the gathered congregations but events dictated otherwise and the godly prince had to be called in. This is not in dispute. But was the question ever asked in the nineteenth century, as to what God was doing with and saying to his church in Germany, in the growth of the new Free Churches? The tragically negative stance of those Free Churches during the Nazi period (see below) in comparison with the Confessing Church, cannot be justified. But it was in part a reflection of the arrogant and high-handed manner in which the Evangelical Church, no less than the state, had treated their forbears a century earlier. During the Church Struggle the Free Church leaders professed an inability to feel much sympathy for those who were now being arrested - in the name of that same Evangelical Church. Then as always, the perspective of minorities can be highly revelatory of aspects otherwise overlooked in the scene at large, as Bonhoeffer himself realized and related in his 1942-43 sayings about 'The view from below.'

On the other hand we are increasingly aware that not *all* history supports the Free Church case. Yes, Free Churches have at times been strongly in the vanguard against social inequities and abuses, and in the promotion of human rights and dignities. A closer examination reveals, however, that most Free Church energies have been expended in these directions where Free Church people themselves have been the most obvious victims (as in nineteenth century England for example). In this respect the 'radical liberalism' of nineteenth century English nonconformity was a powerful movement of self-liberation by the rising (but still heavily disadvantaged) artisan and lower-middle classes. It was never a proletarian movement. It was no less worthy for that. But, having gained their civic, religious and cultural rights, British Free Church people largely lost the broader social view, and since the 1914-18 War increasingly espoused a provincial, bourgeois stance more content to proclaim platitudes than to engage in any searching critique. Indeed a case has been strongly argued by one church historian recently, to the effect that in the 1914-18 War itself, English Free Church 'nonconformity' finally and decisively opted for conformity to the establishment by wholeheartedly supporting the war and abandoning its previous pacifist and internationalist tendencies[24]. The reward was rich: greatly increased public acceptability for the Free Churches who could now be seen to belong in every way to the body politic. The cost appeared to be minimal - after all the Free Churches were still formally as independent of the state as ever. The price however was extracted from the Free Churches' hidden reserves. Less and less could they claim to be offering - as they had early in the nineteenth century - a truly alternative kind of society. The most significant social teachers and prophets in English Christianity since 1918 - one might say the most outspoken 'nonconformists' - have been Anglicans.

Now of course this could simply be as significant of a general historical shift affecting all the British churches, as of any 'decline' in specifically Free Church attitudes. Indeed, concomitant with the growth of ecumenical relationships over the past 80 years has been an increasing awareness among the English churches of a relativization of the distinction between the 'established' and 'non-established' churches. One factor has been the immensely changed position of the

Roman Catholic Church, formerly an alien and somewhat recluse minority in England, now to the forefront in every aspect of public Christianity and ecumenical concern, and representing a massive element in non-established Christianity of a kind quite different from that of the Free Churches. Another factor however has been the almost tacit acceptance by the Free Churches themselves, that for all their formal dissociation from 'establishment' they are nevertheless intimately locked in to much of the apparatus of the state, not least in welfare and educational provision (for instance church youth and community workers may often be paid by the local authority, not to mention the fact that ordinands as a matter of course apply for state funding of their theological training). Seen from the margins of British society, and not least for example from the experience of some of the black-led churches, all the 'mainstream' churches must look pretty well 'established' in terms of their social status and command of available facilities.

This is not to imply that important differences do not remain between the Anglican and other churches in England, and particularly in public attitudes and expectations concerning them. But in a society which is increasingly secularized, the Church of England itself, whatever the persistent formal relationships with the Crown and Parliament, has had to come into a somewhat more self-conscious relationship both to 'the people' at large, to the state, and to other churches. Ecclesia Anglicana is no longer a *Volkskirche* (if it ever was), still less does it now merit the old jibe of it being 'the Conservative Party at prayer.' Indeed, talk of 'confrontation' between church and state has grown in the United Kingdom in recent years as significant church leaders, including a number of Anglican bishops, have been increasingly outspoken in their criticism of many of the policies of the Thatcher Conservative government.

Confessing as a relativizing act

At this point we find Dietrich Bonhoeffer's questions addressed to the Anglo-Saxon Free Churches as sharp as they were when penned fifty years ago. In one respect it is tempting to say that the Free Churches of his native Germany provide the best verifications of his warnings. 'A state-free church is no more protected against secularization than is a state church. The world threatens to break in on the church as much because of freedom as because of association', he wrote reflecting on the churches of the United States in 1939 [25]. No churches were more zealous for their independence from the state than the German Free Churches, yet, by the time of the First World war, none were more socially, culturally and politically assimilated to German nationalism. 'The Baptist Church is not only Evangelical, rather it is also good German,' declared a Baptist writer in 1916.[25] Other examples abound, including an infamous Baptist exposition of Ephesians 4. 4-6 ('one Lord, one faith, one baptism') - applied to the unity of the *German people* ! When the crisis of 1933 arrived the German Free Churches as a whole adopted the quietist 'middle way', not generally supporting the *Deutsche Christen* but on the other hand enthusiastic in their welcome for Hitler, the saviour from godless bolshevism and the total abstainer from alcohol. As far as 'freedom' was concerned, the German Free Churches in the Third Reich had few complaints. Indeed the Methodist Bishop Melle and the Baptist leader Paul Schimdt expressed thanks at the Oxford 1937 Conference on Church and State for the 'unlimited freedom' to pursue their evangelistic and pastoral ministries. There is every reason to believe the authorities were content to allow a continued proclamation which centred on 'Jesus is *my* Lord' rather than 'Jesus is *the* Lord.' Bonhoeffer's dictum needed no clearer exemplification, that 'where thanks for institutional freedom must be rendered by the sacrifice of the freedom of preaching, the church is in chains, even if it believes itself to be free'[27].

Bonhoeffer exposes the vulnerability of a 'free church' to manipulation by extraneous and sometimes sinister forces, at precisely the point where it feels itself to be free from the godless world, just as the national church can complacently assume that by its very existence it is upholding the divine order in the world. In both cases the question of the gathered people, bound to the Lord and to one another, can become the choice to be a church on one's own terms, in order (consciously or otherwise), to serve one's own particular social, political - and religious - interests. It can too readily be an accommodation to the society as it is, rather than providing a critique of it. We have already seen how this has become a temptation to the British Free Churches in their 'suburban captivity'. In terms of freedom, they have been left with relatively little to say to a government which has cleverly based much of its popular appeal on the sanctity of 'personal freedom' interpreted as 'individual choice', while all the time the state apparatus is growing more centralized, more authoritarian and more secretive, and in which an undefined 'national security' or 'national interest' is presented as overriding all other considerations. Will the churches mark time in face of this advance of state power, while Mrs Thatcher, the candle-lighter of freedom in Moscow, continues to speak of 'freedom of choice' as the essence of Christianity?

In South Africa the political struggle as presented by the government is frequently seen as one for 'religious freedom' in the face of 'communism', and once more the churches, and especially those of the Free Church tradition, are susceptible. Again, none are more zealous for 'independence' from the state than are the Baptists. But tragically no denomination has been more illustrative, in its very structure, of apartheid than this denomination for which 'proclaiming the gospel' has been claimed to be of supreme importance. At least now a point of honesty has been reached whereby the black Baptist Convention has disaffiliated itself from the dominant white-led Baptist Union. In fact all the church traditions of South Africa have had to examine the extent to which they are primarily locked into the interests of the particular social groups, whether of the powerful or the powerless. But in particular, claimants to 'free churchmanship' are being brought to the bar for examination as to whether they themselves are truly free, let alone liberating. Is a 'free church' in such a conflict-ridden situation one which is free to be itself, or one which, in costly discipleship, manifests freedom in moving out beyond itself to identify with the oppressed and powerless outside its own circle?

Bonhoeffer questions our Free Churches as to the theological reality of their 'freedom'. Is it truly the freedom which comes *by* preaching the lordship of Christ, the liberating Lord, however costly and unpalatable a word that might be? Or is it only the freedom *to* preach, permitted by the world? That latter freedom is significant. But it is not the final or ultimate freedom for which to pray, and it can obscure the devastatingly simple question: What, or whom, are we preaching? Bonhoeffer faces the Free Church with the question: Are you a confessing church? That question in fact was crucial to him as an aspect of the encounter between the German Confessing Church and the ecumenical movement [28]. The question might be expanded thus: Are you concerned not simply to be gathered in negative fashion, in distinction from the world, but positively under the word of the Lord of the world? Have you a word from the Lord which is significant not only for your own security and sanctity but for the true welfare of the world of which you are a part?

On Bonhoeffer's understanding it is a 'confessing' church which is most truly free, that is, the church which answers the claim of its Lord by putting all rival claims, pressures and possible dangers aside and uttering, not only for itself but for its neighbours on whose behalf it is set in a particular part of the world, the promise and command for that particular hour. In this perspective, the established State Church, the Free Church and the Roman Catholic Church could all become confessing churches - and equally all could be inhibited from becoming so, by blindness, fear or inertia. This is not to make our varied ecclesiological differences irrelevant, but it is to set them in a more significant frame of reference. It certainly means that as history moves on some of us in the Free Churches today are by no means as impatient for the disestablishment of the Church of England as were our parents and grandparents. There simply is little evidence that such a move would of itself 'liberate the Church' to 'speak a word to society' or to 'confront the government'. Put bluntly, the Church of England, no less than the Free Churches, is as 'free' as it wishes to be to say and even to do whatever it really considers to be in the cause of justice, truth and peace. The real question is 'whatever it really considers.' Paradoxically, these days the most strident calls for the disestablishment of the Church of England come from within its own ranks, by those who chafe at the state's role in the appointment of bishops and at the remaining legal controls on liturgical matters. This desire by some Anglicans for greater 'freedom' in the management of 'the Church's own life' would be unexceptionable if it was not also in some cases accompanied by an implicit wish to abandon the public roles with which the Church of England has been endowed - whether one likes it or not - by history. However odd it may seem, this Free Church writer feels uneasy at the tone of some of his Anglican friends' hankering after freedom from responsibilities. Bonhoeffer's word is apposite: 'The ultimate question for a responsible man to ask is not how he is to extricate himself heroically from the affair, but how the coming generation is to live.'[29]

The churches in the United Kingdom are increasingly speaking and acting together on public issues, and as not infrequently happens in history it is the historic occasion, the *kairos*, rather than the prepared programme, which is most capable of creating a new consciousness. In retrospect it is clear that in this regard one of the most significant occasions in the life of modern Britain and the British churches occurred in the summer of 1982, following the successful recapture of the Falkland/Malvinas Islands after the Argentinian occupation. The outcome was marked by a state service of thanksgiving in St Paul's Cathedral, conducted by leaders of the Anglican, Free and Roman Catholic Churches. Much controversy was aroused at the tone of the service, especially the Archbishop of Canterbury's sermon and the prayers which laid heavy emphasis on the need for repentance and reconciliation, and intercession for the Argentinian as well as British casualties. The government and its supporters in the press expressed patriotic anger at this evident betrayal of the Land of Hope and Glory. Vitriol was especially directed at the Church of England leadership, and it is a widely held view that the Prime Minister's continuing unease with the English bishops - whether over their views on inner-cities, or unemployment, or race, or nuclear weapons - owes more to this single unforgivable act than to anything else. However mild and symbolic, it was in a true sense an occasion of confessing the kingdom of God in face of the rampant claims of the kingdoms of this world. And the lesson is not, hopefully, being forgotten in Britain: it was confession because it was ecumenical, and it was truly ecumenical because it was confession. It is perhaps unfortunate that the Archbishop of York, Dr John Habgood, should commit himself to the statement that 'Only the Church of England could have insisted on counter-balancing the nationalistic thrust of the Falklands celebration, precisely because of its relationship to the nation. And the fact that it did so was a direct consequence of its developing relationship with the Anglican communion and other world Christian bodies.' [30] As it stands this statement ignores completely both the logic of the other churches' stances and the actual course of events surrounding that episode. That the Church of England played a crucial public role in countering the uncritically jingoistic mood is not in dispute. That it *would* or *could* have done so without the other churches which were at least as concerned at the chauvinistic attitude is open to question. The stand taken at the St Paul's service resulted also from the independent-mindedness of the Free Church leadership which once again warned that Christianity was not a state monopoly, and also from the inherent internationalism of the Roman Catholic Church - the 'enemy' had after all been a predominately Roman Catholic country.

Confessing Free Churches

At this point we contemporary Free Church representatives may well feel that Bonhoeffer is not so much critical of the Free Church tradition as such, but rather encouraging us to recover those vital elements in our legacy which have tended to be lost in the efforts to ensure Free Church survival and growth as ends in themselves in recent generations. At its most creative points in western society the Free Church tradition has been able to assert both the distinctness of the gathered, believing community (the 'fellowship of believers') and the rightful claim of the lordship of Christ over the whole of secular society. The so-called 'nonconformist conscience' of nineteenth century Britain, summed up in the slogan 'What is morally wrong can never be politically right' may have been simplistic and open to the charge of being hypocritically selective in its priorities, but it did at least witness to the universalistic concern of the local, covenanted *sanctorum communio*. At the turn of this century, for example, it was John Clifford, minister of Westbourne Park Chapel in London, the 'uncrowned king of militant nonconformity', who was both leading the fight against what were felt to be continuing and unjust Anglican intrusions into religious instruction in schools, and at the same time campaigning against sweated labour and against Britain's last great imperialistic adventure in the South African Boer War (several times his chapel was beset by chauvinistic mobs). The Free Churches can indeed point to cherished occasions in their story where they have not merely claimed freedom to exist, but have exhibited freedom in confession.

Bonhoeffer's challenge to the Free Church tradition has another aspect, however. We note his off-hand reference to a 'semi-Pelagian Free Church theology.' Certainly the 'voluntarist' principle can appear to express more self-assertiveness ('Lord, I will follow you wherever you go') than obedience to a given call. Bonhoeffer was justified, in his analysis of the encounter between his Confessing Church and the ecumenical movement, in asking other churches about their confessions:

> There can only be a church as a Confessing Church, i.e. as a church which confesses itself to be for its Lord and against his enemies. A church without a confession or free from one is not a church, but a sect, and makes itself master of the Bible and the Word of God. A confession is the church's formulated answer to the Word of God in Holy Scripture, expressed in its own words. [31]

Certainly Free Churches have at times, especially under the influence of late nineteenth century subjectivism and liberalism, fought shy of any 'credal' emphasis either in their liturgies or their constitutions. Nor has that been without reason, for on occasion they have had bitter experience of the use of creeds by religious and secular authorities attempting to coerce conformity, both spiritual and political. However, Bonhoeffer is not concerned primarily about whether churches have confessions in written or credal form . We note again the reservations in his prison letters about how in the Confessing Church itself personal faith in Jesus Christ had been evaded under cover of the abstract 'faith of the Church' [32]- a criticism which finds more than an echo in much Free Church sentiment. He is more concerned about confessing rather than confession, the obedient act rather than a static piece of theology. He criticizes the attitude which 'knows nothing of the significance of the living confession, but regards the confession as a dead system which is from time to time applied schematically as a standard against other churches.' [33] The first item in confession is a confession of sin, and the first confession is the deed. And the nature of confession is not self-proclamation but response to the given Word of God as it is heard by the church in that particular historical situation. In this dynamic understanding of confessing, as the responsible, obedient answer of the believing community to the claim of the Lord of the church in the particular historical situation (or *kairos*), as revealed in Scripture and enabled by prayer in the Holy Spirit, we are in fact exceedingly close to what some of us will recognize as authentic Free Church theology. A classic exponent was the Scottish Congregationalist P.T. Forsyth (1848-1921), often described in Britain as a Barthian before Barth, thanks to his reaction against liberalism even prior to 1900. In certain respects however he also pre-dates Bonhoeffer's 'dynamic confessionalism' in his repeated insistence that the freedom of the church is a '*founded* freedom', and one moreover with implications for the whole body politic. Thus:

> From first to last . . . Independency has pursued not a dogma but a polity based on a gospel. Its interest has not been pure doctrine through a church so much as a true church through a gospel, *a true church in a true state.* [34] (emphases mine)

Forsyth was acutely aware of the need for a firm anchorage of the Free Church in that which makes it free, the gospel (for which read Bonhoeffer's 'Word'). Thereby he was also more aware than most of his Free Church contemporaries, of the ambiguous possibilities of a universalistic worldly concern. The Independent (that is, including the Baptist) tradition 'has always had that sense of the real world which was so pre-eminent in Cromwell, and it has had the consequent temptation, when its dogmatic base was shaken or dissolved, of becoming the victim of that world.' [35] Not that he was in the least advocating a non-social, apolitical attitude. Forsyth was second to none in his social and political concern, and was an exceedingly acute analyst of the shifting dynamics and polarities on the Edwardian British scene. But he did recognize the problem of how the church as a gathered community can formulate prescriptions, to the extent of a political ethic, for the whole of society. Thereby he anticipates to an intriguing degree a number of the queries raised by Bonhoeffer in the later chapters of the *Ethics* where, we have seen, Bonhoeffer asks how a confessing church community can offer a word to the state, or promote 'solutions' to all the 'problem' areas of life. Forsyth regarded as simplistic the notion that Christianity 'has a direct political ethic', suggesting instead that 'its direct action is to create a moral soul, and thus a social or national ethos, which then creates the political ethic.'[36] That is in fact what happened, he argues, in the contribution of Independency to the creation of western democracy. Whereas the young Bonhoeffer saw the justification of the national church as lying in its ability to become a gathered or confessing church, Forsyth, by a nice converse, saw the justification of congregationalism consisting in the church as free doing what the church as established had failed to do: to relate Christianity to the whole realm of society and politics - an idea which he recognizes as the authentic 'genius' of the idea of establishment. Forsyth's writing, long neglected, can still be highly productive and there are many other parallels with both Barth and Bonhoeffer which would repay exploration.

Dietrich Bonhoeffer, then, with his presentation of an ethically conscious confessing church encourages us, if we are also prepared to face his sharp challenges, to retrace and recover much that is most vital in the Free Church tradition. In the final analysis, one has to admit, there is a sense in which there has to be conceded to Bonhoeffer the last word, even over one such as P.T. Forsyth . Historically, as confirmed by our experiences both in Britain and South Africa (not to mention Germany), it has proved exceedingly difficult for the Free Churches to maintain both their distinctness and their universal social commitment. Forsyth's warning has again been confirmed, that the Free Churches can so easily become the victims of the world they recognize (and even evangelize!). Having proclaimed freedom, too easily they allow the world to give them the freedom to occupy an assigned place which presently becomes a ghetto. But equally, Forsyth's suggestion that the task of the church is to create some kind of moral soul in the body politic, has proved problematic. Something stiffer has to be built into our understanding of the church as the gathered community, to define not only its 'task' but its actual status in relation to the world before God.

As we have seen, in the *Ethics* Bonhoeffer writes of the distinctness of the gathered congregation under the word of God, as clearly as any Free Church theologian could. But no less emphatically does he see the deputyship of the church in relation to the world under God. Such a note counteracts that perennial tendency of the Free Church to conceive itself as gathered apart from the world and thereby privileged in its access to God over against the world. Or, equally, that tendency to moral superiority which tends to see 'witness' in terms of the self-advertisement of virtue. Or, just as pertinent, the assumption that the church already knows what is best for the world. The greater freedom which the Free Church must rediscover, is the freedom to stand with the sufferings and needs of others; and, thanks in no small measure to Bonhoeffer and the Confessing Church, it is being rediscovered. Nowhere is this more evident than in the relatively recent (1977) confession produced jointly by the German-speaking Baptists of the Federal Republic, the Democratic Republic, Austria and Switzerland. The contrast with their earlier pietistic confessions from the nineteenth century and from the Nazi period [37] could not be greater. On the church it states:

The church of Jesus Christ responds to God's reconciling act in praise and worship. Bowing before God *she confesses her guilt* and receives from him forgiveness and the authority for her mission. In evangelization and service the Christian community bears witness to God's salvation for *all men*. She *intercedes in prayer* and in supplication *for all men and nations*.[38] (emphases mine, as below)

Certain paragraphs from Section II, 'Christians in the World', merit quoting in full:

It is the will of God for the Christian church to be the salt of the earth and the light of the world. The church seeks no dominion in society or over society but is called and empowered for worship of God in the everyday life of this world and thus for the development of shared human life by the power of the Holy Spirit. The church as a whole and each of its members are ready for the responsibility of faith. They speak for God and his righteousness, and in their life as brothers and sisters God's gracious rule can be discerned.

... Because Christians rejoice in being accepted by God and called to be his co-workers, they live their faith in bearing witness to Christ personally, *in demonstrating their solidarity with people who are suffering*, in acts of personal assistance, and thus in obedience to the command that we love our neighbours. To take our stand for the truth of Jesus Christ also includes our readiness to accept disadvantage and even persecution.

Because we have our origin in reconciliation with God, we are called also to serve the cause of reconciliation among men . . . [Christians] strive to eliminate any and all discrimination by persons against persons and work for peace in the world. The Christians' calling is to be validated precisely when in substantive issues *they must speak a resounding 'No'*. The readiness for reconciliation works for agreement, but it does not mean capitulation in the face of conflict or the suppression of real problems.

Because we have our origin in God's justification of the ungodly, we are called *to serve the cause of justice among men*. Since Christians live in the liberty for which Christ has set them free, *they oppose every form of dependence that injures human dignity*. In the spirit of Jesus they support corresponding efforts *to liberate men from economic, social and racial oppression*. Accordingly, they contend for the basic freedoms of man, especially for freedom of belief and conscience.

A rediscovery indeed of that 'founded freedom' which manifests itself in liberating others. Note how 'freedom of belief and conscience' is cited *after* the affirmations of the struggles in solidarity for the cause of justice, peace and reconciliation everywhere. This is still very much a Free Church confession. Dietrich Bonhoeffer would not have written it as it stands. But it could hardly have been written without him and the exemplary history of the confessing community he served. Creative figures do not necessarily turn us wholly into their disciples. They also make us reassess and value afresh what is ours already, but what we have perhaps forgotten or as yet hardly recognized. That is what Dietrich Bonhoeffer can do for our Free Church tradition.

7

Sweet Land of Liberty: A Postscript to the American Experience

Dietrich Bonhoeffer was never less than candid, and his frank assessment of North American religion in his 1939 essay 'Protestantism without Reformation' [1] still reads as one of his most penetrating and disturbing writings, not only for Americans but for the British and other citizens of 'western liberal' societies. It is, as we have observed elsewhere [2], a critique of 'freedom' considered as 'individual freedom' and as 'possibility'. The freedom of the church, on this western view, consists in the possible scope of operation allowed to it by its secular environment. So, 'The American praise of freedom is more a praise which is directed to the world, the state and society, than a statement about the church' [3]. And, most forthrightly of all, he declares:

> Whether the churches of God are really free can only be decided by the actual preaching of the Word of God. Only where this word can be preached concretely, in the midst of historical reality, in judgment, command, forgiveness of sinners and liberation from all human institutions is there freedom of the church. But where thanks for institutional freedom must be rendered by the sacrifice of freedom of preaching, the church is in chains, even if it believes itself to be free. [4]

The unqualified assertion of 'freedom' as a 'Christian right' is what Bonhoeffer meant by a 'Protestantism without Reformation'. To be properly 'reformed' as distinct from merely 'Protestant' a church has always to be placing itself under (and thus by implication always distinguishing itself from) the absolute truth of the Word of God by which it is judged, forgiven and renewed. It can never be wholly the advocate of its own cause in the world. (As a historical footnote, it is significant that the term 'Protestant' was not foundational to the

Reformation - certainly not to the theological issues at stake. The word first arose after the course of the Reformation had been running several years, when at the Diet of Speyer in 1529 those German states which had been reforming their churches decided upon a political alliance with each other, in face of the threat from the still-Catholic states and the Holy Roman Emperor).

Bonhoeffer's essay, however, was by no means one-sided in its analysis of American society and the churches' role within it. It fully recognized the impressive energy and diversity of Christian life and community in the United States. In fact the essay is remarkable for its objectivity and rigour, written as it was in one of the most stressful periods of the author's life, those few weeks in the summer of 1939 when he made his momentous decision to return from the security of the 'land of the free' to the perilous situation of a Nazi Germany about to drag all Europe into war. In that decision to return he was about to exhibit the paradox that to accept the costly way of obedience in a situation where politically there was no 'freedom', was itself an act of greater freedom than to remain in a 'free society'. That was fifty years ago. 'Freedom' is still proclaimed as the talisman of the American - and by reflection the British - way of life.

The Oval Office in the White House is won not simply by those with the most well-funded and efficient campaign machines, but by the candidate who can ring the old Liberty Bell with the sweetest tone for the present day. Would Bonhoeffer still make the same criticisms as he made then? Or as Karl Barth made in his American tour of 1962 when he too raised questions about the American emphasis on 'liberty'? A minister attending a Bonhoeffer seminar which I was holding in Philadelphia in 1988 remarked that, on his first reading of it, scarcely a word needed to be changed in 'Protestantism without Reformation' for it to retain its contemporary cutting edge.

It was in fact Philadelphia, home of Independence Hall and Liberty Bell, which provided my own introduction to American perceptions of 'freedom'. It was not, however, the sight of George Washington's silver ink-stand or other historic memorabillia of the War of Independence which made the most impact, but two church services on successive Sundays. In conjunction, they illustrated strikingly how perspectives on 'freedom' differ according to social position and experience, and how the treatment of the Bible by the preacher varies accordingly.

Prayer at midnight: the black gospel

The choir assembled at the rear of the church, splendidly robed. A boy acolyte mounted the sanctuary steps and lit the candles on the communion table. This was not high Anglican or Roman Catholic liturgy, but the start of a service in a black Baptist church in a fairly prosperous suburb of Philadelphia. In the vestibule was a large picture of Jesse Jackson with the caption, 'No-body wins if you don't vote.' The packed congregation grew hushed as the altar boy retreated down the steps, and after a gentle introit the choir of women, men and children started to process down the aisle, singing the song dating from the Civil War:

Walk, O walk! Don't you get weary! Walk, O walk! Don't you get weary! Walk, O walk! Don't you get weary! There's a great camp meeting in the Promised Land!

Walk together children! Don't you get weary! Walk together children! Don't you get weary! Walk together children! Don't you get weary! There's a great camp meeting in the Promised Land!

The singing grew in intensity as the clapping and swaying choristers moved into their stalls, inaugurating a service which defied all classification whether as 'liturgical' or 'charismatic' or 'traditional Protestant'. It was all these and more, the fruit of an evident freedom to embrace whatever kinds of worship seemed appropriate to the congregation, regardless of source or historic association, and quite innocent of the prejudices so often associated with their denomination. It was all skilfully led by the woman President appointed for the day.

The most memorable part however was the sermon, delivered by a guest preacher, a young black minister and homiletics teacher who had been student pastor in the church some years before. He took as his text the story in Acts 16 of the imprisonment of Paul and Silas in Philippi, of their praying in the prison at midnight and the subsequent earthquake. It was superb preaching in every respect, from its simple yet striking language and its well-crafted structure, to its pungent examination of contemporary superstition ('I don't care which stars Mrs Nancy Reagan looks to but I am concerned about how she and her husband do their voodoo economics' - to laughter and prolonged applause from the congregation) and its vibrant delivery. From beginning to end sounded the refrain 'Can a simple prayer change a complex situation? Can a simple prayer *do* at midnight?' Yes, asserted the preacher with utter conviction. Prayer at midnight keeps us together, as it did Paul and Silas. But it is not only the prayer of togetherness. His voice rising in a magnificent, trembling crescendo he declared:

> Prayer also keeps our sense of liberation intact. Paul and Silas prayed and sang praises just as if they were down at the church meeting. No matter where you are, if you call on God you are still free [loud applause]. Our black slave foreparents knew that. In the midst of the incarceration of slavery they refused to let anybody call them slaves. That's why they used to sing:
> *Before I'd be a slave I'd be buried in my grave, And go home to my Lord and be free.*

In the midst of the midnight a simple prayer will keep a liberation agenda in front of us. Jesus' own prayer in the midnight desolation of the cross, 'Father, into thy hands I commit my spirit' was, said the preacher, the final and greatest assurance that prayer at midnight is effective. It was followed by resurrection.

'Nowhere', wrote Bonhoeffer in 1939, 'is revival preaching still so vigorous and widespread as among the negroes [sic], . . . here the Gospel of Jesus Christ, the saviour of the sinner, is really preached and accepted with great welcome and visible emotion.'[5] What I heard that morning was certainly the saving grace of Jesus Christ preached with such power and insight as I have scarcely heard it elsewhere, and for which 'revivalistic' would be too superficial a description. Its main point of interest, however, emerges when compared with what I heard a week later in another church.

Prayer after midnight: the white gospel

The following Sunday I attended a white Baptist church. Again it was a large congregation, but the worship was much closer to the familiar 'Protestant tradition'. It was Independence holiday weekend. The opening hymn was 'America', and the minister chose to preach on 'Freedom'. By a nice coincidence, his text was exactly the same passage from Acts 16 as I had heard the previous Sunday in the black church.

The treatment, though, was different. This sermon focused not on the prayer at midnight, but the situation after the earthquake, after the release of the prisoners. The parallel which the preacher drew was with independent, free America, and the question round which his sermon was built was 'What shall we do with our freedom?' Not the chained prisoners praying and singing, but the released Paul and Silas converting the gaoler, was the focus of the message.

The white congregation was being told that, being Americans, they were free - politically and religiously. The question to which they had to address themselves was how to use this freedom. They should not use it selfishly but in ways that pleased God and benefitted others - as Paul and Silas did. It was a competent, thoughtful homily, and certainly apposite to the national holiday (that very day, immediately preceding Independence Day itself, occurred the tragedy of the shooting down of the Iranian airliner by a United States warship in the Gulf).

Perspectives on liberation

It would be invidious to argue that one of these two sermons was a better or more faithful exposition of the word of Scripture than the other. Nevertheless, it was in listening to the black preacher that I felt more confronted with the sovereign promises and demands of a God who liberates regardless of circumstances, as at the Red Sea, as in Babylon in the sixth century B.C., and above all as in the odd series of events in and around Jerusalem recorded in the New Testament. In the final analysis the white sermon was, in Bonhoeffer's terms, a praise of the world - a reaffirmation of assumptions regarding the social, political and economic context of the congregation summed up in the word 'liberty' - liberty understood as possibility of self-chosen action. It was in the black sermon that I heard most vividly the note that the freedom which God gives is not a freedom dependent upon certain worldly circumstances, but a freedom to transcend and combat those circumstances even when - precisely when - they are at their most oppressive and, humanly speaking, most freedom-denying.

The white preacher assumed a freedom. The black preacher faced people who still - twenty years after Martin Luther King's death - did not feel the complete freedom of belonging to their society. But true freedom does not wait for the dawn, for the release of the shackles. True freedom shows itself precisely by its being claimed when the powers of the age would deny it. That is the black gospel perspective, the viewpoint which reads the scriptural story and identifies with those in prison, not yet released: yet paradoxically it exhibits a greater liberation than those who assume freedom to be their present possession. It is the freedom which denies slavery - 'Before I'd be a slave . . . '

Freedom means living as free people under God (Galatians 5.1), under the freedom God gives, regardless of the freedom donated by the world. It means, on the part of the privileged, being always prepared to listen to those who do not yet feel free, whether as blacks, or women or unemployed people, and being ready to learn again from such people what true freedom means: the liberty of claiming free status at the very points where it is denied them. If Bonhoeffer's comments about the freedom of preaching need modifying at all, it is in the need to complement them with the freedom of *praying* for liberation: praying at midnight, when the shackles are still too tight, when the darkness is still thick, and the gaoler is in charge. Prayer subverts the present oppressive order, and to pray 'Your kingdom come' confesses, even now, who is really in charge. The prison is no longer simply a prison, a place which shuts people in, but a place where people witness. As it happens, of course, Bonhoeffer himself came to know that discipline, suffering and death are themselves stations on the way to freedom, not obstacles to freedom, and he himself knew the strange liberation of the midnight prayer in his prison cell:

Twelve cold, thin strokes of the tower clock
Awaken me.
No sound, no warmth in them
To hide and cover me.
Howling evil dogs at midnight
Frighten me.
The wretched noise
Divides a poor yesterday
From a poor today.
What can it matter to me
Whether one day turns into another,
One that could have nothing new, nothing better
Than to end quickly like this one?
I want to see the turning of the times,

When luminous signs stand in the night sky,
And over the peoples new bells
Ring and ring.
I am waiting for that midnight
In whose fearfully streaming brilliance
The evil perish for anguish
And the good overcome with joy.

The villain
Comes to light
In the judgment.

Deceit and betrayal,
Malicious deeds -
Atonement is near.

See, O man,
Holy strength
Is at work, setting right.

Rejoice and proclaim
Faithfulness and right
For a new race!

Heaven, reconcile
The sons of earth
To peace and beauty.

Earth, flourish;
Man, become free,
Be free!

Bonhoeffer in 1939 had still thought of himself as the preacher who demonstrated freedom in proclaiming the word regardless of circumstance. By early in the war he could no longer deliver public sermons. The conspiracy had taught him the 'view from below', the perspective of the suffering, the outcast and the defenceless. By being banned from the pulpit and joining the oppressed and eventually being imprisoned he was laicized and made Jewish and black. But prayer, no less than preaching, is a measure of the church's freedom - or slavery. Bonhoeffer's last visible act was to kneel, naked among the SS guards, at the foot of the gallows in Flossenbürg. At the end of April 1945, a good fortnight after that death and just days before the unconditional surrender of Germany, the so-called 'Free' Churches of the German Baptists were still issuing public prayers for the preservation and success of the leaders of the Reich, and so witnessing yet again to their enslavement to the powers of this world. And in 1985 nothing so worried the South African government during the State of Emergency as the churches' summons to a day of prayer for the ending of unjust rule. To pray for the kingdom at midnight is indeed to be free.

8
Taking Sides: South Africa and the Cost of Confession

In 1985 a delegation from the British Churches visited South Africa at the invitation of the South African Council of Churches, to take part in an assessment of the crisis in that country, and of the churches' response to it. Among the many observations made in the delegation's report is the following:

> Many South African Christians are growingly disillusioned and impatient with the merely verbal stances of the institutional churches, particularly perhaps the Protestant churches. We may see in the next two or three years the start of an exodus from those churches, of people who feel that their Christian consciences cannot survive within the churches as they are, but only within a fellowship of opposition, however costly, to the tyranny of the present regime.
>
> The parallel to the Confessing Church of Germany will be closer still at that point, for the issue will then become 'Where is the true Church of South Africa?' An outsider cannot comment on the painfulness of that issue for South African Christians, but neither will outsiders be able to avoid all of the pain. For then there will arise the immensely critical question for the Christian communities abroad, as to which community or communities in South Africa they will recognize as representing the one, universal Church of Christ in South Africa. This was an issue never entirely resolved in the German case of 1934-45.[1]

It is not my primary purpose here to describe and analyse the growing confrontation between church and state in South Africa in terms of a 'Church Struggle' parallel to that in Germany during the Third Reich, or as a 'battle for the confession' with which such names as Karl Barth, Martin Niemöller and Dietrich Bonhoeffer are above all associated. The parallels between the South Africa of today and the Nazi Germany of half a century or more ago, and of the churches' respective responsibilities in these situations, have been drawn often enough and will be familiar to any with even a minimal acquaintance with the writings of John de Gruchy, Charles Villa-Vicencio, Allan Boesak and others [2]. Indeed it has become almost a commonplace to speak of 'the church struggle in South Africa'. The main resemblance is that in both historical contexts we see the Christian community under immense pressure to tailor its proclamation and life to serving an oppressive, violent and racist ideology which desires to clothe itself in highly 'religious' terms, and from which the church must therefore - if it is to be authentic - distinguish itself and its gospel with the utmost rigour. There are also of course significant differences. In Nazi Germany a populist dictatorship swung nationalist feeling into racist persecution of a minority, the Jews. In South Africa, a government which at best can represent only about 15% of the total population, maintains and enforces a system which oppresses and dehumanizes the majority, the blacks. And whereas in Nazi Germany the issue of 'confession' predominantly focused on the question of the church (in particular, over whether 'racial' origin could debar one from office or membership), in South Africa the issue of the apartheid society as a whole has always been to the fore, while of course recognizing that the churches themselves have often simply reflected within their own life and structure the divisions and conflicts within the nation at large. At the risk of over-simplifying, whereas in the German case the issue (if it was seen at all) was whether the church and its confession also had a general political reference, in South Africa the typical question is in reverse: whether the socio-political issue is a matter for the church and its gospel.

The matter I wish to address here concerns the implications of the South African church struggle for Christians elsewhere in the world, the *oikumene*. Amid all the comparison-drawing with the German *Kirchenkampf*, one feature of that earlier historical case has gone largely ignored by those of us who watch the South African struggles from abroad, and which has disturbing implications for us if the parallel does indeed extend this far. More than we might recognize from the conveniently safe distance of more than half a century, the German Church Struggle challenged the wider Christian community to take sides in a radical and decisive way. Only now are we in Britain, Europe and elsewhere in the 'west' beginning to feel the sharpness of the parallel challenge from South Africa, and only now are we sensing the pain that this might bring.

This may sound surprising in view of the international concern expended upon South Africa over the past forty years, especially in Christian circles, and the admiration deservedly received from around the world by figures as diverse as Trevor Huddlestone, Joost de Blank, Ambrose Reeves, Byers Naudé and, more recently, by the foremost black Christian leaders such as Desmond Tutu and Allan Boesak. Moreover, international confessional bodies such as the World Alliance of Reformed Churches (which actually suspended the Dutch Reformed Church of South Africa from its membership) and the World Lutheran Federation (which declared apartheid to have brought about a *status confessionis* for the church) have not flinched from controversial stances and decisions, to say nothing of the World Council of Churches which by virtue of its Programme to Combat Racism has long been an ecclesial persona non grata as far as the South African government is concerned. It is significant, however, that hitherto the Christian 'opposition' in South Africa has, from abroad, been seen largely as an opposition to the Nationalist Government in its creation and oppressive maintenance of apartheid - and, alongside the government, its handmaid the Dutch Reformed Church which provided the theological rationale for the doctrine of 'separate development'. Only now is the hard truth biting home, that the 'Christian opposition' of such as Byers Naudé , Allan Boesak, Desmond Tutu and the South African Council of Churches, is equally an opposition to much 'mainstream' Christianity in South Africa, quite apart from the Voortrekker mentality sanctified by the Dutch Reformed Church at its most conservative. Recently a congregation in England was startled to hear a visiting white minister from one of the South African free churches - and not a denomination especially noted for either its political or theological conservatism - declare that in his view Desmond Tutu was 'just a politician in a dog-collar', and an embarrassing one at that. The British Churches' Delegation report recognizes the tensions inherent in the church structures in South Africa, and asks 'whether we are in a breaking process in which the actual leadership is going to be provided by those who, established leaders or not, utter the prophetic word for the hour.' [2]

Let us picture for a moment the visitor, say from Britain, who has decided to go to South Africa for a few weeks to see for himself (we assume a male for no good reason) the 'facts' about South Africa, and to go with an 'open mind' and to 'listen to all points of view'. His early impressions may well be puzzling. He is struck by the natural beauty of the land, and he especially revels in that generous sun and blue sky over the tawny plains, and the exotic birds with flashing wings among the blossoms. He is equally taken with the white people he meets - kindly, courteous and often overwhelmingly hospitable. Yes, many of them admit they haven't got it right yet in their country and many will go so far as to say they 'hate apartheid'. So what do they think about the black political opposition, Nelson Mandela and the African National Congress? The white reaction is not inevitably one of outright hostility. It may well be of overt sympathy towards the black political 'ideals' ; but there are always the 'communists' and 'terrorists' who are eager to exploit them. As for the likes of Desmond Tutu, he too may be a 'sincere' man but is 'playing into the hands of the extremists'. Basically, many whites will say, the problem is that the blacks cannot agree among themselves and therefore for the present there is no real alternative to the present system. Many of these whites will personally be very kind and generous to blacks such as their domestic servants or employees. The sticking point comes when the issue of black political power and rights is raised.

Of course our visitor will meet black people. He may visit Soweto, or Crossroads. He will be shocked by the conditions under which most of the people live. He may possibly be surprised, however, at the 'very nice' houses occupied by some blacks or 'coloureds'. He may see this as evidence that the government 'really is trying' to alleviate the conditions under which blacks live. He may, or may not, be faced with the evidence that such 'good' housing schemes are part of the overall policy of creating and buying off a certain middle-class black stratum which will conveniently soften the radical push from below. He will meet many black people who appear to be 'contented', who have no harsh words about the State President. In his host family's kitchen he may well meet a domestic who thanks God for the security forces which allow her to get back to her township home safely each night without being mugged or raped. And as for those self-same security forces which he has seen in action in such violently lurid detail on his television screen back home or in the film *Cry Freedom*... well, he may see the odd Caspir or Hippo on the edge of Soweto but one would hardly know they are there. If he is specially privileged, he may get an interview with a government representative. He will be plied with courtesy and plausible concern for the blacks, who again (especially the younger population) need protection from exploitation by 'extremists'.

He may well be unnerved by this. Did his previously liberal conscience get it all wrong? Much will depend on which people he meets during his stay. If he spends all his time, effectively, with whites who 'dislike apartheid' but distance themselves from actually identifying with the political struggles of blacks themselves, he is indeed likely to end up feeling that South Africa has been 'misrepresented' in the world media, and that the issues have been 'oversimplified'. Everything depends on whether he is able to sit down with and listen to black people who are carrying on the struggle for their own liberation irrespective of white paternalistic 'concern', and regardless of the cost in terms of harassment, detention, torture and maybe death. If he does have the opportunity and requisite capacity to empathize, he will quickly recognize that in meeting with detainees dependents' organizations, or with black trades unions, or with black students' groups, or for that matter with the white campaigners against conscription into the security forces, he has shifted into a a completely different gear from those whites who 'dislike apartheid' or who even 'abhor it with their whole being' while doing nothing to change the fundamental political status quo.

Perhaps most disconcerting of all, in South Africa he will find that among many 'liberal' whites, and even among many black Christians, there is no assumedly universal support for Desmond Tutu, Allan Boesak and the South African Council of Churches. He will find it unreal to speak of the 'church in South Africa', for there are many churches, with a bewildering diversity of theological, linguistic and cultural composition, and a confusion of tongues on political matters. The single largest wholly black Christian group, the Zionist, is happily apolitical and on one recent occasion invited no less a person than President Botha himself to address its national gathering. Our visitor may well have interviews with major leaders and theologians of the Dutch Reformed Church who seem to be 'revising' the earlier theology of race and nation in an impressively open and creative way. So how 'representative' are those church groups and leaders who have become household names across the world for their 'opposition to apartheid'?

The answer of course is 'not wholly representative' if one is thinking purely in terms of numbers. At the same time, they are more representative numerically than they are often given credit for by either their opponents or cynical observers. On the political front, no responsible assessment would claim that the African National

Congress is the *only* black voice, or that the United Democratic Front unites the whole black population. But, *pace* the supporters (inside and outside South Africa) of Chief Buthelezi's Inkatha organization, the ANC and UDF can justly claim to be the most representative groups of black aspirations. And politics, if it is about 'democracy', is at bottom about allowing power to the groups which are most representative while safeguarding the rights of all. 'Representation' is a more complex concept than a merely numerical approach will allow. But even apart from these considerations, when it comes to the leadership and witness of the Christian Church wholly new issues arise on a theological level which markedly shift the perspective within which 'representation' is viewed and evaluated.

It is clear that since the dramatic events of March 1988 when Archbishop Tutu and other church leaders confronted the government in Cape Town and demanded that in the cause of justice and peace the effective bannings of many black organizations should be lifted, this issue of 'representation' is being highlighted by the authorities as a potentially devastating propaganda weapon against the Christian opposition. Whether or not the government is afraid of what world opinion would say - or perhaps even do - should Tutu, Boesak, Chikane and others be silenced is not clear. But the regime realises that much more effective (and much less expensive in every way) than their detention or expulsion would be their isolation and the discrediting of their claims to 'represent' Christian opinion in South Africa. It is therefore small wonder that we now do have many reports coming out of South Africa that 'there are other positions to which we should pay heed', that 'Tutu is not the only voice we should hear'. Especially, we are being told and will be told even more loudly as time goes on, that as well as the 'extremes' of the 'radicals' like the SACC on the one hand, and the right-wing of the Nationalist Party and the die-hards of the Dutch Reformed Church on the other, there are many 'moderates', many 'reasonable' people. It is this 'middle ground' of people who 'dislike the status quo' but are opposed to anything which 'could make matters worse' (especially any international economic or political pressures from outside the country) whom we should support. Alongside this mild blend of sweet reasonableness with Christian charity towards all, the voice of the 'radicals' sounds increasingly strident - and unnecessary.

Suddenly, therefore, a Christian's involvement in South Africa becomes a fraught matter of taking sides, not simply against the 'apartheid regime' but also seemingly against other Christians. Concern leads not to peace but a sword, and a person's foes are those of one's own church or denominational household. Such a fearful development was recognized most strikingly in the publication of the controversial *Kairos Document* of 1985. This statement, largely but not exclusively the work of black theologians based in Soweto and drawing over 150 signatures right across the ecumenical spectrum, is the starkest call yet issued for a costly Christian opposition to an oppressive state which has made itself into a godless tyranny - all the more evil because it claims divine sanction for its policies and methods. I count it one of the greatest, if fortuitous, privileges of my life to have been present at the public release of their document by the Kairos theologians in Khotso House, headquarters of the South African Council of Churches in Johannesburg (and just a few days' before writing this, shattered by a bomb blast), in September 1985. In front of the press and television cameras, what was so remarkable was the matter-of-fact, almost dead-pan, tone in which the contents were summarized and presented - contents which could hardly have been more passionate:

> The time has come. The moment of truth has arrived. South Africa has been plunged into a crisis that is shaking the foundations and there is every indication that the crisis has only just begun and that it will deepen and become even more threatening in the months to come. It is the KAIROS or moment of truth not only for apartheid but also for the Church. [3]

This was not just a response to the then partial State of Emergency. It was an urgent summons to decision on the part of Christians themselves:

> What the present crisis shows up . . . is that the Church is divided. More and more people are now saying that there are in fact two Churches in South Africa - a White Church and a Black Church. Even within the same denomination there are in fact two Churches. In the life and death conflict between different social forces that has come to a head in South Africa today, there are Christians (or at least people who profess to be Christians) on both sides of the conflict - and some who are trying to sit on the fence! [4]

No less astringent has been the document *Evangelical Witness in South Africa*. Its authors - evangelicals as its title implies - are concerned that theologically 'conservative' responses to *Kairos* must not flinch from examining the highly suspect ways in which enthusiasm for 'preaching the gospel' has in Southern Africa often become a guise for white-led paternalistic structures being perpetuated in the churches and 'missionary' bodies no less than in society as a whole. There is no mistaking its prophetic note:

> To try to extract some 'spiritual' life from a political or economic life, in the name of 'non-involvement' in politics is dualism. This dualism outlook on life is unscriptural. Life is a whole. A 'born-again' Christian was not exempted from carrying a 'pass' book, with its evil accompaniments! This is a political issue. Then why step aside when this miniature symbol of apartheid oppression . . . is attacked? Yet one accepts it without questioning. Perhaps we think of this as a blessed hypocrisy! [5]

Christians in South Africa, then, are being asked to be honest as to where they really stand on the fundamental issues of justice and righteousness in their country, and thereby implicitly to face controversy and conflict among themselves. That is disturbing to those of us who are onlookers, for the question then becomes: who really represents not 'the Christian majority' but 'authentic Christianity' in South Africa? We too in the international Christian family are then faced with painful decision, and it is at this point that we find ourselves looking at a landscape very similar to that of the churches as they contemplated the struggles in Nazi Germany half a century and more ago.

The Confessing Church and the Ecumenical Movement

'The German church struggle marks the second great stage in the history of the ecumenical movement and will in a decisive way be normative for its future' [6] wrote Dietrich Bonhoeffer in his 1935 paper 'The Confessing Church and the Ecumenical Movement'. Bonhoeffer was viewing the ecumenical movement - doubtless sharing with many others the sense of something decisive as having been inaugurated with the Edinburgh International Missionary Conference of 1910 - within a grand historical perspective. First, the churches of the world beginning to meet together. But second, those churches beginning to ask: *On what basis* do we meet together? And, for Bonhoeffer, it is above all the struggle of the Confessing Church for the confession of Jesus Christ as the sole Lord of church and world, which is focusing that question as nowhere else. The Confessing Church was engaged not in mere ecclesiastical politicking or theological refinement, but in reasserting the basis of what it meant for any church to be the church of Christ: belief in Jesus as (in the terms of the Barmen Confession) the one Word of God to be heard, believed and obeyed in life and in death, and in all areas of life and in all circumstances. For Bonhoeffer this meant that there could be no unqualified use of the term 'Christian' any more. 'The confession occupies her [the Confessing Church's] whole sphere'.[7] This carried a stern implication:

> To this confession as it has been authoritatively expounded in the decisions of the Synods of Barmen and Dahlem, there is only a Yes or a No. Thus here too neutrality is impossible, here too an assent to this or that point outside the question of the confession remains excluded. No, the Confessing Church must insist that in any responsible church discussion it is taken seriously enough for this claim to be recognized and accepted. It must further insist that in any conversation with it the solidarity of the churches be shown by the partner in the conversations not entering into discussions with it and with the churches which it accuses of heresy at one and the same time, indeed that even for the ecumenical partner in the conversations the conversations be finally broken off where in its responsibility as a church it declares that they are broken off.[8]

The last sentence, particularly, had harsh implications. An overseas church or ecumenical body could not at one and the same time or on equal terms have fellowship with, or converse with, both the Confessing Church and those groups in Germany - be they never so 'Christian' in claim and appearance - from which the Confessing Church had distinguished itself by virtue of its confession of Jesus Christ as sole Lord of the church and of all human life. That severance was not just with the overtly pro-Nazi 'German Christian' movement, which had tried to 'Germanize' the Protestant faith in a crudely nationalistic manner and had attempted to impose a racial disqualification on Jewish pastors. It was equally with the 'official' Evangelical Church which accepted the authority of the government-sanctioned Reich Church Office and its committees. Many of those who took this 'middle way' had no truck with the 'German Christians'. Equally, however, they could not see the point of the fuss being made on the 'extreme' wing of the Confessing Church. After all, the so-called Aryan Clauses were a peripheral matter, there being relatively very few pastors of Jewish or partly-Jewish descent . But for Bonhoeffer and the 'radicals' of the Confessing Church the issue was all too clear: between those who accepted the decisions of the Barmen and Dahlem Synods and those who, for whatever reason and motive, did not, there was a fundamentally different understanding as to what the Church of Jesus Christ actually was. The ecumenical movement could not have dealings with both.

Bonhoeffer's struggles with the ecumenical movement have been well-documented[9]. To a degree he and his confessing allies had a measure of success with the ecumenical 'Life and Work' Committee, chaired by Bishop George Bell of Chichester who tried to ensure that it was the Confessing Church which was allowed to represent the

'German Evangelical Church' at its conferences and meetings. The high point of this policy was the Oxford Conference on Church and State in 1937. Except for two or three Free Church representatives, no Germans were present. The invitations had gone to the Confessing Church - whose delegates were refused travel documents by the Reich government. With the Faith and Order movement there was less recognition of the Confessing Church's exclusive claims. Leonard Hodgson of Oxford, who was Secretary of Faith and Order and one of the most notable English theologians of the time, steadfastly refused to depart from an even-handed approach to the rival claims coming from Germany. It was not, he held, in the competence of ecumenicals abroad to make a judgment on what was essentially an internal German matter. 'Ecumenical', on this view, meant a comprehensiveness embracing all claims to be 'Christian'. Bonhoeffer's 'second stage' of the ecumenical movement had not, and could not, figure on his horizon.

Indeed, an 'open-minded' visitor to Germany in the late 1930s could well have been at least as nonplussed as his counterpart experiencing South Africa today. Many were. It was perfectly possible to have an enjoyable holiday or business trip or study tour to swastika-draped Germany and to return home convinced that the media image of Germany had been 'unbalanced', that the aggressiveness of Nazism had been 'exaggerated' and that even on the issue of anti-semitism there was 'another side to the story'. Those who had known Germany at the end of the 1920s would contrast the brighter, more orderly towns and people with the drab and dilapidated scenes they remembered in the Weimar Republic. As late as 1938 they could sit in a sunny Berlin tea-garden and even meet some Jews (!) at the next table who did not seem unduly worried by what was happening. Yes, there were some Nazi thugs about but the harrassment could only be a passing phase and Hitler would get things firmly under control again. Yes, there were 'concentration camps' but these were largely filled with communists who would have behaved far more harshly had *they* got into power - and largely thanks to Hitler they had not. In any case, why single out Germany for so much opprobrium? What was happening in Soviet Russia was far worse. On church matters, our visitor might well have become even more puzzled, and have come home writing letters to the religious press, to the effect that the issues were 'not nearly so simple' as some well-meaning but only partly-informed people (with an axe to grind) were making out, who only listened to one quarter in Germany. He had gone to Germany with the example of Martin Niemöller, recently imprisoned, uplifted before him as the spokesman for the freedom of the gospel in face of state tyranny. He had found, however, that the 'Confessing Church' was a steadily decreasing minority within German Protestantism and was certainly not 'representative' of the churches as a whole. There was, he found, a certain arrogance, a self-righteous zeal among some of these Confessing leaders. They were indeed making a fuss out of all proportion to the real issues. He had in fact found hardly anyone in any church who was really 'anti-semitic', though there were 'real problems' created by such a large Jewish element in German life. He was rather impressed by the 'sincere' and 'conciliatory' tone of the official Reich Church leadership who in courtesy and piety were patently Christian and wanting nothing more than that the Church should be able to pursue its spiritual and evangelical work in what was 'admittedly a very difficult situation, which it is difficult for people in Britain to appreciate.' Yes, the Confessing Church people had raised a matter of 'some importance' in protesting about the 'Aryan issue' in the church. But surely it was straining at gnats to worry about a few Jewish pastors when never before had the German Church been offered such an opportunity to find acceptance with the state and the national aspirations of the hour. Freedom of preaching, access to youth, guarantee of church finances and property - surely this was a sign of divine blessing upon their position. In comparison, some of the Confessing Church people were fanatics and pharisees, making dogmas out of abstract principles concerning the 'nature of the church' and so shutting themselves out from the opportunities of unfettered preaching of the gospel. In particular, there were one or two distinctly unhealthy elements promoting division and disunity when what was surely needed was a 'common Christian front' against all 'godlessness and materialism'. And no-one was more blameworthy in this regard, so our visitor might well be told, than a certain young theologian who was director of a preachers' seminary somewhere on the Baltic coast, who was talking loudly about 'costly grace' and 'discipleship' but who could not even manage to make all his students agree with him. Fortunately, a number of these ordinands were 'beginning to see sense' and go along with the Reich Church Committees. Our imaginary visitor is not totally hypothetical. The then Bishop of Gloucester, Dr A.C. Headlam, made some unfortunate forays into German church matters in the 1930s and his disparaging remarks about Martin Niemöller in particular aroused the wrath of many, not least Hensley Henson, Bishop of Durham. As a whole, British and American churchpeople were much impressed with the Confessing Church stand, and the imprisoned Martin Niemöller became an inspiring symbol of Christian resistance throughout the world. Not all the support was informed as to the exact issues. Many in the English-speaking world thought that the Confessing Church was standing up for 'religious freedom', a concept rather unfamiliar to most Germans of any theological persuasion, whereas the Confessing Christians themselves thought it was a matter, as Karl Barth put it, not of the liberty of the Christian conscience but of its binding in obedience to the truth [10]. But the support was no less welcome, or important, for that.

Here in fact we come to one of the chief circumstantial differences between the former German and contemporary South African cases. In the German Church struggle, overseas support for the Christian resistance had a congenial political background. As the 1930s wore on, Hitler's European ambitions became steadily more suspect and threatening to western eyes (though in the view of many not more dangerous than Soviet communism). Support for the Confessing Church did not contradict the growing perception of Nazi Germany as a potential national enemy, and indeed probably reinforced it (although many friends of the Confessing Christians, like Bishop Bell, desperately wanted to avoid war right up to the last). In the contemporary case, there is a massive political and economic linkage between Britain, other western countries and South Africa, to say nothing of close family ties for many people and the emotional factors which are involved. In short, Britain and South Africa are firm allies, as is made clear by the British voting record on sanctions in the United Nations, the Commonwealth and the European Community, and by the continuing, active promotion of trade between the two countries. Taking sides with the Christian opposition in South Africa has to overcome a good deal more political inertia than did solidarity in the German Church Struggle.

This requires that taking sides in the South African struggle must be an even more theologically acute affair than was necessary in the German case. It means being able to state, with clarity as well as with passion, why we should stand with people whose credentials as to their 'representative' status are assailed. We come back to the issue:

representative of what, or of whom?

The costly way

'"Open your mouth for the dumb" (Prov. 31.8). Here the decision will really be made whether we are still the church of the present Christ. The Jewish question.'[11] So Bonhoeffer, according to the notes taken by one of his students at Finkenwalde, brought one of his lectures on preaching to a close. The 'Jewish question', he makes clear, is not simply that of Jews in the church but of Jews in society as a whole, for his immediately preceding remarks are about the requirement of the church to befriend, without exception, the victims of violence and injustice. It is not that in this passage Bonhoeffer is making the definition of the church a matter of socio-political action, of justice and peace, as against a matter of confession (as at Barmen) and proclamation (as in biblical preaching). Rather he is asserting that the action and the confession are two sides of one coin. For him, the Jewish question, the political question, was always implicit in the Confessing Church's very existence, even if, to his sorrow, that Church as a whole failed to open its mouth for the dumb or to protect them when the final peril arose. Confessing Jesus Christ means deciding for him as Lord above all others, and equally deciding for the victims of inhumanity and violence such as he himself embraced and endured on his own cross. 'Here the decision will be made whether we are still the church of the present Christ.' Not whether we are the majority church, or the most popular church, or the most successful church, or the most unified church, but 'the church of the present Christ'. 'Representative' in Christian understanding means, at its deepest, re-presenting Christ himself; which means, on Bonhoeffer's terms, representing and standing for, taking the place of, his most defenceless sisters and brothers. At the very least, that means making these victims visible to the world. It means that in South Africa, and wherever else humanity is oppressed, we have to ask who is 'representing' Christ and those for whom he died, in this way. That can lead us to a very different solidarity from what often passes for 'Christian fellowship'. We are not being asked to decide with whom we think we naturally have most in common, or who are the nicest Christians, or the most spiritual, or the most attractive or impressive 'personalities'. We are being asked who is presenting us with the truth, and painful truth at that, about the situation for only as we do seek the truth wherever it leads can we hope to stand in it before God. That is why the *Kairos* document castigates so severely not just the idolatrous 'state theology' which uses 'God' to justify tyranny, but also the 'church theology' which speaks rather too quickly of 'reconciliation' while ignoring the fundamental inequities and oppression which must be removed - repented of - if 'reconciliation' is to be genuine. In one of its sharpest paragraphs *Kairos* states:

It would be quite wrong to try to preserve 'peace' and 'unity' at all costs, even at the cost of truth and justice and, worse still, at the cost of thousands of young lives. As disciples of Jesus we should rather promote truth and justice and life at all costs, even at the cost of creating conflict, disunity and dissension along the way. To be truly biblical our Church leaders must adopt a theology that millions of Christians have already adopted - a biblical theology of direct confrontation with the forces of evil rather than a theology of reconciliation with sin and the devil. [12]

That is the strongest possible counter to the bland reasonableness which would assure us that with a little more 'restraint' and 'moderation' the problems could be solved, and that the 'middle ground' must be strengthened. To this, we might also address Bonhoeffer 's words:

One is distressed by the failure of reasonable people to perceive either the depths of evil or the depths of the holy. With the best of intentions they believe that a little reason will suffice them to clamp together the parting timbers of the building. They are so blind that in their desire to see justice done to both sides they are crushed between the two clashing forces and end by achieving nothing. Bitterly disappointed at the unreasonableness of the world, they see that their efforts must remain fruitless and they withdraw resignedly from the scene or yield unresistingly to the stronger party. [13]

The question remains, however, of the precise criteria whereby we identify those whose call to solidarity we recognize to be the call of Jesus Christ in the present hour: those who represent the authentic gospel in its two-fold aspect of judgment and grace, demand and succour, the end of the old world and promise of the new. The church situation in South Africa, we have noted already, is vastly more multifarious and complicated than it was in Nazi Germany. A number of 'confessions' have been stated and adopted, but no single one has become a focus of debate and decision as happened with Barmen. Nor is *Kairos* as such a 'confession'. Its intention is not to arrive at a position so much as to mark a direction and to begin a debate within the churches. Rather therefore than looking at this stage for a particular statement, or a single organization, which might embody a 'confessing church' it is more important to seek to discern the features of a confessing movement: of actions and responsibilities undertaken which point towards the decision 'whether we are still the church of the present Christ.' While we take Bonhoeffer's question to be the right and urgent one in relation to our dealings with South Africa, therefore, the answer will not necessarily be in quite the same terms as was his in his own situation.

Discerning the spirits

'No one can say "Jesus is Lord" except by the Holy Spirit' (I Corinthians 12.3). The biblical affirmation can of course be used as a justification for recognizing any credal or confessional statement including this verbal formula as indicating 'authentic' or ' faithful' Christianity. We have the other New Testament warning: 'Not everyone who says to me, "Lord, Lord," shall enter the kingdom of heaven, but he who does the will of my Father who is in heaven.' (Matthew 7.21) Authentic or faithful Christianity confesses the supreme lordship of Jesus Christ, in deed no less than word. And this confession is enabled by the Holy Spirit.

Where, how, among whom, is the Holy Spirit active? Down the Christian centuries the answers to this question have proved notoriously subjective. The Spirit becomes the sanctified cloak for whatever figure, movement or party cause is favourable in our eyes. But criteria there certainly must be, and for Christian faith the supreme criterion is Christ: the Holy Spirit bears and creates the marks of Christ. Indeed, the greatest dangers in an emphasis upon the Spirit stem from an insufficiently trinitarian approach, allowing the Spirit to become a free-ranging entity detached from the Son and unaccountable to the Father. But in turn, what are the marks of Christ?

No apology is made here for turning to insights which I believe are peculiarly apposite to our case, coming as they do from one who has lived both long and deeply in the African context as a missionary, and whose quiet presence on the British Churches' Delegation to South Africa in 1985 meant so much to the whole party. Bishop John Taylor's fine exposition of the mission of the Spirit in his book *The Go-Between God*[14] identifies three fundamental features of the Spirit's work at every level of activity in the cosmos, from the simplest natural processes to the profoundest moments in human history and experience, and supremely in the manifestation of Jesus Christ. These are: creating community; making choices; and accepting sacrifice.

These three criteria do help us to decide, not 'Who is right' in South

Africa (still less the question with which that one is often confused, 'Who is righteous?'), but 'Where do we see and hear the most authentic testimony to the gospel?'

Creating community: We shall take most seriously those persons, groups and churches which are in practice making concerted efforts at partnership and sharing between different communities. As far as whites are concerned, that means those who are making the effort to experience and comprehend what life is actually like for their black neighbours, and to accept black partnership, black initiative and black leadership both in church and political life. On the political level, there can be no evasion here of a commitment to majority rule by one person, one vote, irrespective of colour. Where this is actually happening or being sought, on a basis of true equality, enabling true community to be born, we shall see the Spirit and the 'bonds of peace' (Ephesians 4.3).

Making choices: We shall take most seriously those who have resisted the drifting tide of apathy or resignation which waits for something to turn up, and have actually committed themselves to specific actions towards fundamental change: not simply ameliorating the effects of the status quo, or expressing their dislike of it (Jesus did not say that the blessing of the kingdom rests on those who dislike the status quo, but on those who hunger and thirst for righteousness). It means accepting a life-giving goal in quite specific terms. Responsible choice means choice made in awareness of the truth of the situation (for only the truth makes free), however painful, and the most fundamental choice here is the choice to know what is going on in one's own society. It also means a refusal to tread the path of self-justification in one's actions, and a readiness to acknowledge guilt. A young white Baptist concerned at his denomination's anxiety to present itself as socially caring while increasing numbers of blacks are alienated from its white-dominated structures warns: 'I do not believe that the blessing of God will rest on us if our chief anxiety is to defend our own righteousness. Rather, I believe, the way ahead is in the humble acknowledgment of our sin and complicity with evil and unchristian laws, together with all other white Christians in this country.'[15] It means taking actions which are recognized and validated by the affirmations of the oppressed themselves, not by the self-justification of the privileged who are wishing to demonstrate their 'caring'.

Sacrifice: We shall take most seriously those who are bearing in their own lives the cost of resisting evil, who are risking or actually experiencing harassment, detention and torture, who know that violent death is a daily possibility, or who show their willingness to be identified with and defend and support the victims of such evil. We shall take most seriously the testimony of those who, without seeking to be martyrs, nevertheless carry the cross and walk in its shadow.

There is no single group or church or organization which alone matches these criteria. But the result will certainly not be as inclusive as the term 'Christian'. It will mean a lot of painful heart searching by those churches and denominations with close ties in South Africa. It will lead to much accusation of being 'judgmental' and 'simplistic' in our approach, as we seem to leave out many 'good and sincere Christians'. If, as is still possible, the conflict will sharpen again and become ever more violent, we shall be accused of having helped to 'polarize' the situation even more, instead of 'building bridges'. We shall have taken sides. We shall not thereby claim to have done anything praiseworthy, and in fact will have to confess our own share of the guilt for what has taken place. We shall have to confess that those whom we see as authentic witnesses to the gospel in their fraught context, we recognize as such not because they match what *we* are believing, saying and doing, but because they expose our own unbelief, our own silence and inaction in face of injustice in our own country, and because they prophetically remind and assure us of the possibility of the zeal of our own witness. We shall be unworthy servants, but to become servants is more than enough to dare to pray.

9
How I Love Your Law: Bonhoeffer and the Old Testament

On an infamous night in November 1938, thereafter known as 'Crystal Night' because of the quantity of glass that was smashed, Nazi groups throughout Germany terrorized the Jewish population. Shops were looted, synagogues blazed. Far in the east of Pomerania Dietrich Bonhoeffer, still secretly training ministers for the Confessing Church despite the closure of his seminary the previous year, was in such a remote village that he only found out what had happened a day or so later. When he did hear he turned to his Luther Bible, and to Psalm 74 verse 8: 'They burned all the meeting places of God in the land.' Against those words he pencilled in the date: '9.11.38', and both underlined and placed an exclamation mark against the next verse: 'We do not see our signs, there is no longer any prophet, and there is none among us who knows how long.'

In its time and place it was an unusual reaction for a Protestant pastor and theologian. It was unusual enough for such clear-sighted concern and horror to be expressed at what was happening to the Jews; a perception that it was Germany, not Israel, which was now incurring God's wrath. But it was also somewhat unusual for a Protestant pastor of the time to be so familiar with the Old Testament as to be able to turn to a specific text so readily and to read it as a direct commentary on what was happening in his country there and then. That recognition and identification with the plight of the Jews was to lead him directly into the conspiracy against Hitler and to his death on the gallows at Flossenbürg in 1945.

Bonhoeffer's knowledge and love of the Old Testament was in fact one of the most striking features of his thought, and was to be a powerful ingredient in his search for a new form of Christianity without 'religion' as sketched in the extraordinary letters and papers he wrote while in prison for the last two years of his life[1]. I recall, as a student making the merest beginnings of an interest in theology, being surprised and disconcerted to find Bonhoeffer in his prison writings speaking so ardently of the influence upon him of the Old Testament. I had been told that Bonhoeffer the great Christian hero was the radical prophet and apostle of a new version of Christianity for the modern age - yet what could be more primitive and reactionary than the Old Testament?

I was, perhaps, simply manifesting one form of popular Christian prejudice. I shall always be grateful to J.N. Schofield who at Cambridge began the biblical education of some of us by remarking with disarming but necessary naivety that two-thirds of the Bible is found in the first half. But the question of the relation between the 'Testaments' has of course been under debate ever since the formation of the 'New Testament' canon itself - and even before then. The way the Christian argument often runs is that the finality of Christ implies the provisionality of the law and the prophets, and therewith their dispensability. Even in those understandings and theories of the Old Testament which have been employed to defend the place of the Hebrew Scriptures in the Christian corpus, a certain devaluation of the Old Testament is often implicit (and perhaps always will be so long as we go on referring to *Old*). There is for example the prophetic-proof use of the Old Testament, which sees the main function of the Old Testament consisting in the supply of pre-arranged evidence for the messiahship of Jesus. It all happened 'as prophets foretold', and the fact that the career of Jesus had been foretold so exactly so long ago, must mean that both the prophecies and their 'fulfilment' were of God. Or there is the equally time-honoured typological use of the Old Testament. Jesus is 'prefigured' by certain characters like Isaac, Joseph, Moses, David, in whose careers certain parallels can be detected with incidents in and features of the ministry of Jesus. Moses gives the law from Sinai, Jesus delivers the Sermon on the Mount, and so on. The Old Testament supplies shadowy outlines and sketches, the New Testament fills in the content with reality.

Now there may not be many of us today who would identify wholly with such usages of the Old Testament. But consider their more recent counterparts. For example the theory of progressive revelation which began to be popularized in the nineteenth century is a kind of modern successor to the prophetic-proof attitude. The bloody conquests wrought by the Israelites in the name of Yahweh the God of battles can in retrospect be seen as a rudimentary 'foretelling' of the 'kingdom of God' proclaimed by Jesus in all its spirituality and universality. Or, the old typology has its parallel in that lexicographical and exegetical approach to the Old Testament which sees it basically as a useful quarry of 'background' meanings for New Testament words and concepts. What does 'sacrifice' mean in Romans? Well, look it up in Leviticus - providing of course we can still say that its meaning has been 'refined' or 'transformed' in the New Testament.

All these approaches. ancient and modern, respect the Old Testament in so far as it vindicates and serves the New. And it may be asked, is this not true to the New Testament itself? Do we not read that events took place 'that the saying might be fulfilled . . .'? Yes, but that is rather different from saying that those ancient prophecies were uttered simply in order that a point might be proved several centuries later. Or, does not the writer to the Hebrews evaluate the Mosaic law as a 'shadow of the things which were to come'? Indeed, but the *people* of the old covenant, the heroes and heroines of faith catalogued in Hebrews chapter 11, were no shadows! Change the statement of the question somewhat, from that of the relation of the Old Testament to the New, to that of the Old Testament to *Jesus*, and other elements of the gospels and epistles come into view. According to Matthew, Jesus in his own words comes not to abolish the law and prophets but to fulfil them. In him, says Paul, all the promises of God find their Yes (II Corinthians 1.20) . Jesus vindicates all that the law and the prophets stood for and longed for. There is then a genuine validity which is granted to the Old Testament, both by Jesus and the apostolic preaching, quite apart from any polemical use made of the ancient scriptures to accord validity to Jesus[2].

The most radical Christian way of dealing with the Old Testament has been the attempt to excise it altogether from the Christian canon and from Christian consciousness. The second-century Marcion, who argued for the utter disjunction between the merciful God and Father of Jesus Christ on the one hand, and the wrathful God of the Old Testament on the other, has never been without adherents down the ages whether they recognized themselves as Marcionites or not.

It is in the light of these broader historical attitudes that Dietrich Bonhoeffer's use of the Old Testament takes on more than biographical interest. He provokes us to ask how and why the Old Testament should be used by Christians. He points to the possibility of liberating the Old Testament from the polemical straight-jacket of the past - or perhaps we should say the possibility of our being liberated from the need always to devalue the Old Testament subtly to our own impoverishment - while in no way detracting from the uniqueness and finality of Christ. He does all this while simultaneously, through the witness of his own life and death, facing us inescapably with that question which always accompanies our approach to the Jewish scriptures, of how we relate to the Jewish people .

Bonhoeffer could almost have become a Marcionite. As a student at Berlin he attended the seminar of Adolf von Harnack, the eminent historian of the early church and the most famous living 'Liberal Protestant'. Harnack's version of primitive Christianity typified the Liberal Protestant concentration upon the 'historical Jesus' as a unique teacher of inward piety and personal virtue, quite distinct from his Hebrew precedents and religious contemporaries, Jewish or Hellenistic, not to mention the later Catholicism. Jesus was to be identified precisely in contrast with his Jewish environment.[3] This contrasting was a marked feature of much Liberal Protestantism. The English equivalent to Harnack, the classical historian and lay theologian T.R. Glover of Cambridge, author of *The Jesus of History*[4], vehemently criticized preachers who based their sermons on Old Testament texts, and even depicted Jesus as unlikely to have gained anything of spiritual worth from the synagogue worship at Nazareth. In a rather different way it was also to be true of the existential theology of Rudolf Bultmann, for whom the New Testament kerygma, announcing the possibility of an individual faith-existence 'beyond' temporal history, was in utter contrast to the Old Testament belief in a continuing, corporate, historical existence. But deeply appreciative though he was of Harnack as a historian, Bonhoeffer did not become a neo-Marcionite, nor a Liberal Protestant of any kind. He had already been captivated by the Old Testament. He began learning Hebrew while still at school and diligently attended lectures on the psalms and prophets during his first year of study at Tübingen where one of his acquaintances was Gerhard von Rad, destined to become one of Germany's most illustrious Old Testament scholars.

Influences other than Harnack proved much stronger. For one thing, while at Berlin Bonhoeffer encountered Luther - not surprisingly, it may be thought, in such a Protestant German environment. But in fact a major revival of Luther studies was just then in progress at Berlin led by Karl Holl, whose classes had a decisive effect on the young Bonhoeffer. Bonhoeffer drank deeply from Luther's own works, and whoever takes Luther seriously at first hand must also take the Old Testament seriously. Luther found his doctrine of justification by faith as clearly in the Psalms as he did in Romans and Galatians. Moreover, during the winter of 1924-25 Bonhoeffer encountered, even more decisively, the theology of Karl Barth with his severe Reformed doctrine of the Word of God contained equally in both Old and New Testaments. For the next few years Bonhoeffer's major interests centred on systematic and philosophical theology as seen in the dissertations which became his first published works, *Sanctorum Communio* and *Act and Being*. It was with the rise of Nazism during 1932, Hitler's coming to power in 1933 and the onset of the Church Struggle that Bonhoeffer began to give greater expression to his biblical and exegetical interests, though still in the service of the christocentric theology of revelation which now assumed such immense significance for the Confessing Church. In this context one could hardly open the Bible without raising political issues. Part of the programme urged by the advocates of 'aryanization' upon the church no less than the state, was the purging of all 'Jewish' elements from a properly 'German' Christianity. The most notorious instance was the speech made by a Nazi leader, Dr Krause, at a rally in the Berlin Sports Palace in November 1933, which called for 'liberation from the Old Testament with its Jewish money morality and from these stories of cattle-dealers and pimps.' One might expect a christocentric theology to go along with such an excision of the Hebraic element[5], but for Bonhoeffer (as for Barth) christocentricity did not mean excluding those parts of the scriptures where Christ is not named, but rather reading all scripture in the light of Christ and as a medium of Christ's revelation. It was to see the whole of scripture, in Luther's phrase, 'as the crib wherein Christ lies.' The Old Testament was to be interpreted 'theologically', that is, as a commentary on God's self-revelation in Christ.

Bonhoeffer had already demonstrated this method in the lectures he gave at Berlin University in 1932 on 'Creation and Sin' (now published in English as part of *Creation and Fall*[6]). Here he treats the opening chapters of Genesis as a statement about Christ:

> The creature belongs to the Creator. But the God of the creation and the real beginning is, at the same time, the God of the resurrection. From the beginning the world is placed in the sign of the resurrection of Christ from the dead. Indeed it is because we know of the resurrection that we know of God's creation in the beginning, of God's creation out of nothing. The dead Jesus of Good Friday - and the resurrected Kurios (Lord) of Easter Sunday: that is creation out of nothing, creation from the beginning. [7]

It may well be objected that this is less an exegesis of the Hebrew scripture than an 'eisegesis' - a reading into - of the New Testament faith into Genesis. Rather than a proper respect for the scripture, it manifests yet again an imperialistic Christian invasion of the Old Testament. But we must bear in mind who Bonhoeffer's theological opponents were at this point: not Jews, but those Protestants wishing to make free use of a theology of 'creation' for ideological purposes. For instance, at this time much was being made by nationalistic theologians of the concept of 'orders of creation', that is, structures of human existence which were held to be utterly sacrosanct, ordained by God as essential elements of his purposes for humankind from the beginning and for all time. Pre-eminent among these 'orders', according to the nationalist theologians, were race, people and nation: a theology tailor-made for Nazism. Bonhoeffer was fighting against unqualified assertion of political ambitions which were being consecrated without reference to Christ as the alpha and omega, yet claiming the Christian label.

Bonhoeffer's 'theological' or christocentric interpretation of the Old Testament received powerful reinforcement from the works of Wilhelm Vischer who argued for a certain kind of typological Christian exegesis of all Scripture [8]. It was partly under his influence, but more particularly in the heat of the Church Struggle and when in charge of the seminary at Finkenwalde (1935-37), that Bonhoeffer produced his study *King David* and his expositions of *Ezra and Nehemiah*. These were heavily criticized by Old Testament specialists at the time for doing violence to the meaning of the authors in their own historical contexts, in the service of contemporary ecclesiastical controversy. For example, he turned the refusal of those re-building the walls of Jerusalem to 'build with' the neo-heathen peoples around the city, into a comment on the need for the Confessing Church to keep clear of the 'official' church committees and other compromisers in the struggle. Nor have these studies found many defenders subsequently even among Bonhoeffer's most ardent followers. The only valid point in mitigation is that the struggle of the Confessing Church to maintain its identity had reached a crucial and perilous phase. A recent German study by E.G. Wendel[9] concludes that Bonhoeffer's approach to the Old Testament was based not on any Old Testament study or interest as such, but purely upon his christocentric theology, and his concept of Christ as being revealed through the whole corpus of scripture seen as a unity. Wendel is certainly correct in seeing Bonhoeffer's christology as the centre of his thought : a heavily Lutheran theology of divine condescension in which God and worldly, human reality are united, overcoming all 'thinking in two spheres', and thus providing the basis for the true 'this-worldliness' of faith which emerged in his prison theology. It is also correct to see this christology as informing Bonhoeffer's treatment of the psalms - the prayer-book of Jesus Christ - in which Bonhoeffer sees these Hebrew prayers, precisely in all their awkward humanness, as the prayers which Christ himself offers amongst his people. It is the hidden, incognito Christ who prays in the Old Testament, and who thus validates human prayer. But from this Wendel makes the general conclusion that the Old Testament in itself had very little influence upon Bonhoeffer; that it was his christology which was determinative in his usage of the Bible, and that he deployed the Old Testament solely to expound and illustrate that predetermined christology.

If, however, this was the whole story we would surely expect to find Bonhoeffer always forcing Old Testament texts into an overtly christocentric interpretation and not allowing them to speak for themselves. What we in fact find is that Bonhoeffer, throughout his career, both in preaching and other forms of exposition, deals with an astonishing variety of Old Testament material. If we widen our consideration from what Bonhoeffer *says about* the Old Testament to his *actual use* of the Old Testament in his sermons, his meditation on Psalm 119, and in his prison writings, a far richer and more varied picture emerges. To take but one instance, if Bonhoeffer was so determined simply to find material to express his incarnational christology we would hardly expect to find that in the prison letters and papers Old Testament citations considerably outnumber New Testament ones (93 to 68, to be precise). The weight of evidence points to an intrinsic appeal made to him by the Old Testament, irrespective of any christocentric theories of biblical revelation. The Old Testament had a deeply personal, existential significance for him. Perhaps it was partly a matter of nurture. A useful principle in seeking to understand any theologian is to modify the well-known detective maxim *cherchez la femme* to *cherchez l'enfant*. Every New Year's Eve in the Bonhoeffer household, the father of the family Karl Bonhoeffer (his agnosticism notwithstanding) would read to the assembled company Psalm 90, with its awesome phrases acknowledging the eternity of God who remains faithful through the passing generations, who turns man back to dust, yet who is merciful and who can be entreated: 'establish thou the work of our hands upon us.' Significantly, Bonhoeffer took that psalm as his text when he preached at his grandmother's funeral in 1936. Even at her great age she had been a redoubtable defender of Jewish rights, publicly flouting the boycott of 1933, and Dietrich said of her: 'She was the product of another time, of another spiritual world - and that world does *not* go down with her to the grave.'

New Year's Eve, a funeral: notable rites of passage for individual, family, community; occasions when decisions have to be made, and continuing responsibilities acknowledged in the face of change, uncertainty, challenge and maybe danger. What is striking is how often at crucial points in his own life and in the story of the church with which he was involved, Bonhoeffer's sermons turn to the Old Testament. In 1931, soon after his return to Germany after a year's study in the United States, finding his country sinking ever deeper into political crisis, he preached a harvest festival sermon on that formidable text Psalm 63.3: 'Thy goodness is better than life.' In 1932, the year before Hitler's accession, and when the early indications of a church struggle were stirring, and when Bonhoeffer was increasingly anxious lest the church evade the challenge of a concrete word in face of the crisis, he was gripped by the text II Chronicles 20.12: 'We do not know what to do but our eyes are upon thee.' For the confirmation sermon to his young candidates from the industrial quarter of Wedding in 1932, he took the story of Jacob's encounter with God at the Jabbok. The first sermon he preached after Hitler's accession to power early in 1933, and just before the Reichstag fire, a time when churches were becoming crowded with storm-troopers and many were hailing the Nazi revolution as the hour of revival for the church no less than the nation, was based on the story of Gideon: 'The people with you are too many for me' (Judges 7.2). Three months later, in the prestigious Kaiser Wilhelm Memorial Church in Berlin, as the struggle for control of the church mounted, he preached from Exodus 32, the conflict between Moses and Aaron over the golden calf. It was, said Bonhoeffer, a choice between a church of the Word and a church of the world. For those with ears to hear, Bonhoeffer's message was clear even though he made no explicit contemporary application: 'It is even a pious concern. People are not saying, "Away with gods!", but, "We need gods, religions, make us some." The priest is not driven out, he is told, "Do your duty!" They really want to keep a church with gods and priests and religion, but a church of Aaron - without God.'[10]

One could continue. The historical decisiveness of which Bonhoeffer was aware in his own context drove him to those passages in the Old Testament where such decisiveness and responsibility before God and for others is etched so sharply. And at times Bonhoeffer could invest a seemingly conventional religious occasion with dramatic, disturbing power by his unexpected use of an Old Testament episode. Who on earth, for a Christmas sermon, would preach on Deuteronomy 32.48-52, the story of Moses's final ascent of Mount Nebo and his view of the promised land? Bonhoeffer did, in Cuba during his American tour of 1930-31, asking his hearers to consider what it meant to celebrate Christmas in a world of swarms of unemployed people, millions of suffering children, the starving in China, the oppressed in India 'and in our own unhappy countries' - 'Who, thinking of all this, would wish unconcernedly to enter the promised land?'[11]

Mention of Moses leads us to a still closer relationship between Bonhoeffer and the Old Testament. One of the last surviving items he wrote in prison was the poem 'The Death of Moses', in which Moses and Israel on the one hand, Bonhoeffer and Germany - guilty, ruined but still beloved Germany - on the other, become one:

To punish sin and to forgiveness you are moved,
God, this people I have loved.
That I bore its shame and sacrifices
And saw its salvation - that suffices.

Closest of all Bonhoeffer's Old Testament associates, however, was Jeremiah, his favourite figure even from student days. While pastor of the German congregation in London in 1934 he delivered one of his most impassioned sermons, which Eberhard Bethge describes as virtually a personal confession[12], based on Jeremiah as the prophet whose loyalty to God brands him as a traitor to his people, and who is seemingly also mocked even by God. Again and again in later years he turned to Jeremiah 45, and in prison he confessed he could not get away from that haunting passage where the prophet, whose city and world are collapsing around him, tells his faithful secretary Baruch: 'Thus says the Lord: Behold, what I have built I am breaking down, and what I have planted I am plucking up - that is, the whole land. And do you seek great things for yourself? Seek them not; for, behold, I am bringing evil upon all flesh, says the Lord; but I will give your life as a prize of war into all places to which you may go.' Berlin in the last years of the war seemed very close to Jerusalem in the fourth year of Jehoiakim. This lifelong, increasingly personal and existential attachment of Bonhoeffer to the Old Testament forces us to conclude that it was not simply by applying an abstract christological principle that he dwelt so much on those scriptures. True, he found Christ in the Old Testament, but he also found *himself* there, with his historical situation, the crisis of his church and his country, the plight of the oppressed and the call of responsibility to the future: 'Open your mouth for the dumb!'(Proverbs 31.8)[13]

God's command

But what did Bonhoeffer bring from the Old Testament into his theology? What did the law and the prophets actually contribute to the thinking of the Confessing Church pastor, the political resistance worker and the prophet of 'religionless Christianity'? Brevity permits mention of only two vital Old Testament ingredients in Bonhoeffer's thought. The first is the reinforcement of the biblical command. God requires concrete obedience. In Bonhoeffer's works this found supreme expression in *The Cost of Discipleship* and its exposition of the Sermon on the Mount as the call for practical, unqualified obedience to the word of Jesus. For too long, in Bonhoeffer's view, Protestantism had spoken loosely about 'grace', divorcing it from the concrete following of Christ who carries his cross. 'Obedience' had shrunk from view in face of the accusations of 'unevangelical legalism' or even 'enthusiasm' (a supposed vice of the pietistic sects). Justification by faith had been turned into an evasion of discipleship, countered by Bonhoeffer with his dictum: 'Only those who obey can believe, and only those who believe can obey.'[14]

Now while Bonhoeffer's exposition of discipleship drew largely from the gospels, it was heavily undergirded by the Old Testament understanding of command. On the peace issue, for example, it was

God's command of peace, not its humanistic possibility or desirability, which for Bonhoeffer was the starting point for all Christian consideration of the matter. His own most forthright sermon on the issue at the Fanö Peace Conference in 1934 was based on Psalm 85.8: 'Let me hear what God the Lord will speak, for he will speak peace to his people.'[15] When in 1936 he experimented with preparing a catechism, like Luther he dealt with the Ten Commandments which are there 'so that we may keep them.' Repeatedly he sought to counter falsely narrow and negative pseudo-Lutheran ideas of 'law' and indiscriminately wide applications of the concept 'the forgiveness of sins.' During the war, partly as an ingredient in his *Ethics* and partly as a statement to be used by the churches in the event of a successful overthrow of Hitler, he prepared a confession of the church's own guilt, blunt and specific to the point of ruthlessness, based on each of the Ten Commandments in turn[16].

Bonhoeffer never made that facile differentiation between the Old Testament as a religion of law and judgment, and the New Testament as a religion of grace and salvation. His *Cost of Discipleship* made clear that obedience to the divine command was an essential feature of the gospel. Correspondingly, grace was at the heart of the faith of Israel. This was made abundantly clear by Bonhoeffer in one of his most intriguing and unfinished writings, his meditation on Psalm 119. This, the longest and perhaps to many people the least interesting of the psalms on account of its repetitiveness in confessing the love of God's law, was Bonhoeffer's favourite. In 1935, hearing the Mirfield brothers praying right through this psalm in the course of each day's offices made an unforgettable impression on him. During the winter of 1939-40 Bonhoeffer set some of his students the task of expounding the psalm and made a beginning himself. He only reached verse 21 but there is enough rich food for thought on the old vexed question of the relation between law and gospel. On the one hand Bonhoeffer, good Lutheran that he was, was in no doubt that God's relation with humans begins with grace, even in the Old Testament. He reminds us that in Deuteronomy 6.20ff the ancient Israelite confession, to be repeated from parent to child, as to why the customs and ordinances are maintained, begins with a confession of God's graciousness long ago to the wandering Aramean. 'God's law does not allow itself to be sundered from the act of redemption. The God of the Ten Commandments is the God who led you out of Egypt (Exodus 20.2).

God gives his law to those whom he loves, whom he chooses and has accepted (Deuteronomy 7.7-11). To know God's law is grace and joy (Deuteronomy 4.6-10).'[17]

The gospel of grace in which Christian life has its origin certainly means freedom. But in this meditation Bonhoeffer points out that simply to be concerned with this origin does not spell freedom. There is a self-imposed slavery which seeks ever-renewed assurance about one's new beginning in the gospel. The psalmist however knows about the *way* of God, which means that having once received our new beginning in grace, we are to proceed with God along the way he has set according to his ordinances. Paradoxically it is the commands, the ordinances, which preserve our freedom - our freedom from always wishing to go back and start our Christian life all over again. Is not this, though, to be back in the old state of being 'under the law'? No, says Bonhoeffer. It is not to be *under* the law but to be walking *in* the law of God, that is, walking with him with a whole, undivided self in the assurance of his grace spoken to us once and for all. Bonhoeffer thus frees law and obedience from 'legalistic' connotations, and equally distinguishes grace and freedom from unqualified licence - just as Paul of course wished to do.

The significance of time

The second main ingredient which Bonhoeffer drew from the Old Testament was the validation of time. This found expression at a number of points throughout his career. It became especially important in the writing of his *Ethics* during the early part of the war, and it was to be decisive in his prison writings. It also begins to emerge in his meditation on Psalm 119, especially in his commentary on verse 19, 'I am a sojourner on earth; hide not thy commandments from me!' Bonhoeffer remarks:

> I am a sojourner on earth. By saying that, I acknowledge I cannot stay here, and my time is short. Furthermore, I do not have any claim to possessions or a home. I must gratefully receive all good things that are given to me. However, I must suffer injustice and violence without anyone standing up for me. I find firm support neither in people nor in things. As a sojourner I am subject to the laws of my refuge.
>
> The earth that nourishes me has a right to my labour and my strength. I have no right to scorn the earth on which I earn my livelihood. I owe it faithfulness and gratitude. I must not elude my destiny of having to be an alien and a stranger, and thus God's calling to this pilgrimage, by dreaming away my earthly life thinking about heaven. There is a very godless homesickness for the other world which is certainly not granted a homecoming.[18]

The believing sojourner does not waste strength dreaming of what lies beyond the sojourn, does not 'kill time' but fills time walking in God's ordinances, loving the law which God in his grace gives the sojourner to fulfil. We can see a close connexion between this aspect of 'sojourning' on the earth, and that distinction which at about the same time Bonhoeffer was beginning to emphasize in his *Ethics* between the 'ultimate' and the 'penultimate' things. God's word of justification through Jesus Christ is the last word. The forgiveness of sin and the coming of salvation cut across all human and worldly considerations. But the fact of an ultimate reality, a last word, presupposes a penultimate realm, a next-to-the-last sphere: the so-called ordinary realm, the natural, the social structures in which the world and human life are maintained, and without whose preservation there would be no hearers for the last word. Bonhoeffer sought to re-establish in Protestant thought the rights and claims of the 'natural' dimension in life. The penultimate realm is not to be prematurely written off in face of the ultimate. In the winter of 1942-43, that is shortly before his arrest, Bonhoeffer wrote for his relatives and friends in the resistance an essay 'After Ten Years' in which he made a Christian defence of human optimism. Some people, he states, regard optimism as frivolous or impious in face of present chaos, disorder and catastrophe, and so give up on all responsibility to reconstruct the world for future generations. 'It may be that the day of judgment will dawn tomorrow; in that case, we shall gladly stop working for a better future. But not before.'[19]

It is in his prison writings of 1943-44 that Bonhoeffer's attachment to the Old Testament is at its most uninhibited - and not only in those many textual references referred to earlier, of which the Psalms are by far the most numerous, followed by Proverbs and Jeremiah. Within months of his arrest he reports having read the Old Testament through two and a half times! Then in his letter of December 5 1943 he confesses to Eberhard Bethge that not only has he been reading the Old much more than the New, but that his 'thoughts and feelings' seem to be getting more and more akin to those of the Old Testament. It is only, he says, when one submits to the earth, to the law, to the passing of this life and the world that one then truly longs and believes in resurrection, grace, forgiveness and Jesus Christ himself. 'In my opinion it is not Christian to want to take our thoughts and feelings too directly from the New Testament . . . One cannot and must not speak the last word before the last but one. We live in the last but one and believe the last, don't we?'[20] He goes on to criticize that tendency which treats the Old Testament with its apparently lower ethical standards as an 'earlier stage of religion.' 'That is a very naive way out; it is one and the same God.' The remark about it not being Christian to go too quickly to the New Testament indicates, *pace* Wendel, that a rather different motive for using the Old Testament was operating here than that which simply seeks grist to the christological mill. True, he can say elsewhere that to take the Song of Songs simply as a secular love-poem is the best 'christological' exposition[21] - but that is evidently a display of irony (the word is put in quotation marks). What Bonhoeffer surely means is that to recognize Christ as Lord of the world requires that we affirm the reality and validity of that world. It is the world of human hopes and aspirations, of blessing as well as despair, of achievement as well as death and decay, to which Christ comes. Again, the key is the way in which Bonhoeffer finds his own historicity and humanity affirmed in the Old Testament.

There are other pointers to this recognition by Bonhoeffer. After receiving a visit from his fiancée in December 1943, he writes to Bethge of how she is finding the uncertainty of the indefinite postponement of their marriage. He goes on:

> I sometimes feel as if my life were more or less over, and as if all I had to do now were to finish my *Ethics*. But . . . when I feel like this, there comes over me a longing (unlike any other that I experience) to have a child and not to vanish without a trace - an Old Testament rather than a New Testament wish.'[22]

The fragmentariness of life in face of time and the eternity of God, the longing to be part of a continuing history - all that the New Year's Eve reading of Psalm 90 had imbued in him from earliest days - became almost cruelly pressing upon the imprisoned Bonhoeffer. We should not allow any admiration for his spiritual stature to obscure the degree of psychological trauma brought about by his arrest, expected though it was[23]. How unfortunate it is that the very first essay he wrote in prison, 'The Experience of Time', has not survived. But the title itself indicates what he was striving after: an interpretation of experience and memory whereby what was now lost - family, friendships, freedom, public responsibility - and what was now all too real in the present, could be gathered into a coherent whole. It was seen also in the fiction - a play, a short story and a novel - which he began to write in prison and in which he tried to recreate the kind of society and circle of acquaintances which he most cherished from his own past, and hoped would come in the future: a community of people who were learning what it meant to 'live together' in respect, honesty, justice and compassion. 'Nothing,' he wrote in his letter of February 1 1944, 'sticks fast, nothing holds firm; everything is here today and gone tomorrow. But the good things of life - truth, justice, beauty - all great accomplishments need time, constancy and memory, or they degenerate. The man who feels neither responsibility towards the past nor desire to shape the future is one who "forgets", and I don't know how one can really get at such a person and bring him to his senses.'[24] The recognition of time, of recalling the past and working for a future, so much of which is affirmed in the law, the prophets and the wisdom literature, is what Bonhoeffer felt needed to be reaffirmed in an age of disintegration. It is a call to truly historical existence. Such historical hopes are not to be prematurely written off either by interjecting a 'realized' eschatology which claims that the kingdom of God is already here (in some shape or form) in all its fullness, or by a despairing resignation that nothing can be done until the kingdom comes.

Therefore it is not surprising that the Old Testament plays such a conspicuous part in the explorations, from the end of April 1944, concerning 'Christ for us today' and 'Christianity without religion.' God not on the boundaries of life but at its centre, not in weakness but in strength, not in death and guilt but in life and goodness, 'the beyond in the midst of our life' - 'That is how it is in the Old Testament, and in this sense we still read the New Testament far too little in the light of the Old.'[25] 'Does the question about saving one's soul appear in the Old Testament at all? Aren't righteousness and the kingdom of God on earth the focus of everything? . . . I'm thinking about how we can re-interpret in a "worldly" sense - in the sense of the Old Testament and of John 1 .14 - the concepts of repentance, faith, justification, rebirth, and sanctification.'[26] Unlike other oriental religions the Old Testament is not a 'religion of redemption' - to regard Christianity as such is 'a cardinal error which separates Christ from the Old Testament' and if 'redemption' is to be allowed at all it is a historical redemption - 'Israel is delivered out of Egypt so that it may live before God as God's people on earth.'[27] God's blessing to the patriarchs 'includes in itself all earthly good' and the New Testament is not to be set against this in a superior 'spiritual' sense -'. The only difference between the Old and New Testaments . . . is that in the Old the blessing includes the cross, and in the New the cross includes the blessing.'[28] God as one who loves the world so much that he places himself at its centre, is the preliminary and basis for all that follows in the discussion of a 'worldly' or 'non-religious' understanding of Christianity.

Conclusion

It was said at the beginning of this paper that much Christian doctrine of scripture effectively devalues the Old Testament while insisting on keeping it to serve the purpose of validating the New. Bonhoeffer was one who, whatever we think of his actual interpretation of the Old Testament, saw the inherent contradiction of this position. Perhaps he saw it so clearly because he saw the even greater and more appalling contradiction that it was precisely in a 'Christian' civilization that the present-day representatives of the former covenant were being liquidated. While at times he did approach the Old Testament with a particular christological theory in his hand, he also allowed the Old Testament to speak for itself - and in so doing gained new insights into who is 'Christ for us today': a Christ who meets us in the midst of history and who gives us a new way of being historically responsible. After all, to 'exist for others' includes existing for the coming generation.

10
The Suffering God: A Scottish Resonance with Bonhoeffer

'Only the suffering God can help.'[1] Bonhoeffer's prison statement of 1944 has become a watchword for a generation of theology since the Second World War. Don Cupitt may dismiss the notion as religiously useless[2]. But for theologians of the sophistication of Jürgen Moltmann and Eberhard Jüngel, and equally for many lay Christians, there has been spiritual and intellectual liberation in venturing to believe that, far from residing in impassive detachment from the world, or in direct, omnipotent control over the world (and what a world God is then held to be responsible for!) the source of all being undergoes and bears all the woes that flesh is heir to[3]. The passibility of God the Father was not only considered heretical in the early Christian centuries: for many, reared in the Greek tradition of thought, the notion of a suffering divinity seemed logically contradictory. It was just not possible to believe that the Father - or even the divine constituent of Jesus the Son - could suffer pain and undergo death. Today, many would say they find it equally impossible to believe in a God who does *not* suffer.

Why this modern emphasis upon a suffering God? Bonhoeffer was certainly important and influential in stimulating this trend, but he was not alone[4]. To look at this aspect of Bonhoeffer's prison theology in relation to that of others can be illuminating in two respects. First, it can be shown that Bonhoeffer's radical explorations, while certainly expressed in a uniquely arresting way, were not so singular as to be a curiosity irrelevant except to those interested in exotic intellectual oddities. He was standing on ground common to many others of our age. Second, light can be shed on certain of the factors which have led to a breakdown in the traditional way of formulating the doctrine of God in relation to the world, and particularly to human history. We can better locate the points where traditional religion has stumbled. One particular figure deserves, on a number of counts, to be brought into the picture with the imprisoned Bonhoeffer. At the very same time as Bonhoeffer in Tegel prison was penning those radical questions and affirmations in the summer of 1944, a young chaplain in the Scots Guards was setting down on paper his own highly personal thoughts, at Pirbright Camp in Surrey. The parallel between the thinking of Bonhoeffer and Ronald Gregor Smith at this time - almost to the day - is disconcerting to the point of the uncanny. First, however, certain features of Bonhoeffer's prison writings need to be underlined.

A suffering Bonhoeffer?

It is possible to evade serious encounter with Bonhoeffer by regarding his prison writings as an unfortunate, if understandable, case of pathological thinking under stress. The rigours of prison life, the isolation, the fear of torture (which was never in fact applied to Bonhoeffer) and the likelihood of death (a danger at least as great from allied air attacks over Berlin during 1943-45 as from the Gestapo) all, conceivably, led to a breakdown of nerve and to a theology of agony, if not despair: a continual Gethsemane unrelieved by any Easter. Therefore, all that Bonhoeffer said about the coming of age of the world, about the end of religion, of living without the 'working hypothesis' of God, of radically changing the church to serve the needs of the world rather than preserving itself - all this and much more can likewise be discounted as the meanderings of an overstressed mind producing novelties, paradoxes and conundrums which have a certain interesting quality but no real applicability or relevance outside such an extreme situation as he himself suffered in those months. After all, the church generally is not facing martyrdom. The churches today have to be realistic, must know their way round the stock exchanges and broadcasting studios much more than the catacombs.

Such an evaluation of Bonhoeffer and his situation in prison, however, does not stand up. In the first place, while at times in Tegel there was for Bonhoeffer real and acute suffering, mental and spiritual, remarkably it never took control of his thought and feelings. It was always relativized and kept in place. True, he did confess to Eberhard Bethge that on occasion (perhaps like Luther) he suffered fear, doubt and temptation, to which the antidote was to recite by heart the Psalms of David and the hymns of Paul Gerhardt. True, 'Night Voices in Tegel' is a darkly haunting poem about bondage, guilt and fear [5]. True, he did apparently at one point consider suicide, but that was probably motivated by the desire to protect his fellow-conspirators against any chance of his leaking vital information to the interrogators rather than by any despair at his own suffering. True, he did find separation from his work, his family, friends and fiancée a cruel trial. In her highly perceptive essay on Bonhoeffer's attempts to write fiction while in prison, Ruth Zerner[6] explores the psychology of 'regression' which frequently befalls sensitive people when their lives are savagely disrupted, above all by internment, and points out just how acutely Bonhoeffer felt the isolation from the relationships which had hitherto provided so much of the meaning, stability and hopes of his life. He was, however, through his fictional writings able to create from this regression into his past a new vision of what his own German society might become. True, in one of his most famous poems 'Who am I?' he admits to his inner feelings, 'restless and longing and sick, like a bird in a cage.' But he does not make his immediate feelings the whole and final truth about himself, in contrast to the outward view which others in the prison seem to have of him: an aristocratic, confident person who walks from his cell 'like one accustomed to win.' Bonhoeffer was always suspicious about setting the 'inward' over against the 'outward man', and so the poem leaves open his self-analysis and lets God have the final word - 'Whoever I am, thou knowest , O God, I am thine.'[7]

Bonhoeffer then knew enough about personal anguish to lend authenticity to his statements on suffering. We read them with more respect for knowing whence they came, not as academic musings from a comfortable study but as confessions in a grey prison-cell. But suffering is never glorified by Bonhoeffer for its own sake, as in some forms of Christian asceticism. It is, first, participation in *God's* sufferings in the world that matters. In one of the most famous letters to Bethge, written on July 21 1944, the day after the failure of the atttempt on Hitler's life, he writes:

> By this-worldliness I mean living unreservedly in life's duties, problems, successes and failures, experiences and perplexities. In so doing we throw ourselves completely into the arms of God, taking seriously, not our own sufferings, but those of God in the world - watching with Christ in Gethsemane. That, I think, is faith; that is *metanoia* [repentance]; and that is how one becomes a man and a Christian (cf. Jer. 45!). How can success make us arrogant, or failure lead us astray, when we share in God's sufferings through a life of this kind? [8]

God's suffering had first received specific mention in the prison correspondence five days earlier, when Bonhoeffer drew together the historical development of the 'world come of age' and the biblical picture of the God 'who lets himself be pushed out of the world on to the cross'[9], whose weakness and powerlessness in the world is 'precisely the way, the only way, in which he is with us and helps us'. Bonhoeffer continues:

> Matt. 8.17 ['This was to fulfil what was spoken by the prophet Isaiah, "He took our infirmities and bore our diseases."' RSV] makes it quite clear that Christ helps us, not by virtue of his omnipotence, but by virtue of his weakness and suffering.
>
> Here is the vital difference between Christianity and all religions. Man's religiosity makes him look in his distress to the power of God in the world: God is the *deus ex machina*. The Bible directs man to God's powerlessness and suffering; only the suffering God can help. To that extent we may say that the development towards the world's coming of age... which has done away with a false conception of God, opens up a way of seeing the God of the Bible, who wins power and space in the world by his weakness. This will probably be the starting-point for our 'secular interpretation.'[10]

In dwelling on the theme of the suffering of God, Bonhoeffer was focusing on the ministry and death of Jesus. Thereby he was picking up a theme which he had expounded several years earlier in *The Cost of Discipleship*, where he had written of the Christian's attachment to Jesus in closely similar terms, using the motif of bearing the cross: 'When Christ calls a man, he bids him come and die.' 'If we refuse to take up our cross and submit to suffering and rejection at the hands of men, we forfeit our fellowship with Christ and have ceased to follow him.'[11]

Now, in the prison letters, he is no less insistent that not only does God suffer in the world to the point of the cross, and that faith involves participation in this suffering, but equally this is the way God triumphs in the world. This is not a simplistically triumphalistic theology, but neither is it a grim theology of 'suffering is its own reward', still less a glorification of martyrdom for its own sake. Nor is it a desperate apologetic, a last-chance rescue-mission for Christianity in the modern world. The Word of God makes its own way, and there is a calm assurance, indeed a *hilaritas*, in these writings. Bonhoeffer dismisses the 'clerical' methods of 'smuggling God in', of attacking people at their weakest point so as to show their 'need of God'. 'The importunity of all these people is far too unaristocratic for the Word of God to ally itself with them. The Word of God is far removed from this revolt of mistrust, this revolt from below. On the contrary, it reigns.'[12] Far too unaristocratic! It is not a gloomy spiritual agonizer who is speaking here, but rather one who sees that there are much more important things than personal suffering. And suffering as such, while it must be accepted when appropriate, is not an end in itself but one of the 'Stations on the Way to Freedom', as Bonhoeffer wrote in his poem of that title shortly after the fateful day of July 20, 1944:

> A change has come indeed. Your hands, so strong and active,
> are bound; in helplessness now you see your action
> is ended; you sigh in relief, your cause committing
> to stronger hands; so now you may rest contented.
> Only for one blissful moment could you draw near to touch freedom;
> then, that it might be perfected in glory, you gave it to God.

Suffering *per se* was not wholly determinative of Bonhoeffer's radical prison theology. While it was ineluctably a feature of his prison experience, he never allowed it sovereignty over his existence. What strikes one most forcibly in Bonhoeffer's letters to his family and to Eberhard Bethge, is his determination to recreate in prison as normal a life as possible out of a highly abnormal environment. And for Dietrich Bonhoeffer that means as enjoyable a life as possible. He sees to it that letters can be written and smuggled in and out, as well as the 'official' ones allowed by the censor. He listens to music on the radio, and enjoys Reger organ pieces and Carl Orff's *Carmina Burana*. Bird-song (and still today in summer, the gardens around Tegel resound to more blackbirds per acre than anywhere else I know), flowers, books by the score, poetry, hymns and music remembered by the inward ear, desire for his fiancée, hopes of marriage, memories of Italy and Berlin beer, news of former students and friends, gifts of food, the big cigar from Karl Barth - all these are Bonhoeffer's world in prison. He is very human, and very near us if we are honest enough to admit that life in the body and life on earth and life with others matter to us. Add to all this his quite down-to-earth and practical reports to the prison authorities on safety during air-raids, and one sees just how 'normal' an existence Bonhoeffer sought to create and share in prison. In short, rather than be removed to a lonely eminence of Christian sanctity and martyrdom, the imprisoned Bonhoeffer insists on returning to the world in which most of us live, of food, family, friends, music, care for others, nature, card-games and novels (perhaps mercifully, he was spared the television age).

In the second place, even in his theological explorations Bonhoeffer was not completely alone. We must not overlook the vital role played by Eberhard Bethge as interlocutor (see chapter 2, above). Bethge was far more than just a passive recipient of the letters, as is clear from his own replies and Bonhoeffer's comments on his remarks and questions. The character of the prison material as letters to a a tried and trusted friend, who did not consider himself an academic in the same league as Bonhoeffer, is crucial. Moreover, Bethge himself was already moving towards an attitude well in tune with Bonhoeffer's radical questioning when the theme of ' religionless Christianity' was taken up by Bonhoeffer in the spring of 1944. In fact there is a strange, almost telepathic, relationship between the two at this point. It is in his letter of April 30 that Bonhoeffer first ventures in his new direction, and confesses: 'You would be surprised, and perhaps worried, by my theological thoughts and the conclusions that they lead to; and that is where I miss you most of all, because I don't know anyone else with whom I could so well discuss them to have my thinking clarified.'[13] Then come the remarks about the imminent end of religion in the modern world and the lengthy criticism of 'religion' as untrue to the biblical picture of God in the midst of life, and a very personal confession:

I often ask myself why a 'Christian instinct' often draws me more to the religionless people than to the religious, by which I don't in the least mean with any evangelizing intention, but, I might almost say, 'in brotherhood'. While I'm often reluctant to mention God by name to religious people - because that name somehow seems to me here not to ring true, and I feel myself to be slightly dishonest (it's particularly bad when others start to talk in religious jargon; I then dry up almost completely and feel awkward and uncomfortable) - to people with no religion I can on occasion mention him by name quite calmly and as a matter of course.[14]

This letter took scarcely more than a week to reach Bethge in his army unit in northern Italy. Before it arrived, however, Bethge on May 5 began a letter to Bonhoeffer in which he asks:

Can you tell me anything about the fact that all my feeling and thinking is now really concentrated on personal experience, and that excitement over church affairs, love for its cause, has been caught up in a degree of stagnation? My conscious missionary impulse, which in earlier years was there perhaps more or less naively, has given way to the attempt to understand things, people and circumstances and to grasp them in a 'human' way. A few days ago the lawyer here asked me whether I would like to take my Bible with me on a walk and read him something aloud, gospel and epistle and something else good. And we did that. But I can't record it as anything special or report it with special hopes and exclamations . It was 'very nice'; but matter of fact.[15]

We can understand then, why Bethge was so stirred by Bonhoeffer's letter of April 30 when it arrived on the evening of May 8. Bethge added a hurried coda to his uncompleted letter begun on May 5: 'I'm delighted about the things which, I must say, excite me very much. Some of it is echoed in the questions that I've written above, though they're put more naively and primitively.'[16] While Bethge, as the subsequent correspondence shows, was indeed surprised at some of his friend's arguments, the two were clearly on the same wavelength especially on the need for honest appreciation of how their contemporaries - and they themselves - felt about matters of belief. Theirs was a shared world, and without this sense it is doubtful whether Bonhoeffer would have felt able to explore his questions as radically as he did.

In short, when Bonhoeffer was shut in his cell he was not shut away from the outside world or the 'real world' (whatever that maybe) or the world of 'ordinary people'. Indeed, many of his warders and fellow-prisoners, for the most part young soldiers and flak-operators who had committed relatively petty misdemeanours, were drawn to him, and his reflections on their attitudes and experiences must be counted among the ingredients of his radical theological thinking. The theology of the suffering God grew in the common, public world. Nor was this world simply the extremist context of Nazi Germany. It was found, too, in the less exotic setting of the young Scottish army chaplain at Pirbright.

Ronald Gregor Smith[17]

Ronald Gregor Smith was born in Edinburgh in 1913. His premature death in 1968 was to rob British theology of one of its most original and creative minds in the post-war years just when his thought was flowering into its full maturity. A prize-winning student at Edinburgh, first in English literature and then in theology, he also had a natural gift with languages and was as much a continental European as a Scotsman. Germany, in particular, soon drew him and he spent several periods living and studying there and in Denmark before the outbreak of the Second World War, when he was ordained to the ministry of the Church of Scotland. As a student he was especially excited by the powerful stream of personalist and existentialist thought then flowing in Europe and immersed himself in Kierkegaard. But it was in connexion with the Jewish religious philosopher Martin Buber that he first made his name. Encouraged by John Baillie who had recently returned to the chair at New College, Edinburgh, from Union Theological Seminary in New York, Gregor Smith in 1937 produced the first (and still after 50 years many would say the finest) translation of Buber's classic *I and Thou*[18] . Both in its rendering of an almost impossibly elusive writing to translate, and in its introduction to the significance of Buber's thought for theology and philosophy, it was an astonishingly assured work for one who still had to graduate in divinity.

The student Gregor Smith had a two-fold passion: literature and evangelical faith. While in Denmark in 1938 the problem of resolving a humanistic love of this world with the severity of exclusive faith in Christ - a tension made no easier of course by a devotion to Kierkegaard - presented itself when he tried to map out a possible research programme under the heading 'Faith. Or the New Humanity.' Everything in theology, he states, has to be seen in terms of God's reconciling the world to himself, avoiding artificial distinctions and dichotomies between church and world, and instead dealing with 'God's relation to man in his creation':

That is, all men are to be considered in a real theology: God and the world. Just as a saint on earth never leaves the situation of time so even the bad man is in that situation. The being in the same boatness of all men is greater than any artificial distinction between the church and the world.[19]

The affinity with Bonhoeffer's attempt, shortly to be made in the *Ethics*, to overcome 'thinking in two spheres' in the light of God's reconciliation of the world in Christ, and the assertion that in Christ 'God and reality are united', is striking. Gregor Smith can scarcely have heard of Bonhoeffer, if at all, at this time. The closest link between them would have been John Baillie, who had had Bonhoeffer in his seminar at Union Seminary in 1930-31 and was both impressed and disturbed by this young prophet of Barthianism. (What is possibly the earliest reference to Bonhoeffer in a British theological work is in fact found in a footnote in Baillie's *Our Knowledge of God* (1939).[20]) For Gregor Smith, the tension between the creaturely life and the life of faith was made concrete and personal by his two-fold sense of calling: on the one hand to be a poet and man of letters, and on the other to be a minister of the Word of God. His model lay to hand in the seventeenth century figure of George Herbert, the Anglican poet-priest of Bemerton. So at the outbreak of war Gregor Smith became minister of the Lawson Memorial Church in the quiet border town of Selkirk. His study and garden and the gentle green hills would provide the quietness for scholarship, writing, poetry, and sermon preparation. He was certainly an energetic minister, both as preacher and pastor, and a steady stream of articles for serious and more popular journals flowed from his pen. Verses appeared, and he became a devotee and correspondent of T.S. Eliot. His first book appeared, too, in 1943, *Still Point*[21]. In part this was an expression of a sense of deepening and catastrophic crisis felt by many in the war years, for example by the Anglican writer Melville Chaning-Pearce. In part, also, *Still Point* was an apologia for Gregor Smith's continued manner of life as a studious country minister during that time of crisis. Repeatedly, he had to answer the queries of those who felt that the only proper place for a young minister in wartime was as a chaplain to the forces. His answer, with equal insistence, was that in a time of unbridled secularism, materialism and threatening catastrophe there was a need for some, albeit a few, to preserve that ' life of the Spirit' which constituted the inner core of the life and activity of a responsible society. He was standing for the 'absolute validity' of this life of the Spirit.

Now by this 'life of the Spirit' at the 'still point of the turning world' (to quote T.S. Eliot), though it was contemplative rather than active, Gregor Smith did not mean an existence of untrammelled tranquillity. The decision to remain there had to be won over and over again. It was a kind of continued suffering - the kind which he felt the contemporary church was avoiding in its desire for bland self-preservation. He writes:

> So I perceive the need for all human institutions to come under the doom of the eternal spirit: the church must learn again what dying means, must be aware, as it is not at present aware, of the inadequacy of all its ways. Only a dying church is adequate for life. Only a community which has no hope in itself is ready to derive hope from the only source of hope, that is, from the eternal spirit active in the forms and traditions of history.[22]

The theme of suffering, of life through death, also had a strong christological reference. Among his many articles written at this time, was a piece for the *British Weekly*, 'What Christ Shows Us of God'. The obstacle to faith in Christ's divinity, he asserts, is our assumption as to what divinity is - as for example in the 'succession of absolutes' in the Westminster Confession. But the human , humiliated Jesus presents us with a very different picture of God from the immutable and eternal. Christ is God's Word spoken out of darkness, and thereby we know that God's real life is not static omnipotence or immutability, but 'simply what Christ is':

> What we discover in the life of Christ, then, is not any remote and mighty idea about God's life, but a living, acting, suffering God: a God in action. The God whom Christ shows us is not One who scorns the stress of action, but he is in the midst, ceaseless, restless, ever pouring out of the strength of his beneficence, out of the bottomless ocean of his liberality, ever spending himself to the last in pure self-giving. Only in this way does the cry of Christ on the cross sound with meaning in our ears: I THIRST; never was God more clearly God to our mortal faith than when he found himself then at the end of his resources: and it was then that the world was won to his true life in him. This is his omnipotence, if you choose to call it so: his almighty self-giving, without stint and without end, without any possibility of failure.[23]

Gregor Smith was still deeply under Kierkegaard's influence in these war years, and of course the theme of the suffering and humiliation of Christ was central to Kierkegaard, especially for example in his book *Training in Christianity*. But whereas Kierkegaard stresses the offence of Jesus' suffering humanity, the absurd paradox of the crucified God-man, Gregor Smith simply points to the 'fact' of the humanity of Jesus as the sign and explanation of his divinity. Gregor Smith is not asking for acceptance of an absurdity, but for a reversal of the assumptions which make for absurdity - and by so doing was coming close to the very Lutheran christology which the imprisoned Bonhoeffer was shortly to re-emphasize with such powerful effect as in his 'Outline for a Book':

> Who is God? Not in the first place an abstract belief in his omnipotence etc. That is not a genuine experience of God, but a partial extension of the world. Encounter with Jesus Christ. The experience that a transformation of all human life is given in the fact that 'Jesus is there only for others'. His 'being there for others' is the experience of transcendence. It is only this 'being there for others', maintained till death, that is the ground of his omnipotence, omniscience, and omnipresence. Faith is participation in this being of Jesus (incarnation, cross, and resurrection).[24]

The Gregor Smith-Bonhoeffer parallel is already striking. It was however to become even more so, thanks to sudden and scarcely expected developments in Gregor Smith's life.

The turning point

The Selkirk minister seemed determined to resist all invitations and entreaties to take up a forces chaplaincy and, outwardly, maintained his poise. Inwardly, however, other pressures were at work. One was loneliness. Before the war he had fallen in love with and become engaged to a German doctoral student in English literature, Käthe Wittlake. War prevented their plans for marriage and the pain of separation grew as the war dragged on with little opportunity for communication apart from occasional letters via the Red Cross. Gregor Smith was eminently sociable but a bachelor minister inevitably felt an outsider to much of the family life of his parish. Then too war took its toll of some of the best of his friends and parishioners. He grew daily more sickened by the puerility of much wartime propaganda, and even more so by the conservatism and self-complacency of his own Church of Scotland, which seemed more concerned with legalism and rectitude than with the realities of grace and the crisis of the hour. Doubts about his own understanding of the ministerial vocation began to arise. His people did not always see, as he did, the 'extraordinary' nature of the Christian life. A sense of all pervading pessimism at the futility of much that was being maintained and fought for in the war, crept over him. By autumn 1943 he was approaching despair and wrote in his journal: 'I am obsessed with death. Everywhere I see the falling leaf. My finest parishioners are the first to go. . . This age is quickly dying. I am oppressed with the futility of the makeshift schemes of life.' All he could do was hold out in faith for the future, turning again and again (note another parallel with Bonhoeffer) to Jeremiah for inspiration. He expressed his pain in a poem as simple as it is moving:

Breaking, pain-torn, through the growth
Tangled with sighs. I nothing loth
Won free, and saw a star
With wheeling course afar
From love's strict tears
Beckoning my years:
But as I rose the star raced down
And lit a circuit like a crown
Round a low thorn, and hung adoring there.
In grief I read the secret of that star
And all its cosmic peers, and sun
And earth from which I sought to run,
That to suffering in love there is no alternative.

Exactly what precipitated the move we do not know, but in the early summer of 1944 Gregor Smith, all that he had previously written notwithstanding, became a chaplain in the Scots Guards and began two years' service at Pirbright Camp in Surrey. Evidently the increasing loneliness and frustration of the winter 1943-44 reached a breaking-point. Whatever the motives, it was to prove a momentous step, and he had not been long at Pirbright when he began to set down further reflections on his life. These took the form of letters to an imaginary friend (again note the parallel with Bonhoeffer's prison writings, except that Eberhard Bethge is far from imaginary) to be called, significantly, *Turning Point: Reflections on the Ministry*. It never got further than the autobiographical introduction, but this proves of extraordinary interest, especially in his evaluation of his parish ministry. He had begun at Selkirk with the intention of living as a modern George Herbert. But now he sees that a love of this ideal had two faults. First, it ministered to his pride, encouraging him to see himself as the centre of the spiritual life. He had assumed that as a minister in this tradition he would be respected, honoured and admired. Second, pursuit of this ideal had assumed what could no longer be assumed, namely, the existence of a stable society with an acknowledged hierarchy of values: 'This is, approximately, the ideal which I elaborated in *Still Point*... yet at that time I was still sufficiently sentimental in my ideas to make a careful and obstinate selection of those fragments of my experience which I *wanted* to be the whole truth. *Still Point* is thus the nearest I was able to reach, in modern circumstances, to Herbert's exposition of the priestly life.'[25]

The manuscript is dated August 22 1944. It was almost exactly a month earlier, in the great letter of July 21, that Bonhoeffer had laid bare his own hard-won discovery that 'the Christian is not a *homo religiosus*, but simply a man, as Jesus was a man', and the difference between wanting to be a 'saint' and having faith:

> I thought I could acquire faith by trying to live a holy life, or something like it. I suppose I wrote *The Cost of Discipleship* as the end of that path. Today I can see the dangers of that book, though I still stand by what I wrote.
>
> I discovered later, and I'm still discovering right up to this moment, that it is only by living completely in this world that one learns to have faith. One must completely abandon any attempt to make something of oneself, whether it be a saint, or a converted man, or a churchman (a so-called priestly type!), a righteous man or an unrighteous one...[26]

'Making something of oneself', is precisely what Gregor Smith, for his part, realises he has been attempting to do for the past few years, in cultivating the image and pattern of a modern George Herbert. And as Bonhoeffer was having some reservations about *The Cost of Discipleship* so Gregor was now dubious (in fact much more so) about his own *Still Point*. Along with this more mature self-awareness went a new appreciation of personal faith in Jesus, set in the context of human need:

It has taken me five years in the ministry, and another year [sic] as a chaplain in the Forces, to disengage myself from all the unexamined prejudices, the masquerade of dogmas, the layers of easily-acquired ideas, which so easily and stubbornly lie across the path of the would-be believer. Even now I cannot be sure that I have reached anything like the centre of Christian meaning; but at least I believe I have reached a kind of tolerance, a respect for other people's ways of thought, and a lasting pity for the condition of humanity. I cannot claim that I am now able to see the historical Jesus without prejudice, but I do claim that in discarding much of the accumulated dogmas of the Church I am nearer than before to proper faith.[27]

The tone is highly redolent of Bonhoeffer's relief at feeling able to ask himself:

What do we really believe? I mean, believe in such a way that we stake our lives on it? The problem of the Apostles' Creed. 'What must I believe?' is the wrong question; antiquated controversies, especially those between the different sects; the Lutheran versus Reformed, and to some extent the Roman Catholic versus Protestant, are now unreal. They may at any time be revived with passion, but they no longer carry conviction . . . Karl Barth and the Confessing Church have encouraged us to entrench ourselves persistently behind the 'faith of the church', and evade the honest question as to what we ourselves really believe. That is why the air is not quite fresh, even in the Confessing Church.[28]

In both Gregor Smith and Bonhoeffer, awareness of the human world outside the churches was relativizing dogmatic considerations and sharpening a dissatisfaction with the institutional church and its tendency to see its self-preservation as the sum of its purposes. Bonhoeffer's criticism of even his own Confessing Church is well-known. In the end, it had defended itself against the state rather than defended the victims of state oppression. The church is its true self only when it exists for others, for it is the church of Christ, who is there only for others. Gregor Smith for his part exclaims:

The shock of Jesus' life, full of many contradictions as the sea is of waves, has been buffered and softened so that the reality of his being no longer blazes out in its light and its shadows, its flaming purity and its terrible disregard of the usual rules and conventions. Indeed there are still contradictions, shocking contradictions, between his way and this church of would-be followers . . . But they are not the contradictions which he allows and expects people to hold within the fierce struggle of faith: they are other, pride-begotten, fear-reared contradictions, which miss altogether the absolute demand of faith. Jesus talked with a woman of Samaria; he consorted with outcasts and harlots; he was accused of wine-bibbing and gluttony. . . What a man! the despair of the proper; the perplexity of the sinner; the undoing of the wise. What is this life? What is here that is not in the churches? What is the secret of this freshness, gaiety, abandon, which characterizes his whole handling of people and of problems? In one word, I should call his secret *humility*. That is the startling gift of God.[29]

In both writers' cases, the critique of the church is based on a christology: the liberating solidarity of Jesus with all people, without reserve and in complete freedom. Gregor Smith goes on to criticize the failure of the churches to understand the humility of God and 'all those other magnificent dialectical insights of Jesus which flow from this teaching, about strength in weakness, wisdom in folly, victory by means of the death of the cross, gain through loss, life through death.' Luther's paradox, that we are sinners yet justified, has been lost. It is by faith alone that the omnipotent Lord 'may be worshipped as suffering Love - no understanding can penetrate this.' And it was exactly the preceding day, August 21, that Bonhoeffer wrote of the need to base all our understanding of God on 'quiet meditation on the life, sayings, deeds, sufferings, and death of Jesus' in contrast to what God as we imagine him could and ought to do. He too referred to the paradoxes, that 'our joy is hidden in suffering, and our life in death'.[30] It is almost as if Gregor Smith and Bonhoeffer were using the same daily lectionary from the Pauline epistles. Then two days later, on August 23, in the last surviving letter to Bethge Bonhoeffer spoke of his own personal belief in the forgiving mercy of God seen in the crucified Christ.

Thus Gregor Smith's situation, while not nearly as extreme or dramatic as Bonhoeffer's, led to astonishingly similar thoughts, and in an oddly close coincidence of time. Actually, not all the thoughts were new to Gregor Smith - as we have seen in his parish period he had written very effectively of a doctrine of God based on the crucified Jesus. But then too, in his prison theology Bonhoeffer likewise was retrieving certain fundamental themes of christology and sociality from much earlier in his career, but casting them in a much more world-oriented, rather than churchly, form. What happened to Gregor Smith in moving from manse to army barracks was a kind of liberation in which the theology towards which he had been previously struggling now acquired a context, a concreteness of life, in which he could live and breathe freely. He had previously written of the impending crisis coming upon western society which only some massive spiritual change could avert. Now, the turning-point has come - but it is he himself who has turned. He who had wanted to be the still point of the turning world, had turned to the world - and not primarily in condescension but for his own salvation. He had stepped out of an idealised world of spiritual self-cultivation, to share in faith the lot of his fellows. In that essay written in Denmark in 1938 he had spoken of the 'being in the same boatness' of all people. Now at last he has stepped into that same boat. In so doing, his Christ becomes much more vividly real, and he himself attains a new freedom.

Gregor Smith managed to get back to Germany in 1946, as administrator of Bonn University for the Allied Control Commission. He was reunited with his fiancée, and Karl Barth (no less) conducted their wedding ceremony in a little church on the banks of the Rhine. He returned to England in 1947 to work for the Student Christian Movement Press, of which he became Managing Director and Editor in 1950. In 1956 he moved back to his native Scotland, to the Primarius Chair of Divinity at Glasgow University where he remained until his death. It was in 1951 that Gregor Smith first read the newly published German edition of Bonhoeffer's prison writings and could scarcely contain his excitement at the discovery of such a kindred spirit whom he had previously known only as author of *The Cost of Discipleship*. He immediately secured the English language rights for the SCM Press, and *Letters and Papers from Prison* appeared in 1953. That year, too, Eberhard Bethge arrived in London as pastor of the German congregation in Sydenham, which Bonhoeffer himself had served in 1933-35, and a close friendship between the Gregor Smiths and the Bethges quickly grew. Along with Buber, Kierkegaard, J.G. Hamann and Rudolf Bultmann, Bonhoeffer now took his place as a figure whom Gregor Smith interpreted with great artistry for the English-speaking world, and adopted as one of the crucial mentors for his own theology. Gregor Smith's *The New Man* (1956) was the first British theological attempt to make serious use of Bonhoeffer, along with Bultmann, Buber and Tillich, for the sake of a theology which saw history unreservedly as the place where God's transcendence is encountered. His *Secular Christianity* (1966) [31] was not, as its title might imply, yet another brash attempt typical of those years to 'update' Christian belief, but a highly original exploration of what it means to take Christianity seriously as utterly historical. At the time of his death he was preparing *The Doctrine of God*[32] which, for all its incompleteness (a final parallel with Bonhoeffer) is one of the most intriguing attempts to earth God in the secularity of human relationships and responsibilities, while preserving the mystery of God's transcendence and freedom.

Much could be written of Gregor Smith as an interpreter of Bonhoeffer, but in conclusion let us return to the significance of the striking parallel between them in that fateful summer of 1944.

The suffering God: a response to dislocation

Between, on the one hand, the theologian who was to the fore in the struggle of the Confessing Church and who subsequently did not spare himself in political resistance and conspiracy, and on the other the quiet, self-effacing scholar-pastor ('a soul like an aspen-leaf, full of good will, but much too refined for this world', was Karl Barth's description of him in Bonn[31]), there might seem to be a great gulf fixed. Bonhoeffer's position might seem so unique, both in his character, gifts and career, as to remove him totally from any relation to the more 'normal' existence that is the lot of most of us. But the parallels were there, as we have seen. In each case a liberating view of Christ as the manifestation of the suffering of God in the world, and a new vision of what the church might be in the light of this Christ, broke through. A new awareness and acceptance of the world as it is, not as we would wish it to be, but as the world God loves, emerged; and all this as part of a new stage in personal self-awareness of what it meant to be a Christian, contemporary with the needs and tasks of one's neighbours. A figure like Gregor Smith is significant in making Bonhoeffer more accessible. The army barracks is, after all, a little nearer reality for most of us than a Nazi military prison cell. If Bonhoeffer represents a lonely peak of spiritual eminence, Gregor Smith was at least an outcrop of the same geological material. Or, to change the metaphor, Gregor Smith may represent a kind of step-down transformer enabling people living relatively undramatic lives to plug in to Bonhoeffer's theology without blowing a fuse. Some people find martyrs and saints off-putting and demoralising by virtue of their moral stature. Gregor Smith himself realised this when he once felt led to defend T.S. Eliot's play *The Cocktail Party* against a critic who claimed that it offered nothing that could not be found outside the teaching of the church. Gregor Smith answers the charges of triviality in the play's setting (an upper middle-class London flat), and of superficiality in the characters' interests (except for Celia, who becomes a missionary martyr), with the comment that it is precisely in such concrete realism that Eliot offers his spiritual insight. Not everyone can be a Celia, or a Kierkegaard. But:

> There is life to be lived, choice to be made, death to be died, also in the fashionable flats of London - or in the midst of any routine where the morning separates and the evening brings together. The life of 'tolerance', without 'excessive expectation', of 'the people who know they do not understand one other' is also a life in which Christ (and therefore the church and theology) may enter. [39]

But the most conspicuous stratum common to Bonhoeffer and Gregor Smith is the suffering God. Both sought to ground their doctrine of God in the humanity of Jesus the crucified one. But this was more than an abstract theological interest to be accounted for by a common attachment to a Lutheran-type doctrine of condescension (Gregor Smith, it should be noted, was becoming increasingly fascinated even during the war years by the eighteenth century figure of J.G. Hamann for whom this element in Lutheran christology was crucial). It was far more existential to both of them. Only the suffering God can help, asserted Bonhoeffer. To suffering in love there is no alternative, either for God or humankind, said Gregor Smith. Perhaps we can discern at least one crucial factor in their circumstances and experiences which led to this considerable revision of the conventional notion of God.

Both cases were marked by what can best be described as the experience of dislocation. By this I do not mean simply the respective experiences of Bonhoeffer's imprisonment and Gregor Smith's moving to the army, though in each respective case these undoubtedly were catalytic experiences. For Bonhoeffer, as was seen earlier, imprisonment when it came was by no means unexpected and, though it was a disruptive experience, it was one which he refused to allow to determine his existence negatively. He rebuilt as normal and creative a life as he could in the abnormal and threatening circumstances. For Gregor Smith, the army and the officers' mess provided a kind of humanising liberation[35]. Rather, in connexion with these personally disruptive experiences each theologian was able to register a much wider process of dislocation occurring in their respective churches and societies. Put in the most general terms, the dislocation is the failure of moral and spiritual idealism either to predict, prevent or cope with tragedy, which has been the fundamental problem of individuals, churches and societies living in the twentieth century.

In Germany the most philosophically educated and culturally aware classes had not been able to prevent the rise of Nazism, and indeed they had acquiesced in it, for all their expressions of distaste. Nor had the churches found the courage to open their mouths for the dumb. Even the Confessing Church, when it came to it, had been more anxious to demonstrate its patriotism in supporting the war against atheist, bolshevist Russia than to defend the human brothers and sisters of Jesus, the Jews, from murder. In one of his most powerful passages in

Ethics, Bonhoeffer catalogues the failures of reason, conscience, assertion of individual freedom and private virtuousness, to cope with the depths of evil[36] in the contemporary world. Each of these stances can simply be crushed, ignored or manipulated by the greater evil (as was repeatedly demonstrated by the Nazi tyranny). One cannot ethically theorize in the abstract, argues Bonhoeffer, nor work from general 'principles' to the 'real' world. Rather, with one's eyes fixed on Jesus Christ, in whom God and the world are reconciled in a single reality, one must throughout deal with concrete reality - however unpalatable - combining simplicity and wisdom. This was the voice of one who was prepared to throw conventional scruples about personal innocence to the winds, in responsibility to God. For Bonhoeffer personally this meant accepting complicity in the conspiracy rather than acquiescing in effective complicity in the holocaust.

But even the conspiracy proved a failure, and rather than removing Hitler and saving the Jews, it simply wrought even more suffering as the regime took its revenge. It was after that failure, on July 21, that Bonhoeffer spoke most personally about faith meaning participation in the sufferings of God in the world. There is no direct visible triumph of the good in the world, no immediate omnipotence of righteousness. But righteousness is real, and must be apprehended in hope. How can there be continuity between this reality of righteousness, the world as it is now, and the hope? If God really is the 'beyond in the midst' - this midst - and exhibiting his transcendence in the midst of history, then it can only be in the form of a suffering which is wholly identified with the afflictions of the world. Yet, in so identifying, it contains a promise. As the form of God's actual presence, it is the assurance of God's utter commitment to the world and his eventual reign over it, and belief in it is concretized in the life of a church which exists for others.

Thus the theme of the suffering God relates intimately to the form of the church in the world. Bonhoeffer's church had for generations represented a privileged group with an assumed authoritative role in teaching members of society. But its moral authority had collapsed totally, and it would have to begin learning all over again what faith means. That would mean a readiness for silence where the great doctrines could not readily be communicated in their traditional form, and a 'secret discipline' of prayer and righteous action out of which new teaching and proclamation would emerge. The omnipotence of God had, traditionally, been an intimate partner of a privileged, authoritarian church upholding a stratified social order. What was right, true and good simply had to be taught, applied and put into effect, downwards from above. But shortly before his arrest, Bonhoeffer wrote of the 'experience of incomparable value' for himself and his family and friends in the conspiracy: 'We have for once learnt to see the great events of world history from below, from the perspective of the outcast, the suspects, the maltreated, the powerless, the oppressed, the reviled - in short, from the perspective of those who suffer'. 'We have to learn that personal suffering is a more effective key, a more rewarding principle for exploring the world in thought and action than personal good fortune.'[37] The dislocation of the assumed role of the social elites had thus been realised, accepted and used creatively. And the old God of power - only *apparent* power because this 'power' was in fact at the mercy of those wishing to obtain religious sanction for their own power and privilege - was thus dethroned in this new perspective. As Bonhoeffer would later write in prison, faith means 'taking seriously, not our own sufferings, but those of God in the world - watching with Christ in Gethsemane' [38]. Or, as he put it in his poem 'Christians and Pagans':

Men go to God when he is sore bestead,
Find him poor and scorned, without shelter or bread,
Whelmed under weight of the wicked, the weak, the dead;
Christians stand by God in his hour of grieving.[39]

The theme of the suffering God thus enabled Bonhoeffer to find continuity, meaning and hope in his personal life, and to believe in a continuing purpose for the wider world, precisely when the conventional supports for belief were crumbling. In a letter in April 1944 he speaks of his conviction that 'however strange it may seem - my life has followed a straight and unbroken course, at any rate in its outward conduct. It has been an uninterrupted enrichment of experience, for which I can only be thankful.'[40] The suffering God is not helpless but enables people to become new persons, and new strands of a providential understanding of life become discernible from this point. For Gregor Smith, likewise, the theme of God as suffering love and of faith as the humble response to it, enabled a new start to be made, and a hope to arise for a new meaning both to his own life and ministry, and of the church in the contemporary world. Again, it meant beginning from below, in humility. The most strongly held ideals of culture and spirituality could not be imposed on society, and one's own idealism and enthusiasm for them had no more guarantee of success than the activities of the traditional church unaware of its own decline. There seemed no way that human programmes, however well-meant, could insure against failure. Indeed, the more idealistic they were, the more they seemed to precipitate their own collapse. That was the tragedy of the earnest young minister.

It was also, he realised, the tragedy of an age which still believed that the kingdom of God could be programmed in some direct, politically managed scheme. Instead, he discovered, there had to be a venture in service to real people and their real problems, which meant an experience of a kind of helplessness, a letting-go of the self-controlled life in which one had looked at the needs of the world in detached, superior wisdom. Both Bonhoeffer and Gregor Smith, then, stood on that same fault-line which runs through the modern western consciousness, which detects that it is no longer possible to make a simple link of the ideal to successful accomplishment, whether in terms of an omnipotent God, or an omnicompetent state, or an omniscient church. Temptations to find a short-cut escape route from this dilemma are clear enough. Pietists would solve the problem by denying any real connexion between God and the world at all. All will be well in the kingdom beyond, or all is now well in the kingdom within. The world as it is is dismissed. The ideologues state the problem as consisting solely in the failure to implement their solutions completely. The world as it is, is despised. For Bonhoeffer and Gregor Smith there is a profound sense of alienation from the traditional church and contemporary society, but a deep sense of the need nonetheless for solidarity with the actual people who are suffering. It is out of that solidarity with humanity, they believe, that answers *will* come, for the true embodiment of that solidarity, maintained to the cross, is Jesus.

Only the suffering God can help - by keeping hope open amidst the realities of the world as it now is. And not only Bonhoeffer and Gregor Smith have stood on that line. The tremors have been particularly apparent in time of war, when the degree of suffering has eventually placed too heavy a burden upon the simple moral idealism with which the conflict was entered initially. It is notable, for example, how in the First World War the suffering God made an appearance not only in sermons at home, and in theodicies such as those of P.T. Forsyth[42], but even more eloquently in the poetry written in the trenches, from the popular ballad-style of Studdert Kennedy [43] ('The Sorrow of God' for example) to the haunting lines of Wilfred Owen. This young officer-poet, killed just before the armistice, had experienced the dislocation of conflicting ideals as the war progressed. 'He had come to see the war as absolutely evil in the agonies and senseless waste it caused: on the other hand, only as a combatant could he conscientiously and effectively speak for the men who were suffering from it.'[44] Before the war he had been a Christian believer considering entering the priesthood , but had evidently lapsed from his faith. Christ, however, insistently reappears in his poems written in the trenches. 'Christ is literally in no man's land. There men often hear his voice' he once wrote in a letter. And one of his poems, written after seeing a roadside Calvary near the battle front, is not at all dissimilar in style and content to Bonhoeffer's 'Christians and Pagans' - though more bitter about the way in which the churches have betrayed Christ by succumbing to mindless national chauvinism:

> One ever hangs where shelled roads part.
> In this war he too lost a limb,
> But his disciples hide apart;
> And now the soldiers bear with him.

The emphasis upon the suffering God can be expected wherever and whenever the traditional and conventional links between ideal and accomplishment, between churchly authority and spiritual authenticity, between God and directive power, are dislocated in people's experience. In their own way, many men and women of our own time stand on the same fault-line as Bonhoeffer, Gregor Smith and Owen (Simone Weil could be brought in as another Second World War witness). They do so in families on the point of disintegration, in hospital wards fighting cancer, in factories threatened with closure, in inner cities struggling to maintain community, in squatter camps defying apartheid. They see no easy answers, and refuse easy platitudes. They refuse to disengage from the situation, and they do not give up hope, because they sense that it is precisely in the brokenness of the world that the God of the cross has placed himself, the God of resurrection who has a future which is worth looking for. They will suffer with God now, and rejoice with God at the end. Already, they begin to register in their experience that sharing the sufferings of God means their own liberation. 'This is the end, for me the beginning'.

Appendix: The International Bonhoeffer Society

The International Bonhoeffer Society for Archive and Research exists to promote study of the life and work of Dietrich Bonhoeffer and to present his continuing significance for theology, church and human responsibility in society. International conferences have been held at four-yearly intervals in Geneva (1976), Oxford (1980), Hirschluch, German Democratic Republic (1984) and Amsterdam (1988). The next is planned for 1992 in New York. These occasions not only provide stimulating opportunities to hear the latest fruits of research into Bonhoeffer, his historical context and relevance for today, but also enable encounters between people from widely different contexts in the present-day world who find Bonhoeffer apposite to their situation, not to mention the chance to meet personally a number of close acquaintances of Bonhoeffer and survivors from his circle.

The Society has an English-speaking Section administered in the United States, which issues a regular newsletter. A major project being initiated by the Section is a new and complete English edition of all Bonhoeffer's writings, based upon the critical German edition now in process of publication. Anyone seriously interested in Bonhoeffer (not necessarily on an 'academic' level) and wishing to further their understanding of his life and thought is encouraged to join through one of the regional groupings. Details as follows:

United Kingdom:
The Secretary, International Bonhoeffer Society (British Section),
The Vicarage,
Barton,
Cambridge CB3 7BG.
(Meets twice-yearly and issues newsletter)

United States:
The Managing Editor,
International Bonhoeffer Society
(English Language Section),
c/o Lynchburg College,
Lynchburg, VA 2451-3199.
(Meets during annual gathering of
the American Academy of Religion)

South Africa: International Bonhoeffer Society,
c/o Department of Religious Studies,
University of Cape Town,
Private Bag, Rondebosch 7700.

NOTES

Abbreviations

Works of Dietrich Bonhoeffer cited in the text are abbreviated in these notes as follows:

SC *Sanctorum Communio*, Collins 1963.

CT *Creation and Temptation*, SCM Press 1966.

C *Christology*, Collins Fontana 1971.

CD *The Cost of Discipleship*, SCM Press 1959.

E *Ethics*, SCM Press 1971.

LPP *Letters and Papers from Prison*, SCM Press 1971.

NRS *No Rusty Swords: Letters, Lectures and Notes 1928-36*, Collins 1965.

WTF *The Way to Freedom: Letters, Lectures and Notes 1935-39*, Collins 1973.

FFP *Fiction from Prison: Gathering Up the Past*, Fortress Press 1981.

Also:

B Eberhard Bethge, *Dietrich Bonhoeffer*, Collins 1970.

Chapter 3: Peacemaker and Liberator

1 B, p516.

2 E, p327.

3 Storm Jameson, *Last Score*, White Lion 1975, p118.

4 LPP, p303.

5 ibid. p310f.

6 Bonhoeffer, 'Gedenken für den Prediger am Volkstrauertag', *Gesammelte Schriften* Band IV, Chr. Kaiser 1965, pp197ff.

7 ibid.

8 CD, p102.

9 E, p102.

10 NRS, p290.

11 E, p67.

12 Jan Milic Lochman, 'The Quest for God and Human Identity in Central Europe', *Cross Currents* 7 (1988) p47. See also his *Christ and Prometheus? A Quest for Theological Identity*, WCC 1988.

13 NRS, p169f.

14 *The Kairos Document. Challenge to the Church. A Theological Statement on the Political Crisis in South Africa,* Catholic Institute for International Relations and British Council of Churches 1985, p12.

15 LPP, p17.

16 E, p210.

17 Lila Watson, quoted in Patricia J. Patterson, 'Liberations Bound Together', *In God's Image* June 1988, p11.

18 FFP.

19 ibid. p121.

20 Lev. 25.23, Ex. 22.21, 23.9 etc.

21 E, p70. 22 C, p111.

Chapter 4: The Confessing Church Tradition and Its Relation to Patriotism in a Nuclear Age

1 The most significant statement of recent years to appear in the 'confessing' tradition in South Africa is the *Kairos* statement of September 1985 (see chapter 3 above, n14).

2 Reinhold Niebuhr, *Moral Man and Immoral Society,* SCM Press 1963, p83.

3 J.S. Conway, 'The Struggle for Peace Between the Wars: A Chapter from the History of the Western Churches, *Ecumenical Review* Vol. 35 (January 1983), p40.

4 Quoted in W. Shirer, *The Rise and Fall of the Third Reich,* Pan Books 1964, p111.

5 From Bonhoeffer's final letter to Reinhold Niebuhr, summer 1939. See WTF p246.

6 From a recent translation of the Barmen Declaration by D.S. Bax in *Journal of Theology for Southern Africa* Vol. 47 (June 1984), pp78-81.

7 H. Vogel, 'Christ the Centre', *Journal of Theology for Southern Africa* Vol. 47 (June 1984) p9.

8 Vogel, ibid.

9 NRS p290. See p above.

10 *British Weekly* April 22, 1937.

11 Cf. Jeremiah 29.7.

Chapter 5: Religious Liberty or Christian Freedom? Bonhoeffer, Barmen and Anglo-Saxon Individualism

1 Bonhoeffer, NRS p104.

2 G. Kitson Clark, *The English Inheritance: An Historical Essay,* SCM Press 1950, p174f.

3 *The Mistery of Iniquity,* 1612.

4 Bonhoeffer, op. cit.

5 ibid.

6 See K.W. Clements, 'A Question of Freedom? British Baptists and the German Church Struggle', in Clements (ed.), *Baptists in the Twentieth Century*, Baptist Historical Society 1983.

7 J.C. Carlile, *Baptist Times*, August 2, 1934.

8 See chapter 4 above, p

9 *Fifth Baptist World Congress*. Official Report, ed. J.H. Rushbrooke, London 1934, p182.

10 See D.S. Batchell, 'Freedom in Bonhoeffer' in A.J. Klassen (ed.), *A Bonhoeffer Legacy: Essays in Understanding*, Eerdmans 1981, pp330-344.

11 Victor Gollancz 1938.

12 Some years ago the Revd John Wright, a student at Richmond College at the time of Bonhoeffer's visit, gave me a copy of the notes he made of Bonhoeffer's lecture.

13 *British Weekly*, April 22, 1937.

14 ibid.

15 ibid.

16 Bethge, DB p298.

17 LPP p158.

18 TP p113.

19 ibid. p112.

20 FPP p121. See chapter 3 above, p64

21 LPP p381

22 ibid. p382.

Chapter 6: The Freedom of the Church: Bonhoeffer and the Free Church Tradition

1 Cited in E.A. Payne, *The Free Church Tradition in the Life of England*, SCM Press 1944, p34.

2 LPP, p382f.

3 See G. Balders, *Ein Herr, ein Glaube, eine Taufe. 150 Jahre Baptistengemeinden in Deutschland 1834-1984*, Oncken Verlag 1985.

4 *Die Soziallehren der Christlichen Kirche und Gruppen* (1911). English edition, The *Social Teaching of the Christian Churches*, Allen and Unwin 1931.

5 ibid. p993.

6 ibid. p819.

7 SC, p151.

8 ibid. p152.

9 ibid.

10 ibid.

11 ibid. p153.

12 E, p187.

13 SC, p187f.

14 ibid. p190.

15 Bonhoeffer in 1933 was strongly tempted by 'the idea of the Free Church' as a strategy in the Church Struggle, but was dissuaded from this by Karl Barth. See B, p239. The battle was to be fought over the identity of the German Evangelical Church in both its legal and theological constitutions, not in the formation of 'another' church.

16 E, p263.

17 ibid. pp252-267.

18 ibid. pp258-267.

19 ibid. p264.

20 ibid. p265.

21 ibid. p266.

22 Balders, op. cit. pp95-97.

23 See e.g. G. Limouris (ed.), *Church, Kingdom, World. The Church as Mystery and Prophetic Sign*, Faith and Order Paper No. 130, WCC Geneva 1986.

24 A. Wilkinson, *Dissent or Conform? War, Peace and the English Churches 1900-1945*, SCM Press 1945.

25 'Protestantism without Reformation' in NRS, p103.

26 Balders, op. cit. p73.

27 NRS p105.

28 'The Confessing Church and the Ecumenical Movement', NRS pp326-344.

29 'After Ten Years', LPP p7.

30 J. Habgood, *Church and Nation in a Secular Age*, Darton Longman and Todd 1983, p10. For some British reflections on the Falkl ands episode and related issues of national loyalty, see K.W. Clements, *A Patriotism for Today. Love of country in dialogue with the witness of Dietrich Bonhoeffer*, Collins 1986.

31 NRS, p105.

32 e.g. LPP p381.

33 NRS p337.

34 P.T. Forsyth, *Faith, Freedom and the Future*, Independent Press edition, 1955, p112.

35 ibid.

36 ibid. p126.

37 See e.g. W.L. Lumpkin, *Baptist Confessions of Faith*, Valley Forge 1969.

38 English version in G.K. Parker, *Baptists in Europe. History and Confessions*, Broadman Press 1982. Note the reference to the confession by the church of its own guilt. In 1984 at the European Baptist Congress in Hamburg, the Baptist Unions of both the German Federal Republic and the German Democratic Republic made a public act of confession and repentance for the failure of their churches to speak and act against the iniquities of the Third Reich. This occasion was the fiftieth anniversary of the Congress of the Baptist World Alliance meeting in Berlin in 1934 (see Chapter 5, above), at which the German Baptists

had made clear their welcome of Hitler's accession. See K.W. Clements, 'A Question of Freedom? British Baptists and the German Church Struggle', in *Baptists in the Twentieth Century* (ed. Clements), Baptist Historical Society 1983.

Chapter 7: Sweet Land of Liberty: A Postscript to the American Experience

1 NRS, pp92-118.

2 See chapters 5 and 6 above.

3 NRS p105.

4 ibid.

5 ibid. p113.

6 LPP, pp

Chapter 8: Taking Sides: South Africa and the Cost of Confession

1 *Whose Rubicon? Report of a visit to South Africa by representatives of the British Churches*, British Council of Churches and Catholic Institute for International Relations 1986, p48.

2 See e.g. J.W. de Gruchy and C. Villa-Vicencio (eds.), *Apartheid is a Heresy*, Eerdmans 1983; J.W. de Gruchy, *The Church Struggle in South Africa*, 2nd edition W.B. Eeerdmans 1986, and *Bonhoeffer and South Africa*, Eerdmans 1984; C. Villa-Vicencio, *Reading Barth in South Africa* and (ed) *Theology and Violence*. The South African Debate ; A. Boesak, *If This is Treason I am Guilty*, Collins Fount 1988.

3 *The Kairos Document* (see chapter 3 above n14), p4.

4 ibid.

5 *Evangelical Witness in South Africa. A Critique of Evangelical Theology and Practice by South African Evangelicals themselves*, Evangelical Alliance 1986, p5. p5.

6 NRS p326.

7 NRS p329.

8 NRS p329f.

9 See esp. B, chapters 8, 9, 10, 11.

10 See chapter 5 above, p .

11 NRS p325.

12 *Kairos*, p13.

13 E p47. Cf also LPP p4.

14 J.V. Taylor, *The Go-Between God. The Holy Spirit and the Christian Mission*, SCM Press 1972.

15 Kevin Roy, 'Baptists in South Africa', *Concern* No 1 (Baptist Concern for Southern Africa) November 1988.

Chapter 9: How I Love Your Law: Bonhoeffer and the Old Testament

1 The definitive study on this aspect of Bonhoeffer's theology is that by the East German scholar Martin Kuske, *The Old Testament as the Book of Christ. An Appraisal of Bonhoeffer's Interpretation*, Westminister Press, Philadelphia 1976.

2 See the chapter 'The Kingdom of God and Historical Process' in T. Gorringe, *Redeeming Time: Atonement through Education*, Darton, Longman and Todd 1986.

3 See especially the influential book by the most famous German Liberal Protestant Adolf Harnack, *What is Christianity?* Norgate 1901.

4 SCM Press 1917. On Glover, see K.W. Clements, *Lovers of Discord. Twentieth century theological controversies in England*, SPCK 1988, chapter 5.

5 See R. Ericksen, *Theologians Under Hitler: Gerhard Kittel, Paul Althaus and Emanuel Hirsch*, Yale University Press 1985.

6 CF,See bibliography.

7 ibid. p17f.

8 Wilhelm Vischer, *Das Christuszeugnis des Alten Testaments. Volume 1, Das Gesetz (The Law)* appeared in 1934. Bonhoeffer met Vischer in 1933 and had lengthy discussion with him (Kuske, op. cit. p9).

9 E.G. Wendel, *Studien zur Homiletik Dietrich Bonhoeffers*, J.C.B. Mohr/Paul Siebeck 1985.

10 NRS p245.

11 B, p111.

12 ibid. p259.

13 NRS p325.

14 CD p60.

15 NRS pp289-292.

16 E, p93.

17 *Gesammelte Schriften IV*, p509 (own translation).

18 Translation by Daniel Bloesch, 'God's Guest', Sojourner 26/May 1984.

19 LPP p15f.

20 ibid. p156.

21 ibid. p303.

22 ibid. p163

23 See Ruth Zerner, 'Dietrich Bonhoeffer's Prison Fiction: A Commentary', FFP.

24 LPP p203.

25 ibid. p282.

26 ibid. p286f.

27 ibid. p336.

28 ibid. p374.

Chapter 10: The Suffering God: A Scottish Resonance with Bonhoeffer

1 LPP p361.

2 D. Cupitt, *Taking Leave of God*, SCM Press 1980, p112f: 'The god of the modern patripassian believer is nothing but Humanity, the god of Comtist humanism. . . it gives no permanent victory and no salvation.'

3 J. Moltmann, *The Crucified God*, SCM Press 1974, and *The Trinity and the Kingdom of God*, SCM Press 1981; E. Jüngel, *God as the Mystery of the World. On the Foundation of the Theology of the Crucified One in the Dispute between Theism and Atheism*, T. and T. Clark, 1983.

4 For a recent survey and discussion of the theme, see P. Fiddes, *The Creative Suffering of God*, Clarendon Press 1988.

5 LPP pp349-356. See chapter 7 above, p .

6 R. Zerner, 'Dietrich Bonhoeffer's Prison Fiction: A Commentary' in FFP, pp139-167.

7 LPP p357f.

8 LPP p370.

9 LPP p360.

10 LPP p360f.

11 CD p79f.

12 LPP p346.

13 LPP p279.

14 LPP p282.

15 ibid.

16 LPP p284.

17 To date the only full-length study of Gregor Smith's thought is K.W. Clements, *The Theology of Ronald Gregor Smith*, E.J. Brill (Leiden), 1986.

18 T. and T. Clark, 1937 (and recently re-issued). Another translation by W. Kaufmann was published in 1970 , but Gregor Smith's has subsequently been re-issued.

19 Clements, op. cit p20.

20 J. Baillie, *Our Knowledge of God*, Oxford University Press 1939, p70n - a reference to Dietrich Bonhoeffer's *Akt und Sein*. The English edition (*Act and Being*) did not appear until 1962 - published by Collins and largely at Gregor Smith's instigation .

21 *Still Point*, Nisbet 1943 under pseudonym Ronald Maxwell.

22 ibid. p42.

23 Clements, op. cit p35.

24 LPP p381.

25 Clements, op. cit. p40.

26 LPP p369.

27 Clements, op. cit. p40.

28 LPP p382.

29 Clements, op. cit. p41.

30 LPP p391.

31 Collins 1966.

32 Collins 1970.

33 See E. Busch, *Karl Barth. His Life from Letters and Autobiographical Texts*, SCM 1975.

34 Clements, op. cit. p53.

35 Gregor Smith reflected on his army experiences, though not on as profound and self-revealing a level as the 'Turning Point' notes, in *Back From the Front*, under pseudonym Sam Browne 1946.

36 E pp46-50.

37 LPP p17.

38 LPP p370.

39 LPP p348f.

40 LPP p272.

41 Cf Bonhoeffer's critical comments on the threat to humanity from 'organization',LPP p380.

42 P.T. Forsyth, *The Justification of God*, Duckworth 1916.

43 See esp. 'The Suffering God' and 'The Sorrow of God' in G.A. Studdert Kennedy, *The Unutterable Beauty*. later issued as *The Rhymes of G.A. Studdert Kennedy*, Hodder and Stoughton 1940.

44 *The Collected Poems of Wilfred Owen*, edited with Introduction and Notes by C. Day Lewis and memoir by Edmund Blunden , Chatto and Windus 1963.

Index